A-Z MANSFIELD

CONTENTS

Key to Map Pages	2-3
Map Pages	4-67
Index to Streets, Towns, Villages, Hospitals and selected Places of Interest	68-88

REFERENCE

Motorway	M1	Car Park (selected)	P
A Road	A617	Church or Chapel	†
B Road	B6030	Fire Station	■
Dual Carriageway		Hospital	H
One-way Street		House Numbers (A & B Roads only)	57 44
Traffic flow on A roads is indicated by a heavy line on the driver's left.	→	Information Centre	i
Restricted Access		National Grid Reference	³60
Pedestrianized Road		Police Station	▲
Track		Post Office	★
Footpath		Toilet	▽
Residential Walkway		with facilities for the Disabled	♿
Railway	Station Heritage Sta. Tunnel Level Crossing	Educational Establishment	⌐
		Hospital or Hospice	⌐
Built-up Area	OAK ST	Industrial Building	⌐
Local Authority Boundary	–·–·–	Leisure or Recreational Facility	⌐
Postcode Boundary	––––	Place of Interest	⌐
		Public Building	⌐
Map Continuation	34	Shopping Centre or Market	⌐
		Other Selected Buildings	⌐

SCALE

1:19,000

0   ¼   ½ Mile
0   250   500   750 Metres   1 Kilometre

3 ⅓ inches (8.47 cm) to 1 mile
5.26 cm to 1km

Copyright of Geographers' A-Z Maps Company Limited

Head Office :
Fairfield Road, Borough Green, Sevenoaks, Kent TN15 8PP
Tel: 01732 781000 (General Enquiries & Trade Sales)

Showrooms :
44 Gray's Inn Road, London WC1X 8HX
Tel: 020 7440 9500 (Retail Sales)
www.a-zmaps.co.uk

Ordnance Survey
© Crown
Edition
Copyright

D1493834

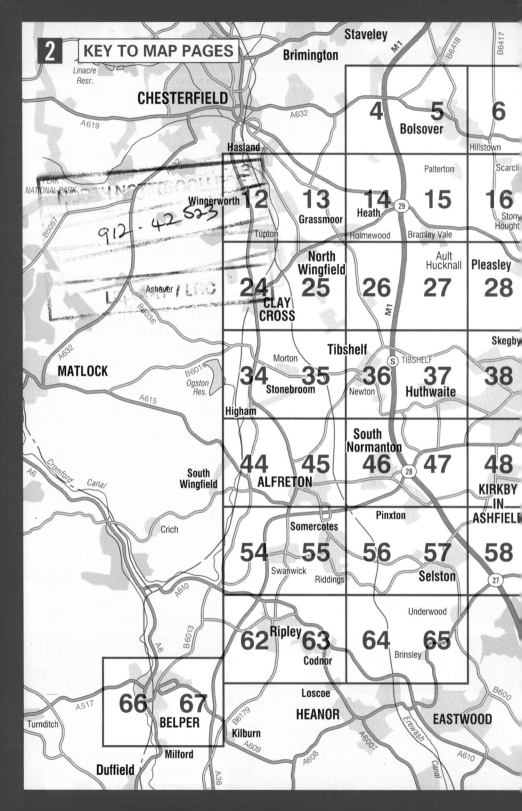

2 **KEY TO MAP PAGES**

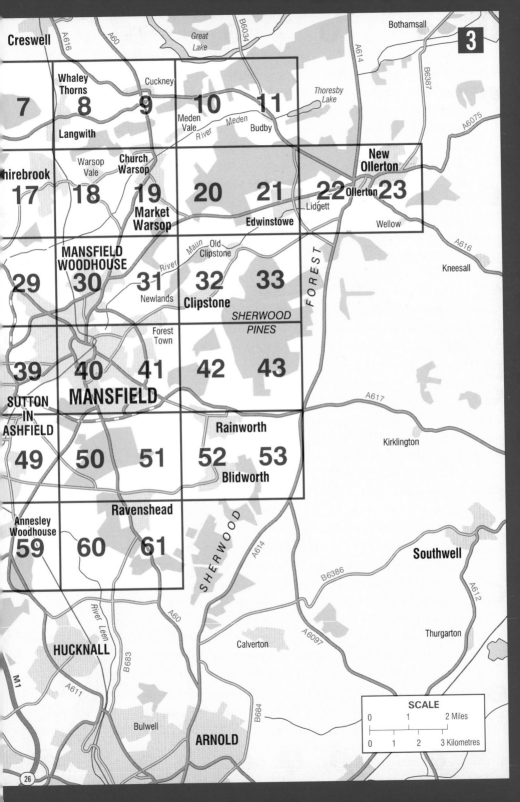

Creswell

Whaley Thorns

Cuckney

7

8

9

10

11

Langwith

Meden Vale

River Meden

Budby

Great Lake

Thoresby Lake

B6034

A616

A60

B6387

A614

A6075

Bothamsall

hirebrook

Warsop Vale

Church Warsop

New Ollerton

17

18

19

20

21

22 Ollerton **23**

Market Warsop

Edwinstowe

Lidgett

Wellow

A616

Kneesall

MANSFIELD WOODHOUSE

River Maun

Old Clipstone

FOREST

29

30

31

32

33

Newlands

Clipstone

SHERWOOD PINES

Forest Town

39

40

41

42

43

MANSFIELD

A617

SUTTON IN ASHFIELD

Rainworth

Kirklington

49

50

51

52

53

Blidworth

Ravenshead

SHERWOOD

Southwell

Annesley Woodhouse

59

60

61

A614

B6386

A612

Thurgarton

River Leen

A60

A6097

Calverton

HUCKNALL

B683

M1

A611

B684

Bulwell

ARNOLD

SCALE

0		1		2 Miles

0	1	2		3 Kilometres

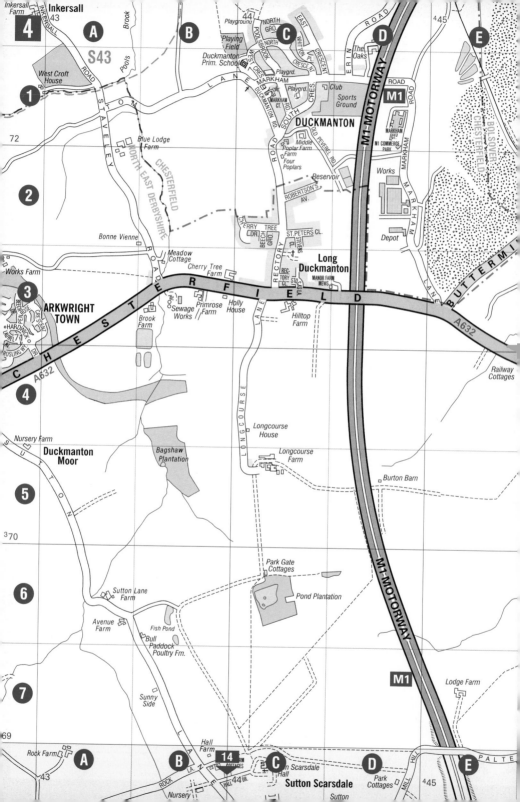

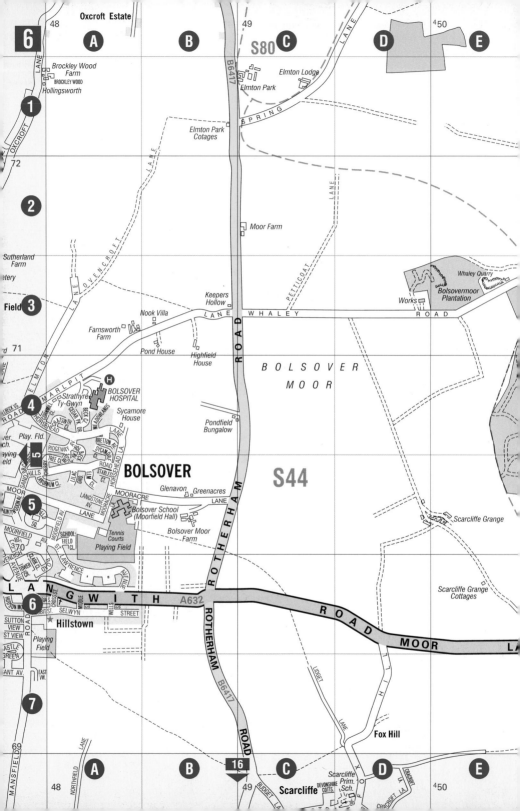

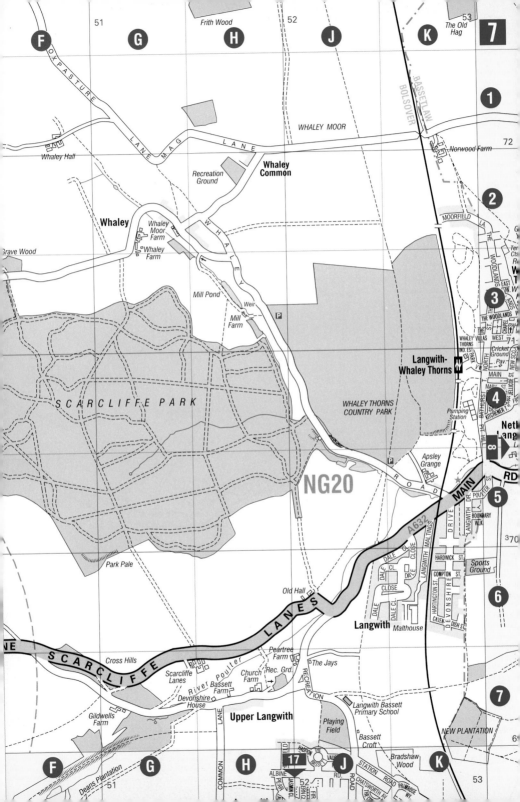

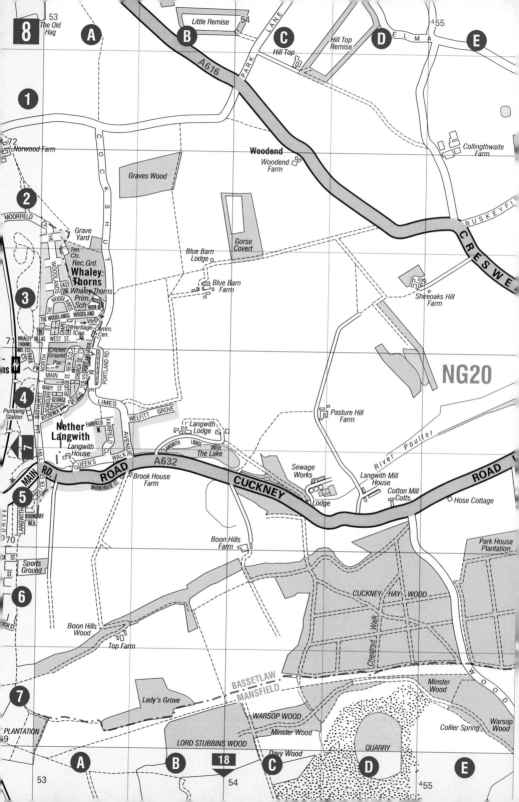

8

53 The Old Hag
54
455

A **B** **C** **D** **E**

Little Remise

Hill Top
Hill Top Remise

PARK LANE
A616
DELMA

1

72
Norwood Farm

Woodend

Woodend Farm

Collingthwaite Farm

Graves Wood

BUSKEYFI

CRESWE

2

MOORFIELD

Grave Yard

Blue Barn Lodge

Gorse Covert

Ten. Cts.
Rec. Grd.
Whaley Thorns
Whaley Thorns Prim. Sch.

Blue Barn Farm

Shireoaks Hill Farm

3

THE WOODLANDS

WOODLAND

Vic.
Heritage Comm. Cen.

71

WHALEY THORNS IND. EST.

WEST ST.

Cricket Ground Pav.

NEW ST.

NG20

Pasture Hill Farm

4

MAIN

MARY ST.
GEORGE

LIMES

WELFITT GROVE

Langwith Lodge

Pumping Station

FAIRFIELD

Nether Langwith

Langwith House

FAIRFIELD CL.
FAIRFIELD

LODGE DRIVE

The Lake

Sewage Works

Langwith Mill House

River Poulter

7

AVENUE
QUEEN'S
WALK

ROAD
A632
CUCKNEY

Lodge

Cotton Mill Cotts.

ROAD

5

MAIN RD.

Brook House Farm

BROOKHOUSE CT.

Hose Cottage

LANGWITH
BOUNDARY WLK.

370

Boon Hills Farm

Park House Plantation

6

CK ST.

Sports Ground

ISH ST.

Boon Hills Wood

Top Farm

CUCKNEY HAY WOOD

Chestnut Walk

Minster Wood

WOOD

Warsop Wood

7

PLANTATION

Lady's Grove

BASSETLAW
MANSFIELD

WARSOP WOOD

Minster Wood

LORD STUBBINS WOOD

Davy Wood

QUARRY

Collier Spring

Warsop Wood

A **B** **18** **C** **D** **E**

53
54
455

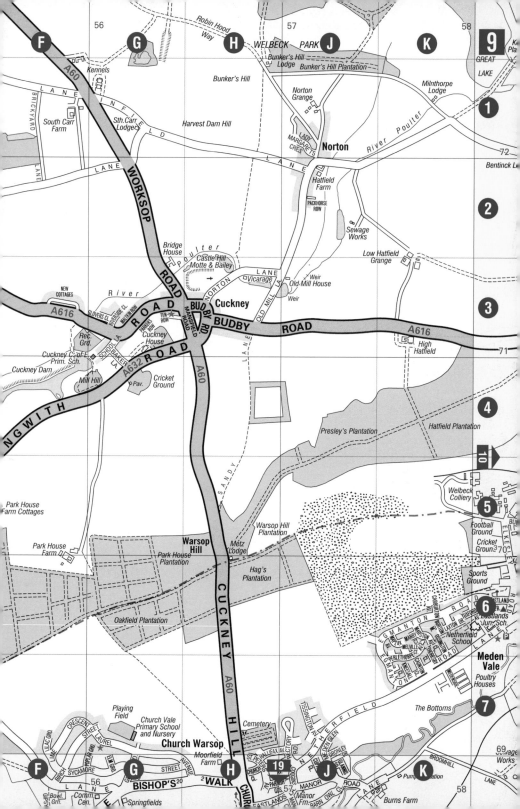

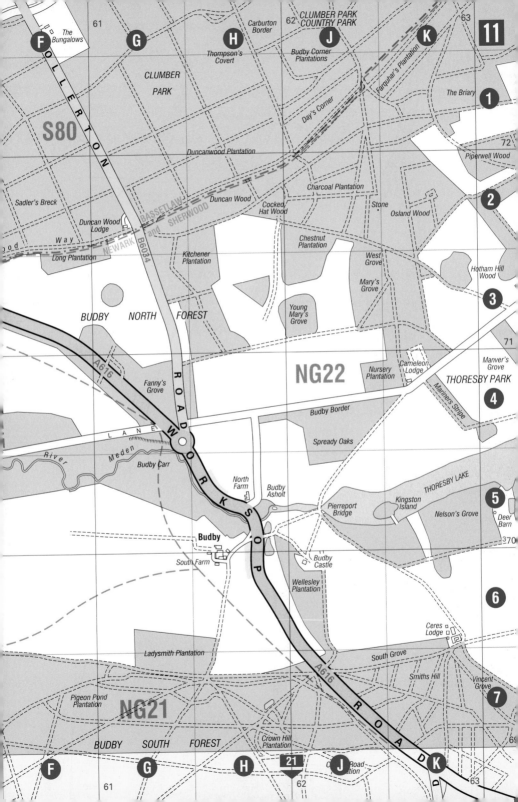

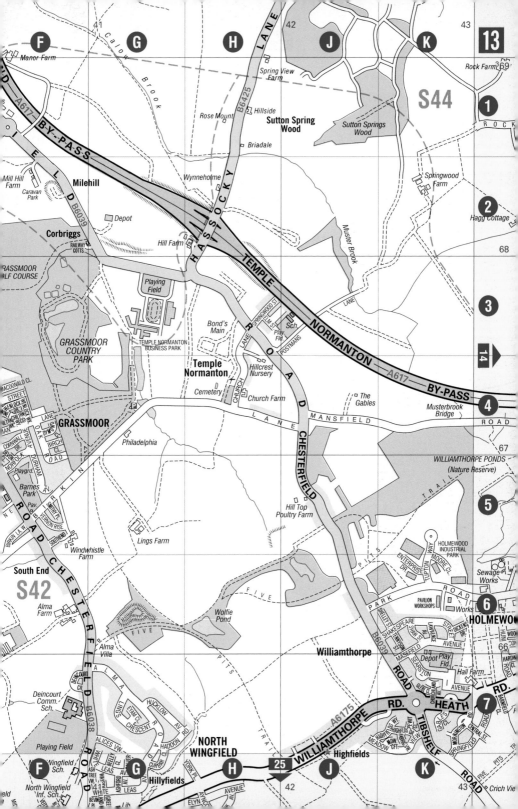

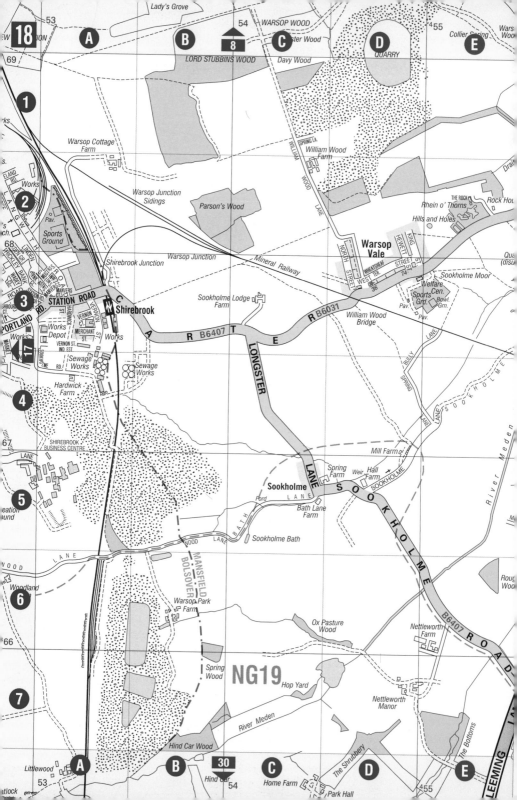

20

58   **A**   Assarts Hill Plantation   **B**   **↑ 10**   **C**   Gleadthorpe New Plantation   **D**   460   **E**

69 BROOMHIL

Sewage Works

BROOMHILL   LANE

1

Hanger Hill Wood

2

Sod Wall Plantation

NG20

68

Sunnyside Wo

Hanger Hill

Hanger Hill

Jerusalem Plantation

Railway Pie

Ling Plantation

3

THE LINGS

Fox Den Plantation

↑ 19

Warsop Quarter

LANE

4

Turner's Plantation

Bottom Vals Hill

Cabin Plantation

Blackpool Plantation

Norman's Plantation

Top Vals Hill

Black Pool

67

LANE   LING

Blakeley Hill

5

Blakeley Hill Plantation

Rough Piece

The Sarts

Clipstone Old Qu

arm

BLAKELEY

Bradmer Hill

6

Market Warsop Towermill   Depots

FOREST

B6035   **ROAD**   **A6075**

Windmill Plantation

M

PEAFIELD   LANE

GORSETHORPE

Broomhill Grange

366

Gorseybrecks

Broomhill Gose

7

Broomhill Gorse

Gorsethorpe

LANE

A   Sherwood Forest Farm Park   **B**   **▼ 32**   **C**   **D**   460   **E**

58   Lamb Pens Farm   59

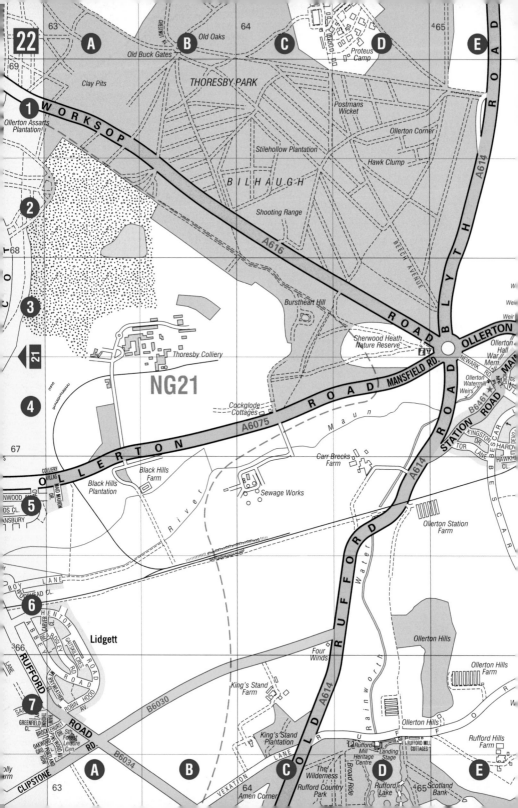

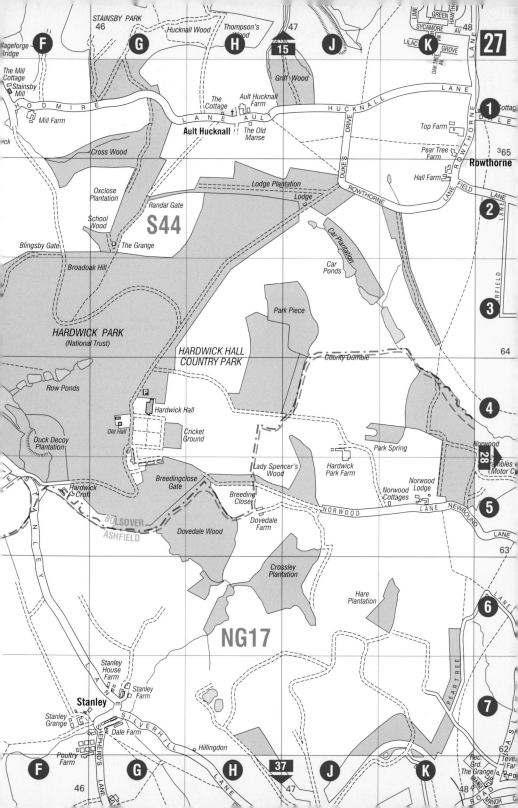

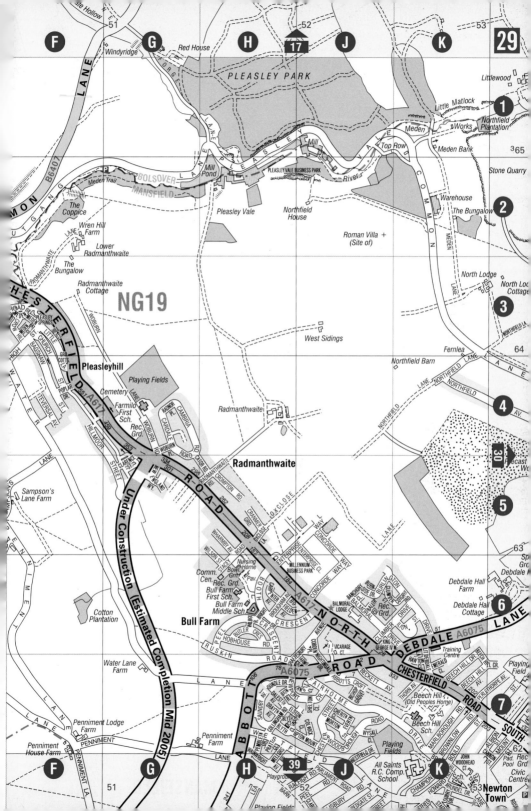

58 | A | 59 | B | 20 | C | Gorsethorpe | D | 460 | E

Gorsethorpe

Sherwood Forest
Farm Park

1

365

Lamb Pens
Farm

Lawn Hills

Sherwood Forest
Caravan Park

Vic

Maun

Cavendish
Lodge

SQUIRES

2

Cavendish Wood

HOLBROOK CRES

OLD BARN CT.

Old
Clipstone

King John's
Palace
(Remains of

River

DRIVE

LANE

Birklands

DRIVE

B6030

WATERWORKS

Pumping
Station

DR.

Chestnut
Screed

• Mast

3

64

gh Rocks

Intake Wood

Waterfield
Farm

NG21

HIGHFIELD
RD.

WOODLAND
CL.

CLIPSTONE

4

INFIELD
RD.

HIGHFIELD

BAULKER

Baulker
Farm

Cemetery

HIGHFIELD
INTAKE
ROAD

GORSEWAY

KING JOHN'S
RD.

JOHN'S RD.

GREENDALE CR.

LANE

Works

31

Ply
Fld.

Newlands
Junior
School

Playing
Field

Lib.
Sch.

FIRST

AVENUE

NTH. CRES.
STH. CRES.

Clipstone
Colliery

Forestry
Holdings

D

5

Clipstone

GREENWAY

John T. Rice
Inf. Sch.

BRAEMAR

VIN. FIR TREE

FOREST ROAD

FOURTH

FIFTH

THIRD

ROAD

Play Fld.

SECOND

AVE.

AVENUE

Slurry
Pond

GARIBALDI

TREE CRES

WILLOW FIR TREE

Garibaldi
School
Playing
Field

SIXTH AVENUE

SEVENTH

CHURCH

CHURCH ROAD

Play
Fld.

Pav.

MAIN

AVENUE

F
I
E
L
D
S

6

Lido

Sports
Ground

Pav
Football
Grd.

VICARS CL.

Pav.

Vicar Water
Country Park

Vicar Pond

CLIPSTONE RD. EAST

B6030

LIDO

EDMONTON RD.

CENTRAL DRIVE

SHAFTON ST.

VICARS CT.

EASTFIELD
CL.

P

Subway

Clipstone Colliery
Junction

CLI

NEWLANDS

Road

Vicar

Water

NG19

7

Newland's
Farm

Road

NEWARK and SHERWOOD

MANSFIELD

SHER

NG18

62

Vicar
Water

F

58 | A | 59 | B | 42 | C | 59 | D | 460 | E

Long Planta

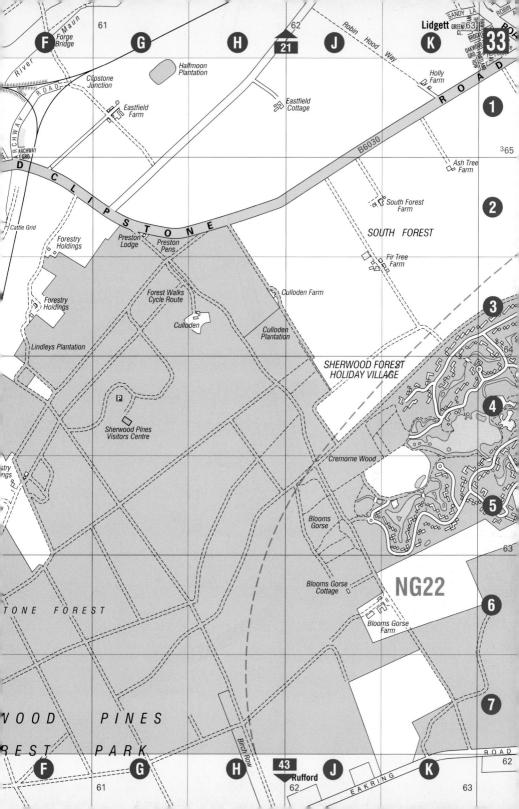

F Forge Bridge **G** **H** △21 **J** Robin Hood Way **K** Lidgett SANDY LA GREENF 63 **33**

61 62

River Maun

Clipstone Junction

Halfmoon Plantation

ARCHWAY GRO

ROAD

Eastfield Farm

Eastfield Cottage

B6030

Holly Farm

ROBIN

ROAD

1

Ash Tree Farm

³65

South Forest Farm

2

CLIPSTONE

Cattle Grid

Forestry Holdings

Preston Lodge

Preston Pens

SOUTH FOREST

Fir Tree Farm

Forestry Holdings

Forest Walks Cycle Route

Culloden Farm

3

Culloden

Culloden Plantation

³64

Lindleys Plantation

SHERWOOD FOREST HOLIDAY VILLAGE

4

P

Sherwood Pines Visitors Centre

Cremorne Wood

estry ngs

Blooms Gorse

5

NG22

63

TONE FOREST

Blooms Gorse Cottage

6

Blooms Gorse Farm

WOOD   PINES

7

REST   PARK

ROAD

62

F **G** **H** ▽43 Rufford **J** **K**

Birch Row

EAKRING

61 62 63

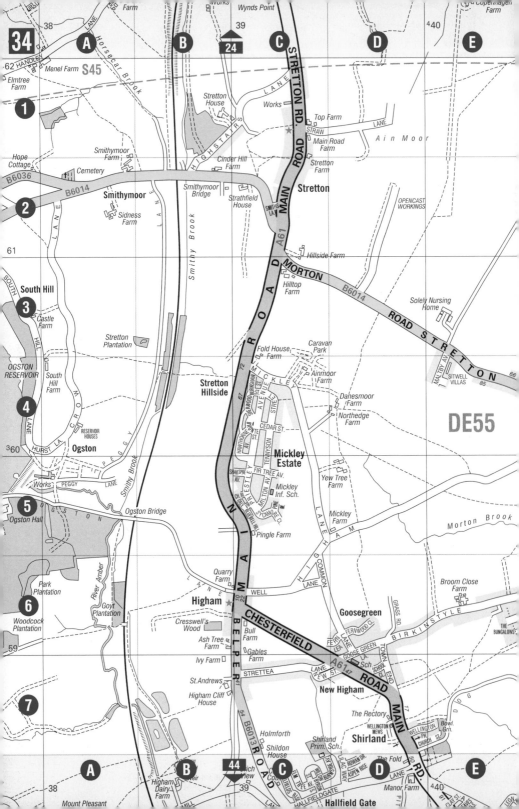

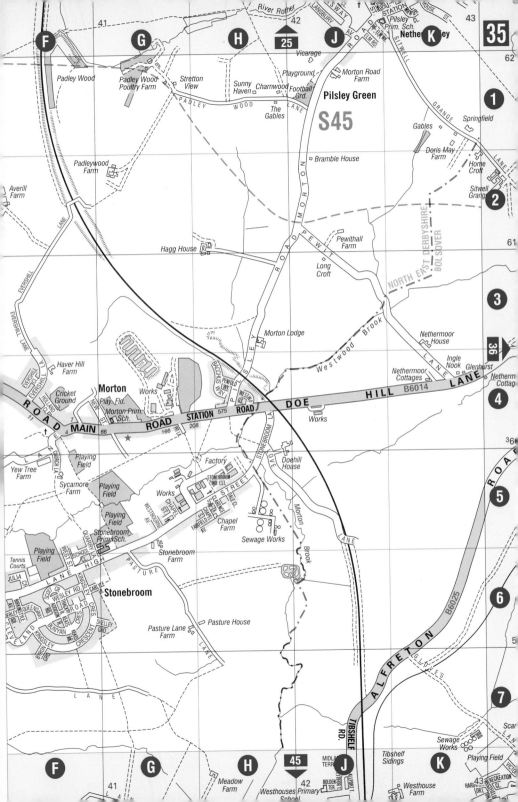

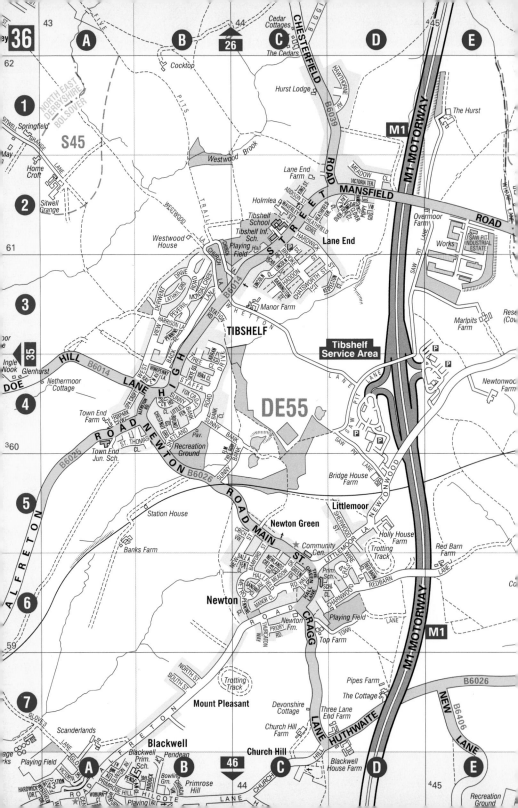

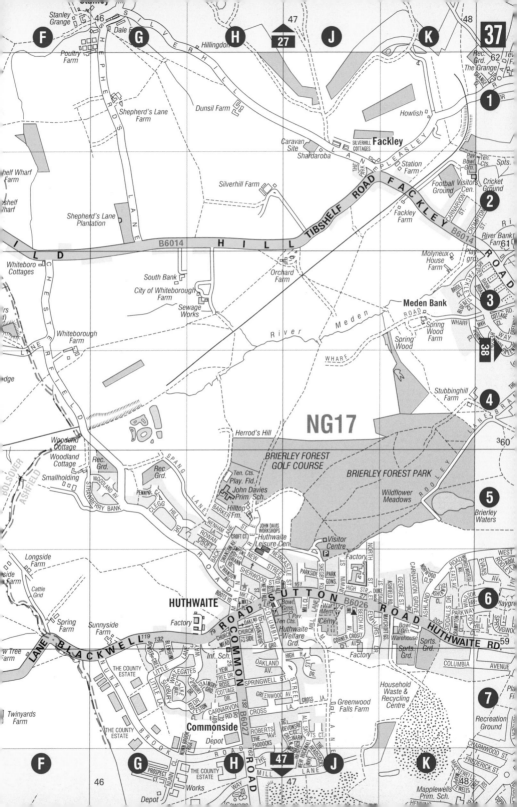

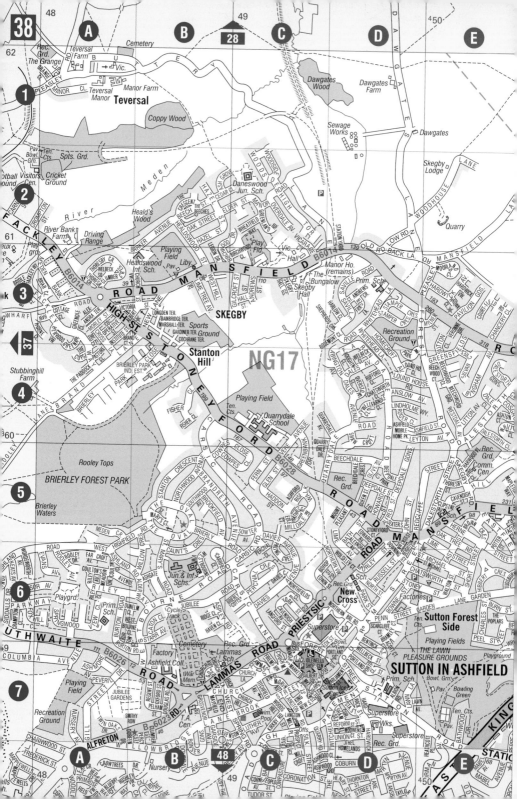

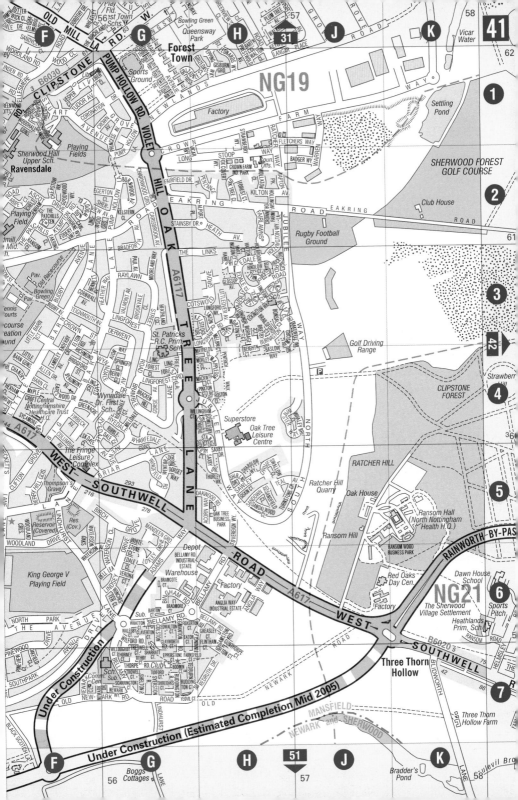

58   59   460

A   B   **32**   C   D   E

62 Vicar
Water

1

NG18

SHERWOOD FOREST
GOLF COURSE

S H E R W

F O R E

Long Plantation

2

MANSFIELD
NEWARK and SHERWOOD

E   K   R   N   G

61

3

41

CLIPSTONE FOREST

Strawberry
Hill

4

Slurry
Pond

NG21

Coal Stocking
Area

60

5

6

Dawn House
School

Sports
Pitch

Heathlands
Prim. Sch.

9

RANSOM   ROAD

Works

Rainworth
Nursery

Nursery
Cottage

WOODLANDS PARK
HOMES

Spring Hill

Filter
Beds

Sewage
Works

Water

Rainworth

R A I N W O R T H

BIRCHWOOD PARK
HOMES

A617

7

Three Thorn
Hollow Farm

SOUTHWELL

B6020

THE CLOSE

HELMSLEY

LEEWAY CL.

LARGE CL.

FARNSWORTH AV.

FIRST AV.

SECOND AV.

THIRD AV.

PAXTONS

FOURTH AV.

ROAD

Heathlands
First Sch.

Works

Bishopshill Plantation

EAST

CHURCHFIELD

B Y - P A S S

K I R

A   B   **52**   C   D   E

Foulevil Brook

58   KIRKLINGTON   ROAD   460

Hall   Python
Hill Jun

RUFFORD

LIME TREE
PL.

FOREST

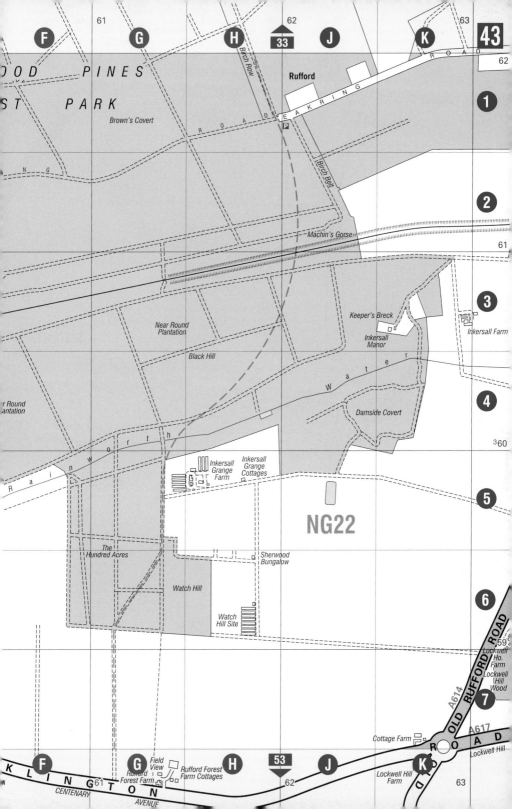

43

F   G   H   ▲33   J   K

61   62   63

62

Rufford

OOD   PINES

ST   PARK

Brown's Covert

Birch Row

EAKRING ROAD

ROAD

1

N G

Birch Belt

2

61

Machin's Gorse

3

Keeper's Breck

Inkersall Farm

Near Round
Plantation

Inkersall
Manor

Black Hill

Water

4

Damside Covert

³60

Round
antation

R   a   i   n   w   o   r   t   h

Inkersall
Grange
Farm

Inkersall
Grange
Cottages

5

NG22

The
Hundred Acres

Sherwood
Bungalow

6

Watch Hill

OLD RUFFORD ROAD

Watch
Hill Site

Lockwell
Ho.
Farm

59

Lockwell
Hill
Wood

7

A614

A617

Cottage Farm

ROAD

Lockwell Hill

F   G   Field
View   H   ▼53   J   K

Rufford Forest
Farm Cottages

Lockwell Hill
Farm

KLINGTON

Rufford
Forest Farm

61

62   63

CENTENARY
AVENUE

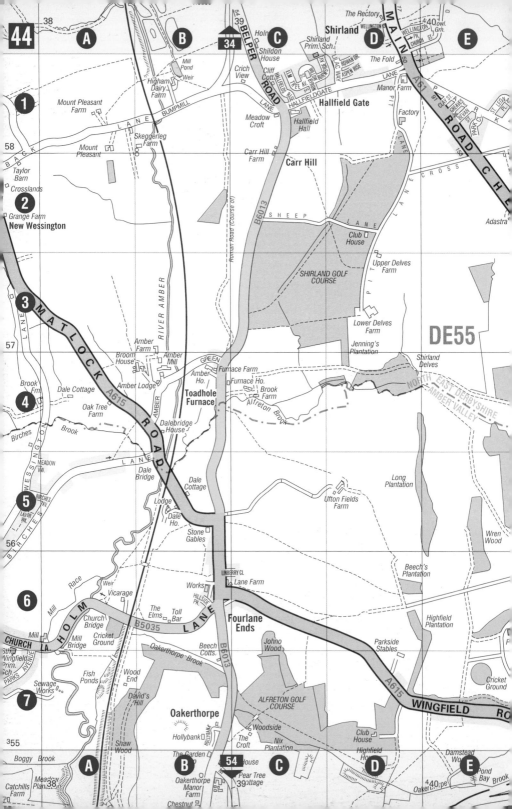

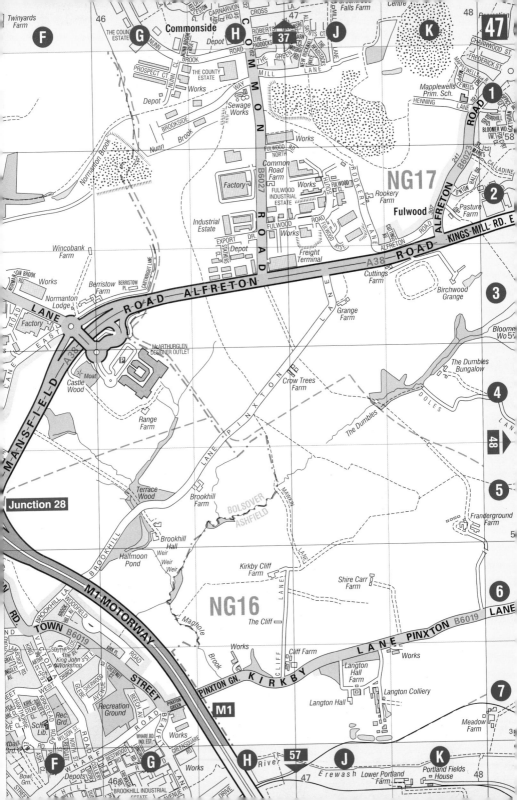

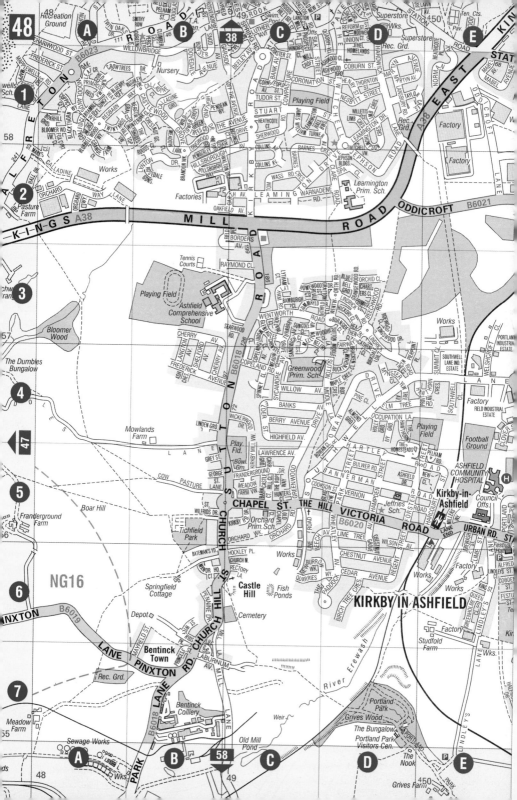

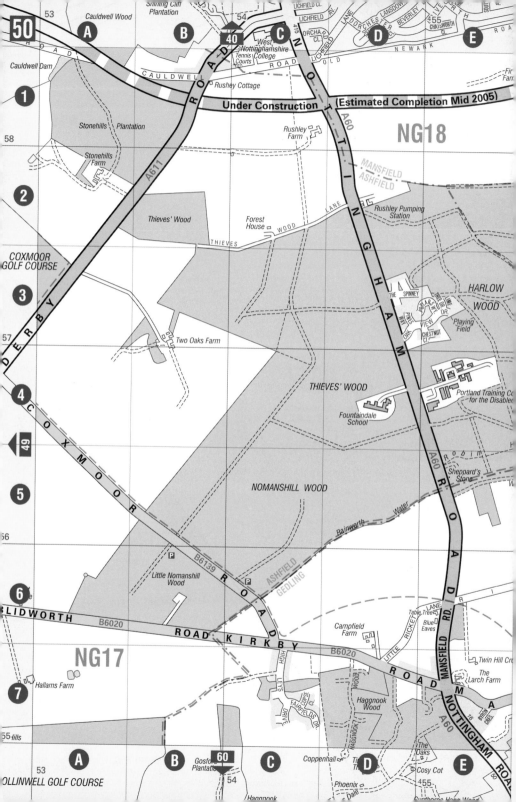

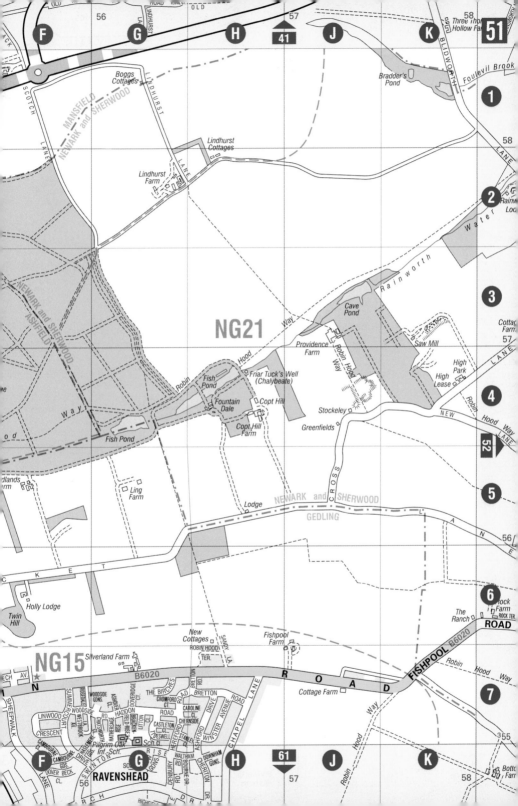

Grid references (top): F 61 G H 62 [43] J Cottage Farm K OLD ROAD 63 **53**

Grid references (right, top to bottom): 1 58 2 3 57 4 5 56 6 7 355

Grid references (bottom): F G 61 H 62 J OLLERTON RD. NG25 K 63

Labels on the map

- LINGTON
- CENTENARY AVENUE A617
- Field View
- Rufford Forest Farm
- Rufford Forest Farm Cottages
- Lockwell Hill Wood
- Lockwell Hill
- Lockwell Hill Farm
- A614 RUFFORD ROAD
- Little Allamoor Farm
- Allamoor Farm
- Cattle Grid
- The Court House
- Forest Farm
- Farnsfield House
- White Post Modern Farm Centre
- Nursery Cottage
- **NG22**
- White Post
- Boundary Farm
- Lurcher Farm
- Hood Way
- Hill House Farm
- Robin
- Sewage Works
- Hill Top Site
- Poultry Houses
- Forest Farm
- A614
- P
- FAULKER LANE
- LONGLAND LA.
- Longland Farm
- Baulker Farm
- Warren Hill
- RUFFORD ROAD
- A614 OLD ROAD
- OLLERTON RD.
- A6097
- **NG25**
- Combs Farm
- Settlement
- ROB LA.
- Haywood Oaks Forest Walks

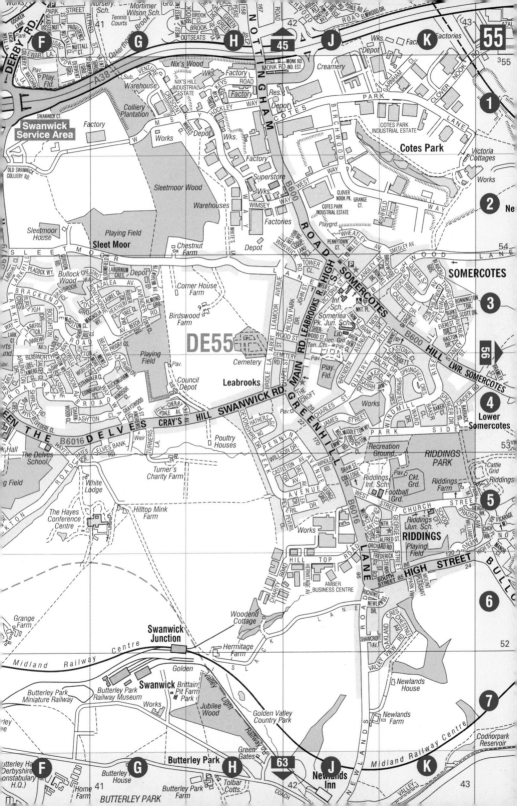

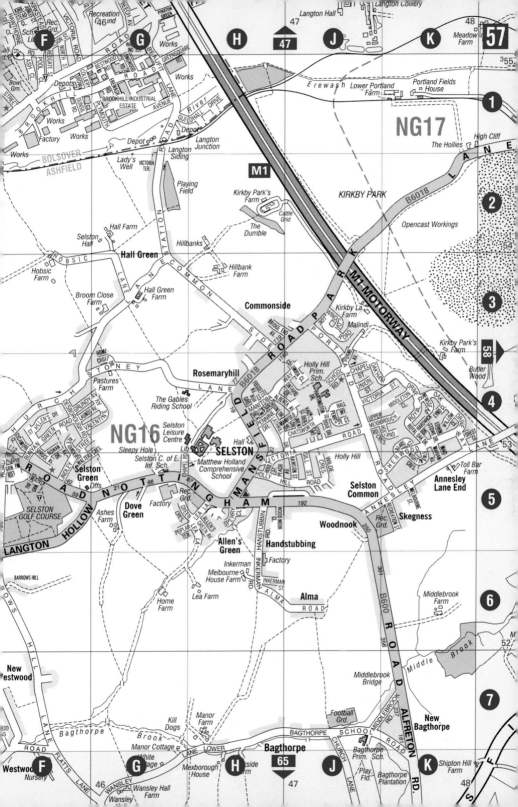

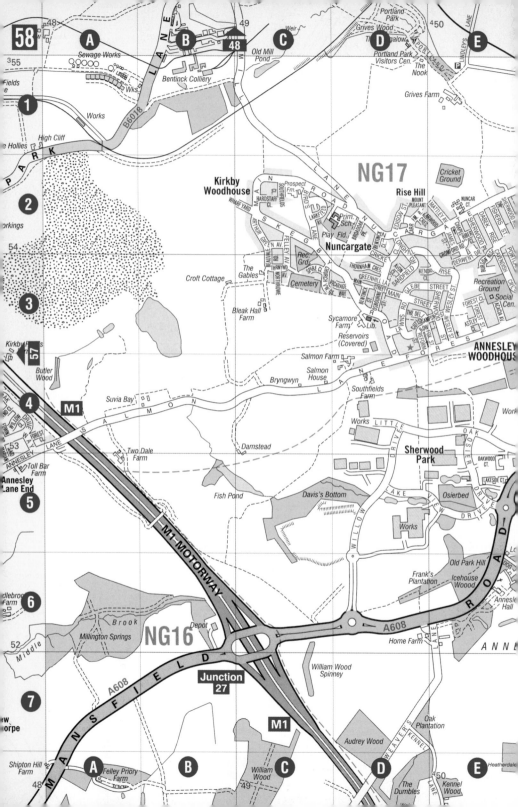

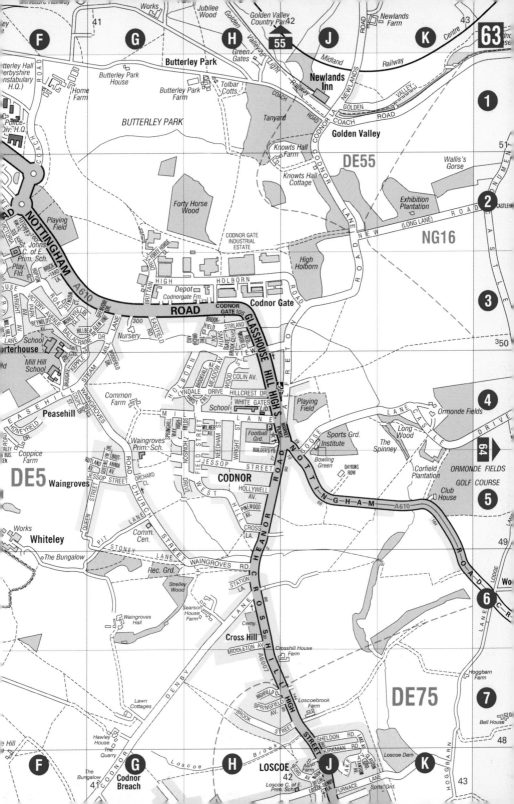

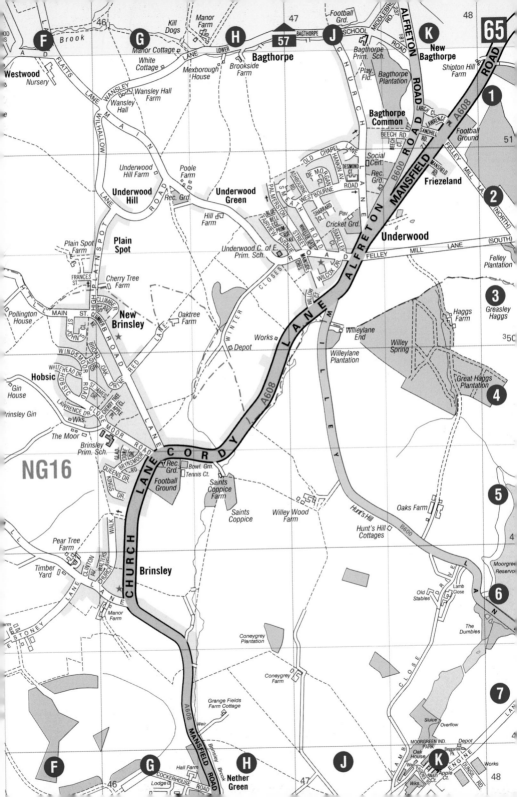

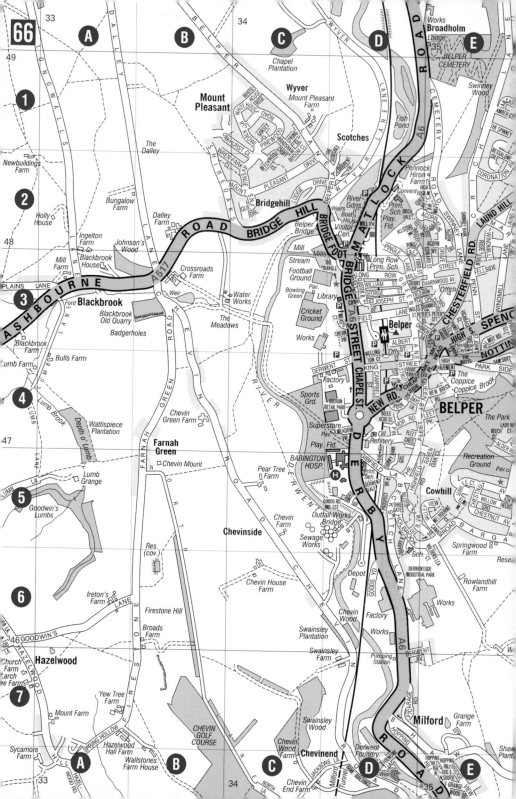

INDEX

Including Streets, Places & Areas, Hospitals & Hospices, Industrial Estates,
Selected Flats & Walkways and Selected Places of Interest.

HOW TO USE THIS INDEX

1. Each street name is followed by its Posttown or Postal Locality and then its map reference; e.g. Abbey Rd. *Blid* . . . .5D **52** is in the Blidworth Postal Locality and is to be found in square 5D on page **52**. The page number being shown in bold type.

2. A strict alphabetical order is followed with Abbreviations in Italics with the thoroughfare to which it is so on) are read in full and as part of the street name; e.g. Amberley Ct. appears after Amber Heights but before Amber Pl.

3. Streets and a selection of flats and walkways too small to be shown on the maps, appear in the index in *Italics* with the thoroughfare to which it is connected shown in brackets; e.g. *Bk. Wyver La. Belp* . . . .2D **66** (off Wyver La.)

4. Places and areas are shown in the index in **blue type** and the map reference is to the actual map square in which the town centre or area is located and not to the place name shown on the map; e.g. Alfreton 6G 45

5. An example of a selected place of interest is Alfreton Heritage Cen. 6G 45

6. An example of a hospital or hospice is ASHFIELD COMMUNITY HOSPITAL 5E 48

GENERAL ABBREVIATIONS

All : Alley	Ct : Court	Lit : Little	Rd : Road
App : Approach	Cres : Crescent	Lwr : Lower	Shop : Shopping
Arc : Arcade	Cft : Croft	Mc : Mac	S : South
Av : Avenue	Dri : Drive	Mnr : Manor	Sq : Square
Bk : Back	E : East	Mans : Mansions	Sta : Station
Boulevd : Boulevard	Embkmt : Embankment	Mkt : Market	St : Street
Bri : Bridge	Est : Estate	Mdw : Meadow	Ter : Terrace
B'way : Broadway	Fld : Field	M : Mews	Trad : Trading
Bldgs : Buildings	Gdns : Gardens	Mt : Mount	Up : Upper
Bus : Business	Gth : Garth	Mus : Museum	Va : Vale
Cvn : Caravan	Ga : Gate	N : North	Vw : View
Cen : Centre	Gt : Great	Pal : Palace	Vs : Villas
Chu : Church	Grn : Green	Pde : Parade	Vis : Visitors
Chyd : Churchyard	Gro : Grove	Pk : Park	Wlk : Walk
Circ : Circle	Ho : House	Pas : Passage	W : West
Cir : Circus	Ind : Industrial	Pl : Place	Yd : Yard
Clo : Close	Info : Information	Quad : Quadrant	
Comn : Common	Junct : Junction	Res : Residential	
Cotts : Cottages	La : Lane	Ri : Rise	

POSTTOWN AND POSTAL LOCALITY ABBREVIATIONS

Alf : Alfreton	*E'ly* : Edingley	*Mans W* : Mansfield Woodhouse	*Scarc* : Scarcliffe
Ambgt : Ambergate	*Edwin* : Edwinstowe	*Mare* : Marehay	*Sels* : Selston
Ann : Annesley	*Farn* : Farnsfield	*Med V* : Meden Vale	*Shire* : Shirebrook
Ark T : Arkwright Town	*For T* : Forest Town	*Milf* : Milford	*Shirl* : Shirland
Asvr : Ashover	*Glap* : Glapwell	*Mort* : Morton	*Shot G* : Shottle Gate
Askh : Askham	*Gras* : Grassmoor	*Neth L* : Nether Langwith	*Skeg* : Skegby
Bagt : Bagthorpe	*Grn L* : Green Line Ind. Est.	*N Hou* : New Houghton	*Sook* : Sookholme
Belp : Belper	*Har W* : Harlow Wood	*New O* : New Ollerton	*S Norm* : South Normanton
B'thpe : Bilsthorpe	*Has* : Hasland	*News V* : Newstead Village	*S Wing* : South Wingfield
Black : Blackbrook	*Haz* : Hazelwood	*Newt* : Newthorpe	*Stanf* : Stanfree
B'wll : Blackwell	*Heage* : Heage	*Nwtn* : Newton	*Stan H* : Stanton Hill
Blid : Blidworth	*Heath* : Heath	*New T* : New Tupton	*Stav* : Staveley
Bsvr : Bolsover	*Hghm* : Higham	*Nix H* : Nixs Hill Ind. Est.	*Ston* : Stonebroom
Boug : Boughton	*Hilc* : Hilcote	*N Wing* : North Wingfield	*Stre* : Stretton
Brac : Brackenfield	*Holb* : Holbrook	*Nor* : Norton	*Sut A* : Sutton-in-Ashfield
Brins : Brinsley	*Hlmwd* : Holmewood	*Oake* : Oakerthorpe	*Sut S* : Sutton Scarsdale
Bud : Budby	*Hors* : Horsley	*Old C* : Old Clipstone	*Swanw* : Swanwick
But : Butterley	*Hors W* : Horsley Woodhouse	*Old T* : Old Tupton	*Temp N* : Temple Normanton
Cal : Calow	*Huth* : Huthwaite	*Oll* : Ollerton	*Tev* : Teversal
Ches : Chesterfield	*Iron* : Ironville	*Oxt* : Oxton	*Tib* : Tibshelf
Chur W : Church Warsop	*Jack* : Jacksdale	*Pal* : Palterton	*Turn* : Turnditch
Clay C : Clay Cross	*Klbrn* : Kilburn	*Pap* : Papplewick	*Up L* : Upper Langwith
Clip V : Clipstone Village	*Kirk A* : Kirkby-in-Ashfield	*Pent* : Pentrich	*Und* : Underwood
Cod : Codnor	*Lan M* : Langley Mill	*Pils* : Pilsley	*Wain* : Waingroves
Cor : Corbriggs	*Lang* : Langwith	*Pinx* : Pinxton	*Wars* : Warsop
Cow L : Cowers Lane	*Lang J* : Langwith Junction	*Ple* : Pleasley	*Wars V* : Warsop Vale
Cuc : Cuckney	*Lea* : Leabrooks	*Ple V* : Pleasley Vale	*W'low* : Wellow
Dane : Danesmoor	*L'by* : Linby	*Pool* : Poolsbrook	*Wess* : Wessington
Den : Denby	*Los* : Loscoe	*Pye B* : Pye Bridge	*Westh* : Westhouses
Den V : Denby Village	*Lwr H* : Lower Hartshay	*Rain* : Rainworth	*W'wd* : Westwood
Doe L : Doe Lea	*Lwr K* : Lower Kilburn	*R'hd* : Ravenshead	*Wing* : Wingerworth
Duck : Duckmanton	*Lwr P* : Lower Pilsley	*Ridd* : Riddings	
Duf : Duffield	*Mak* : Makeney	*Rip* : Ripley	
E'wd : Eastwood	*Mans* : Mansfield	*Ruff* : Rufford	

A

Abbeydale Dri. *Mans* 6D **40**	Abbey Rd. *News V* 5J **59**
Abbey Rd. *Blid* 5D **52**	Abbots Gro. *Belp* 2E **66**
Abbey Rd. *Edwin* 6K **21**	Abbott Lea. *Mans* 1H **39**
Abbey Clo. *S Norm* 5D **46**	Abbey Rd. *Kirk A* 5G **49**	Abbott Rd. *Alf* 7H **45**
Abbey Ct. *Mans* 2F **41**	Abbey Rd. *Mans* 2E **40**	Abbott Rd. *Mans* 2G **39**

Abbotts Cft. *Mans* 7J **29**
Aberconway St. *Blid* 5C **52**
Abington Av. *Sut A* 4D **38**
Acacia Av. *Kirk A* 3E **58**
Acacia Ct. *For T* 7E **30**

Acacia Dri.—Bathurst Rd.

Acacia Dri. *Lwr P* 5H **25**
Acer Clo. *Pinx* 7E **46**
Acorn Bus. Pk. *Mans* 3B **40**
Acorn Dri. *Belp* 2E **66**
Acorn Ridge. *Shire* 2H **17**
Acorn Way. *Belp* 2E **66**
Acorn Way. *Mans* 5H **41**
Acreage La. *Shire* 5J **17**
Acres Rd. *Lwr P* 5H **25**
Acres, The. *Lwr P* 4H **25**
Acre, The. *Kirk A* 7F **49**
Adams Way. *Mans* 6G **41**
Addison Dri. *Alf* 6H **45**
Addison Rd. *Ston* 6F **35**
Addison St. *Tib* 2C **36**
Adelaide Wlk. *Iron* 7B **56**
Adlington Av. *Wing* 5C **12**
Adrians Clo. *Mans* 4E **40**
Alandale Av. *Lang J* 2K **17**
Albany Clo. *Mans W* 7C **30**
Albany Dri. *Mans W* 7C **30**
Albany Pl. *Mans W* 7C **30**
Alberta Av. *Sels* 4H **57**
Albert Av. *Jack* 7D **56**
Albert Clo. *Kirk A* 2G **59**
Albert Rd. *Rip* 2C **62**
Albert Sq. *Mans W* 4C **30**
Albert Sq. *Sut A* 7C **38**
Albert St. *Belp* 3D **66**
Albert St. *Iron* 6B **56**
(in two parts)
Albert St. *Lea* 3H **55**
Albert St. *Mans* 3B **40**
Albert St. *Mans W* 4C **30**
Albert St. *Rip* 3E **62**
Albert St. *S Norm* 4C **46**
Albert St. *Stan H* 3A **38**
Albert St. *Wars* 2H **19**
Albine Rd. *Lang J* 1H **17**
Albion Rd. *Sut A* 7D **38**
Albion St. *Mans* 7A **30**
Albion St. *Rip* 3E **62**
Alcock Av. *Mans* 2D **40**
Aldercar. 7D 64
Aldercar La. *Lan M* 5B **64**
Alder Clo. *For T* 7E **30**
Alder Clo. *Shire* 2H **17**
Alder Ct. *Sut A* 4H **39**
Alder Gro. *Mans W* 3B **30**
Alder Gro. *New O* 2H **23**
Alder Rd. *Belp* 4E **66**
Alder Way. *Shire* 2H **17**
Alder Way. *Sut A* 6B **38**
Alexander Av. *Sels* 4F **57**
Alexander Ter. *Pinx* 2E **56**
Alexandra Av. *Mans* 5B **40**
Alexandra Av. *Mans W* 4B **30**
Alexandra Av. *Sut A* 5D **38**
Alexandra St. *Kirk A* 4F **49**
Alexandra St. *Wars* 2G **19**
Alexandra Ter. *Stan H* 3A **38**
Alfred Ct. *Mans* 2B **40**
Alfred Rd. *Klbrn* 7K **67**
Alfred St. *Alf* 7F **45**
Alfred St. *Kirk A* 6E **48**
Alfred St. *Pinx* 6E **46**
Alfred St. *Ridd* 5K **55**
Alfred St. *Rip* 2E **62**
Alfred St. *S Norm* 5B **46**
Alfred St. *Sut A* 5D **38**
Alfreton. **6G 45**
ALFRETON GOLF COURSE. 7D 44
ALFRETON HERITAGE CEN. 6G 45
ALFRETON LEISURE CEN. 6F 45
Alfreton Rd. *Alf* 4F **45**
Alfreton Rd. *B'wll & Tib* 7J **35**
Alfreton Rd. *Cod* 4J **63**
Alfreton Rd. *Huth* 3H **47**
Alfreton Rd. *Pinx* 6E **46**
Alfreton Rd. *Pye B & Sels* 5C **56**
Alfreton Rd. *S Norm* 5A **46**
Alfreton Rd. *Und* 7K **57**
Alices Vw. *N Wing* 7G **13**
Allcroft St. *Mans W* 4C **30**
Allendale Rd. *Rain* 2D **52**
Allendale Way. *For T* 7E **30**
Allen Dri. *Mans* 4F **41**
Allen's Green. **5H 57**
Allen's Grn. Av. *Sels* 5H **57**
Allington Dri. *Mans* 2H **39**
Allissa Av. *Rip* 5E **62**
Allport Ter. *Westh* 1J **45**
All Saints Ct. *Huth* 7J **37**
Allstone Lee. *Belp* 2D **66**
Allwood Clo. *Mans* 1E **40**
Alma. 6J 57
Alma Rd. *N Wing* 7G **13**
Alma Rd. *Sels* 6H **57**
Alma St. *Alf* 6G **45**
Alma St. *N Wing* 2E **24**
Alma St. *Rip* 1D **62**
Almond Av. *Rip* 4D **62**
Almond Av. *Shire* 2J **17**
Almond Gro. *Kirk A* 4D **48**
Almond Gro. *Swanw* 3G **55**
Almond Ri. *For T* 7E **30**
Alport Clo. *Belp* 2F **67**
Alport Pl. *Mans* 2H **41**
Althorp Clo. *Swanw* 4F **55**
Alton Rd. *Belp* 3G **67**
Amber Bus. Cen. *Ridd* 6J **55**
Amber Clo. *Rain* 1E **52**
Amber Ct. *Belp* 1E **66**
Amber Grn. *S Wing* 4B **44**
Amber Gro. *Alf* 1F **55**
Amber Heights. *Rip* 2C **62**
Amberley Ct. *For T* 6K **31**
Amber Pl. *Clay C* 4A **24**
Ambleside. *New O* 2G **23**
Ambleside Dri. *Bsvr* 5H **5**
Amethyst Clo. *Rain* 1E **52**
Andover Rd. *Mans* 3G **39**
Andrew Dri. *Blid* 6C **52**
Angela Av. *Kirk A* 2F **59**
Anglia Way. *Mans* 6H **41**
Anglia Way. Ind. Est. *Mans* 6H **41**
Ankerbold Rd. *Old T* 7D **12**
Annesley. 3F 59
Annesley Cutting. *Ann* 3F **59**
Annesley La. *Sels* 5J **57**
Annesley Lane End. **5K 57**
Annesley Rd. *Ann* 5F **59**
(in two parts)
Annesley Way. *Mans* 3H **39**
Annesley Woodhouse. **3D 58**
Anslow Av. *Sut A* 4D **38**
Appian Way. *Clay C* 6B **24**
Appin Rd. *Mans* 4H **39**
Appleby Rd. *N Hou* 2D **28**
Appleton Dri. *Belp* 1F **67**
Appleton Rd. *Blid* 5D **52**
Appleton St. *Wars* 3H **19**
Applewood Clo. *Belp* 2F **67**
Arbour Clo. *Ches* 1D **12**
Arcadia Av. *Shire* 2J **17**
Archway Gro. *Old C* 1F **33**
Archway Rd. *Old C* 1F **33**
Argyle Clo. *Wars* 2F **19**
Argyle St. *Mans* 3D **40**
Argyll Pl. *Rip* 2E **62**
Argyll Rd. *Rip* 2E **62**
Arkwright Av. *Belp* 1G **67**
Arkwright Town. **3A 4**
Arlington Av. *Mans W* 5E **30**
Arlington Dri. *Swanw* 4F **55**
Armstrong Rd. *Mans* 2H **39**
Arran Ct. *Tib* 4B **36**
Arran Sq. *Mans* 4H **39**
Arthur Grn. Av. *Kirk A* 2C **58**
Arthur St. *Alf* 5G **45**
Arthur St. *Mans* 3C **40**
Arthur St. *Pinx* 7F **47**
Arthurs Vw. *Iron* 7B **56**
Arun Dale. *Mans W* 5D **30**
Arundel Dri. *Mans* 1K **39**
Ascot Clo. *Kirk A* 7G **49**
Ascot Dri. *Mans* 2F **41**
Ash Acre. *Belp* 3H **67**
Ashbourne Av. *Clay C* 3A **24**
Ashbourne Ct. *Shire* 3K **17**
Ashbourne Rd. *Turn & Cow L* 3A **66**
Ashbourne Rd. *Und* 2J **65**
Ashbourne St. *Shire* 3K **17**
Ashby Av. *Mans W* 3D **30**
Ash Clo. *Pinx* 1F **57**
Ashcourt Gdns. *Sut A* 5F **39**
Ash Cres. *Kirk A* 4B **48**
Ash Cres. *Rip* 4D **62**
Ashcroft Ct. *Sut A* 5F **39**
Ashdene Gdns. *Belp* 2G **67**
Asher La. *Pent* 5C **54**
Asher La. *Rip* 7D **54**
Ashfield Av. *Mans* 1B **40**
Ashfield Av. *Som* 2K **55**
ASHFIELD COMMUNITY HOSPITAL. 5E 48
Ashfield Dri. *Kirk A* 5D **48**
Ashfield Mobile Home Pk. *Sut A* 4D **38**
Ashfield Precinct. *Kirk A* 5F **49**
Ashfield Rd. *Huth* 6K **37**
Ash Fields. *Belp* 5E **66**
Ashfield St. *Sut A* 4D **38**
Ashford Av. *N Wing* 1G **25**
Ashford Dri. *R'hd* 7H **51**
Ashford Ri. *Belp* 1G **67**
Ashford Ri. *Sut A* 5C **38**
Ashgate. *Sut A* 6B **38**
Ash Gro. *Brins* 4F **65**
Ash Gro. *Sels* 4H **57**
Ash Gro. *Shire* 2H **17**
Ash Gro. *Sut A* 2B **38**
Ashland Rd. *Sut A* 6A **38**
Ashland Rd. W. *Sut A* 6K **37**
Ashlands Clo. *Sut A* 6K **37**
Ashleigh Way. *Mans W* 6G **31**
Ashmore Av. *Sut A* 7A **38**
Ashop Rd. *Belp* 2H **67**
Ashover Clo. *R'hd* 7G **51**
Ashover Rd. *Clay C & Old T* 2A **24**
Ashover Vw. *Westh* 1J **45**
Ashton Clo. *Swanw* 4F **55**
Ashton Ct. *Sut A* 4E **38**
Ashton Gdns. *Old T* 2B **24**
Ashton Rd. *Dane* 4E **24**
Ashton Way. *Belp* 3H **67**
Ashtree Av. *Mans W* 3C **30**
Ash Tree Vw. *N Wing* 1G **25**
Ashwell Av. *Mans W* 3E **30**
Ashwell Ter. *Blid* 6B **52**
Ashwood Av. *Kirk A* 4G **49**
Ashwood Clo. *Mans W* 3E **30**
Ashwood Clo. *Sut A* 1C **48**
Ashwood Gro. *Sut A* 1C **48**
Ashworth Dri. *Mans W* 4E **30**
Askew La. *Wars* 4G **19**
Aspen Ct. *For T* 7E **30**
Aspen Ri. *Shirl* 1D **44**
Aspley Rd. *Sut A* 6B **38**
Asquith M. *Mans* 3E **40**
Asquith St. *Mans* 3E **40**
Astley Clo. *Kirk A* 3E **58**
Astlow Dri. *Belp* 1F **67**
Astwith. **3C 26**
Astwith Clo. *Hlmwd* 6B **14**
Astwith La. *Pils* 3C **26**
Atkin La. *Mans* 6B **40**
Attlee Av. *For T* 7G **31**
Audrey Cres. *Mans W* 3B **30**
Ault Hucknall. **1H 27**
Ault Hucknall La. *Doe L* 1H **27**
Austin Clo. *Mans* 1E **40**
Austin St. *Shire* 3A **18**
Avenue, The. *Belp* 5D **66**
Avenue, The. *Mans* 6D **40**
Avenue, The. *Sut A* 1B **48**
Averham Clo. *Mans* 3H **39**
Avon Clo. *Kirk A* 3D **58**
Avondale. *Mans* 2E **40**
Avondale Rd. *Bsvr* 6J **5**
Avon Way. *Mans* 4G **41**
Ayncourt Rd. *N Wing* 1H **25**
Azalea Av. *Swanw* 3G **55**
Azalea Clo. *Som* 7A **46**

B

Babbington St. *Tib* 3C **36**
BABINGTON HOSPITAL. 5D 66
Babworth Ct. *Mans* 2D **40**
Bacchus Way. *Mort* 4H **35**
Back Cft. *Dane* 6E **24**
Back La. *Glap* 6K **15**
Back La. *Huth* 6H **37**
Back La. *Oll* 4F **23**
Back La. *Pal* 1K **15**
Back La. *Pent* 5C **54**
Back La. *Pils* 6J **25**
Back La. *Sut A* 3D **38**
Back La. *Tib* 4B **36**
Back La. *Wess* 2A **44**
Bk. Wyver La. Belp *2D 66*
(off Wyver La.)
Bacon La. *Rip* 5B **54**
Bacon's Spring. 7B 24
Badger Way. *For T* 2J **41**
Baggaley Cres. *Mans* 7B **30**
Bagshaw St. *Ple* 3F **29**
Bagthorpe. 7J 57
Bagthorpe Common. **1K 65**
Bailey Cres. *Mans* 2J **39**
Bainbridge Rd. *Bsvr* 5H **5**
Bainbridge Rd. *Wars* 3H **19**
Bainbridge Ter. *Huth* 3B **38**
Baker Clo. *Som* 4K **55**
Baker La. *Cuc* 3G **9**
Baker Rd. *Mans W* 2C **30**
Bakewell Wlk. *Mans* 3J **41**
Balderton Ct. *Mans* 2J **39**
Baldwin Clo. *For T* 6H **31**
Balfour St. *Kirk A* 6G **49**
Balkham La. *Mans* 5E **16**
Ballacraine Dri. *Rip* 3F **63**
Ballater Clo. *Mans* 6J **29**
Ball Hill. *S Norm* 4D **46**
Balls La. *Kirk A* 1F **59**
Balmoral Clo. *Mans W* 3E **30**
Balmoral Dri. *Mans* 6J **29**
Balmoral Lodge. *Mans* 6J **29**
Bamburgh Clo. *Kirk A* 3C **48**
Bamford Av. *N Wing* 1F **25**
Bamford Dri. *Mans* 3H **41**
Bamford St. *Nwtn* 6C **36**
Bamford St. *Rip* 5D **62**
Banchory Clo. *Mans* 6J **29**
Bancroft Ho. Mans *2A 40*
(off Connexion, The)
Bancroft La. *Mans* 2K **39**
Bank Av. *Sut A* 1C **48**
Bank Bldgs. *Milf* 7D **66**
Bank Clo. *Bsvr* 3J **5**
Bank Clo. *Shire* 3K **17**
Bank Clo. *Tib* 4B **36**
Banks Av. *Kirk A* 4C **48**
Bank St. *Som* 3J **55**
Bannerman Rd. *Kirk A* 5D **48**
Barbers Wood Clo. *R'hd* 2G **61**
Bargate. 6G 67
Bargate Clo. *Belp* 6G **67**
Bargate Rd. *Belp* 5E **66**
Barker Av. *Jack* 7D **56**
Barker Av. *Sut A* 3B **38**
Barker St. *Huth* 5H **37**
Barley Cft. *Belp* 5F **67**
Barley Cft. *S Norm* 6D **46**
Barley M. *Mans W* 2E **30**
Barn Clo. *Mans* 4F **41**
Barn Ct. *Kirk A* 5C **48**
Barnes Cres. *Sut A* 2C **48**
Barnfield Clo. *Hlmwd* 7A **14**
Barn Owl Clo. *Chur W* 1J **19**
Barons Dri. *Boug* 1K **23**
Barrack Yd. *Som* 4K **55**
Barringer Rd. *For T & Mans* 6E **30**
Barrowhill Wlk. Mans *3H 41*
(off Beeley Clo.)
Barrows Green. 6E 56
Barrows Hill. *W'wd* 6F **57**
Barrows Hill La. *W'wd* 6F **57**
Barton Clo. *For T* 7H **31**
Barton Ct. *Mans* 6G **41**
Barton Knoll. *Belp* 4H **67**
Barton Knowle. *Belp* 3H **67**
Baslow Way. *Mans* 4H **41**
Bassett, The. *Lang J* 1J **17**
Bateman's Yd. *Kirk A* 6B **48**
Bath La. *Mans* 2C **40**
Bath La. *Sook* 5C **18**
Bath St. *Mans* 3B **40**
Bath St. *Sut A* 5D **38**
Bathurst Rd. *Bsvr* 6G **5**

Bathurst Ter. *Lang* 4K **7**
Bathwood Dri. *Mans* 4J **39**
Bathwood Dri. *Sut A* 7E **38**
Batley La. *Ple* 3C **28**
Baulker La. *Blid* 6F **53**
Baulker La. *Clip V* 4D **32**
Baum's La. *Mans* 4B **40**
Baxter Hill. *Ple* 5D **28**
Baysdale Dri. *For T* 7F **31**
Beackden Clo. *Belp* 3J **67**
Beacon Ct. *New O* 4H **23**
Beacon Dri. *Kirk A* 4G **49**
Beardall St. *Mans* 2A **40**
Beardsley Rd. *Edwin* 6A **22**
        (in two parts)
Beauchief Gdns. *Som* 3K **55**
Beaufit La. *Pinx* 7G **47**
Beaulieu Way. *Swanw* 3G **55**
Beauly Dri. *Mans* 4H **39**
Beaumont Av. *Mans* 4F **41**
Beaumont Clo. *Belp* 3H **67**
Beaurepaire Cres. *Belp* 2F **67**
Beauvale Rd. *Kirk A* 3C **58**
Beazley Av. *Mans* 2K **39**
Beck Clo. *Bsvr* 4A **6**
Beck Cres. *Blid* 6C **52**
Beck Cres. *Mans* 2J **39**
Beckett Av. *Mans* 7J **29**
Beckingham Ct. *Mans* 2J **39**
        (off Kelham Rd.)
Beck La. *Blid* 6C **52**
        (in three parts)
Beck La. *Sut A* 3F **39**
Becksitch Ct. *Belp* 5D **66**
        (off Becksitch La.)
Becksitch La. *Belp* 5D **66**
Bedford Av. *Mans* 2E **40**
Beech Av. *Alf* 5G **45**
Beech Av. *Huth* 6J **37**
Beech Av. *Kirk A* 5C **48**
Beech Av. *Mans* 3B **40**
Beech Av. *New O* 3G **23**
Beech Av. *Oll* 2D **22**
Beech Av. *Pinx* 7G **47**
Beech Av. *R'hd* 7F **51**
Beech Av. *Rip* 2C **62**
Beech Clo. *Belp* 4E **66**
Beech Ct. *Mans* 3H **39**
Beech Ct. *Mans W* 3B **30**
Beech Ct. *Und* 1K **65**
Beech Cres. *Glap* 7K **15**
Beechdale Av. *Sut A* 5D **38**
Beechdale Cres. *Sut A* 5D **38**
Beechdale Rd. *Alf* 7J **45**
Beechdale Rd. *Mans W* 6G **31**
Beech Dri. *Ark T* 3A **4**
Beeches, The. *Sut A* 2B **38**
Beech Gro. *Blid* 5E **52**
Beech Gro. *Duck* 2C **4**
Beech Gro. *S Norm* 5D **46**
Beech Hill Av. *Mans* 7K **29**
Beech Hill Cres. *Mans* 6K **29**
Beech Hill Dri. *Mans* 7K **29**
Beech Rd. *Und* 1K **65**
Beech St. *Sut A* 2B **38**
Beech Ter. *Shire* 3K **17**
Beech Tree Av. *Mans W* 3B **30**
Beech Way. *Mans* 6E **24**
Beechwood Clo. *Belp* 2C **66**
Beechwood Clo. *For T* 7G **31**
Beechwood Clo. *Sut A* 4E **38**
Beechwood Ct. *Sut A* 4E **38**
Beechwood Gro. *Sut A* 4E **38**
Beechwood Rd. *Kirk A* 3D **48**
Beeley Av. *Sut A* 1C **48**
Beeley Clo. *Belp* 1G **67**
Beeley Clo. *Mans* 3H **41**
Beeley Clo. *N Wing* 1G **25**
Beggarlee Pk. *Newt* 7K **65**
Beighton Ct. *Mans* 4H **41**
Beighton St. *Rip* 3E **62**
Beighton St. *Sut A* 6D **38**
Belfit Dri. *Wing* 5A **12**
Belfry Clo. *Kirk A* 3C **48**
Belgrave Clo. *Belp* 2G **67**
Bellamy Rd. *Mans* 6G **41**
        (in two parts)
Bellamy Rd. Ind. Est.
  Mans 6G **41**

Belle Acre Clo. *Belp* 4D **66**
Belle Vue Av. *Rip* 7C **62**
Belle Vue La. *Blid* 5C **52**
Belmont Clo. *Mans W* 6G **31**
Belmont Rd. *Kirk A* 2F **59**
Belper. 3E **66**
Belper La. *Belp* 1B **66**
Belper Rd. *Belp & Holb* 6G **67**
Belper Rd. *Klbrn* 5J **67**
        (in two parts)
Belper Rd. *Shirl* 6C **34**
Belper St John's Chapel
  Heritage Cen. 3E **66**
Belper St. *Mans* 2D **40**
Belper Way. *Mans* 2D **40**
Belpher Sports Cen. 3H **67**
Belton Dri. *Rip* 3E **62**
Belvedere Clo. *Swanw* 4F **55**
Belvedere Ho. *Mans* 2A **40**
        (off Connexion, The)
Belvedere St. *Mans* 3B **40**
Belvoir Way. *Som* 2J **55**
Benjamin Outram Bus. Cen.
  . . . . .4E **62**
Bennett Av. *Mans* 3F **41**
Bennington Wlk. *Mans W* 4E **30**
Bennison Gdns. *Dane* 5D **24**
Bentinck Clo. *Boug* 1J **23**
Bentinck St. *Kirk A* 2D **58**
Bentinck St. *Kirk A* 3D **58**
Bentinck St. *Mans* 3D **40**
Bentinck St. *Sut A* 6D **38**
Bentinck Ter. *Wars* 4H **19**
Bentinck Town. 7B **48**
Bentley Clo. *Alf* 7H **45**
Beresford Clo. *Dane* 6D **24**
Beresford Rd. *Mans W* 2C **30**
Beresford St. *Mans* 3D **40**
Bernard Av. *Mans W* 3B **30**
Bernard Rd. *Mans* 1H **39**
Berristow Grange. *Sut A* 1A **48**
Berristow La. *S Norm* 2E **46**
Berristow Pl. *S Norm* 3G **47**
Berry Av. *Kirk A* 4C **48**
Berry Hill. 5D **40**
Berry Hill Clo. *Mans* 5C **40**
Berry Hill Gdns. *Mans* 5F **41**
Berry Hill La. *Mans* 6C **40**
Berry Hill M. *Mans* 5D **40**
Berry Hill Rd. *Mans* 4C **40**
Berry Pk. Lea. *Mans* 6D **40**
Berry St. *N Wing* 2E **24**
Bertrand Av. *Clay C* 5D **24**
Berwick Av. *Mans* 1H **39**
Bescar La. *Oll* 4E **22**
Bessalone Dri. *Belp* 1E **66**
Besthorpe Ct. *Mans* 2J **39**
Bestwood Dri. *Clay C* 5C **24**
        (in two parts)
Bestwood Park. 5D **24**
Bestwood Pk. *Clay C* 5C **24**
Bestwood Rd. *Pinx* 1G **57**
Bethel Ct. *Mans W* 4C **30**
Beulah Rd. *Kirk A* 6F **49**
Bevan Clo. *Rain* 2D **52**
Bevan Rd. *Dane* 6D **24**
Bevan St. *Shirl* 1E **44**
Beverley Dri. *Kirk A* 7G **49**
Beverley St. *Mans* 7D **40**
Bevin Pl. *N Wing* 1G **25**
Bideford Clo. *Rip* 2C **62**
Big Barn La. *Mans* 4F **41**
Biggin Clo. *Dane* 7D **24**
Biggin La. *Tib* 7C **26**
Bilborough Rd. *Mans* 2D **40**
Billingsley Av. *Pinx* 7F **47**
Bingham Av. *Sut A* 4E **38**
Bingham Rd. *Mans* 6G **41**
Birch Av. *Rain* 1E **52**
Birch Clo. *Alf* 5G **45**
Birch Clo. *Gras* 4F **13**
Birch Clo. *R'hd* 2G **61**
Birch Clo. *Rip* 4D **62**
Birch Cft. Dri. *Mans W* 6G **31**
Birchen Holme. *S Norm* 6C **46**
Birches Av. *S Wing* 5A **44**
Birches La. *S Wing* 5A **44**
Birches, The. *R'hd* 7G **51**

Birch Gro. *Mans* 5F **41**
Birch Gro. *Shire* 2H **17**
Birchlands, The. *For T* 7F **31**
Birch Rd. *New O* 3G **23**
Birch St. *Chur W* 1F **19**
Birch Tree Clo. *For T* 5K **31**
Birch Tree Cres. *Kirk A* 6D **48**
Birch Va. *Belp* 2D **66**
Birchview Clo. *Belp* 5F **67**
Birchwood Clo. *R'hd* 2H **61**
Birchwood Clo. *S Norm* 6C **46**
Birchwood Cres. *Sut A* 3C **38**
Birchwood Cres. *Som* 3K **55**
Birchwood Dri. *R'hd* 2G **61**
Birchwood Dri. *Sut A* 3B **38**
Birchwood La. *Som* 3K **55**
Birchwood La. *S Norm* 7B **46**
Birchwood Pk. *For T* 5J **31**
Birchwood Pk. Homes.
  Rain 7B **42**
Birchwood Rd. *Alf* 7J **45**
Birchwood Way. *Som* 1J **55**
Bird Clo. *Mans* 6C **40**
Birdholme. 1B **12**
Birding St. *Mans* 7B **30**
Bird's La. *Kirk A* 2C **58**
Birkdale Av. *New O* 1H **23**
Birkdale Dri. *Kirk A* 4D **48**
Birkin Av. *New T* 6C **12**
Birkin La. *Gras* 5F **13**
Birkin La. W. *Gras* 5F **13**
Birkinstyle Av. *Ston* 6B **36**
Birkinstyle La. *Shirl* 6D **34**
Birkland Av. *Mans W* 5D **30**
Birkland Av. *Wars* 2H **19**
Birkland Dri. *Edwin* 4J **21**
Birklands Av. *New O* 1G **23**
Birklands Clo. *Wars* 2H **19**
Birkland St. *Mans* 3D **40**
Birks Rd. *Mans* 2H **39**
Bishops Hill. *Rain* 1B **52**
Bishop St. *Alf* 5G **45**
Bishop St. *Mans* 4B **40**
Bishop St. *Sut A* 6D **38**
Bishop's Wlk. *Chur W* 1G **19**
Bishopway. *Klbrn* 5K **67**
Blackberry Row. *Belp* 6G **67**
Blackbrook. 3A **66**
Blackburn Vw. *New O* 1H **23**
Blackmires Way. *Sut A* 5F **39**
Black Scotch La. *Mans* 6E **40**
        (in four parts)
Blacks La. *N Wing* 1F **25**
Blacksmiths Clo. *Glap* 6A **16**
Blackstone Clo. *Som* 4K **55**
Blackthorne Clo. *Klbrn* 5K **67**
Blackthorn Way. *Sut A* 1K **48**
Blackwell. 1A **46**
Blackwell Rd. *Huth* 7F **37**
Blake Cres. *Mans* 2D **40**
Blakeley La. *Wars* 5K **19**
Blakeney Ct. *Mans W* 4E **30**
        (off Brackenfield Av.)
Blakeney Dri. *Mans* 5C **40**
Blake St. *Mans W* 6B **30**
Blankleys Yd. *Chur W* 1H **19**
Bleak Hills. 5J **39**
Bleak Hills La. *Mans* 6J **39**
        (in two parts)
Bleak Hill Way. *Mans* 5J **39**
Bleasby Cres. *Sut A* 1F **49**
Blenheim Av. *Swanw* 3G **55**
Blenheim Clo. *For T* 7D **30**
Blenheim Ct. *Belp* 2H **67**
Blenheim Pl. *Huth* 6G **37**
Blidworth. 5C **52**
Blidworth Bottoms. 7C **52**
Blidworth Ind. Pk. *Blid* 4C **52**
Blidworth La. *Rain* 7K **41**
Blidworth Rd. *Kirk A* 6J **49**
Blidworth Towermill. 6B **52**
Blidworth Waye. *Pap* 5E **60**
Blind La. *Bsvr* 3H **5**
Blisworth Way. *Swanw* 4F **55**
Bloomer Wood Vw. *Sut A* 1A **48**
Bloomfield Rd. *Swanw* 3G **55**
Bluebell Clo. *Shire* 4H **17**
Bluebell Clo. *Som* 1A **56**
Bluebell Clo. *Stan H* 3K **37**

Blue Bell Clo. *Und* 2H **65**
Bluebell Gro. *Kirk A* 3D **48**
Bluebell Hill. *Stre* 5C **34**
Bluebell Pl. *Mans W* 4F **31**
Bluebells, The. *Sut A* 1F **49**
Bluebell Wood Way. *Sut A* 2A **48**
Blueberry Cft. *Sut A* 1A **48**
Blyth Clo. *Mans* 7H **29**
Blyth Ct. *Mans* 7H **29**
Blyth Rd. *Oll* 3E **22**
Boarhill Gro. *Sut A* 1A **48**
Boat La. *Jack* 5B **64**
Bobbin Way. *Belp* 2F **67**
Bodmin Ct. *Mans* 7G **41**
Bolden Ter. *Westh* 1J **45**
Bolsover. 5J **5**
Bolsover Bus. Pk. *Bsvr* 4G **5**
Bolsover Castle. 4J **5**
Bolsover Clo. *Rip* 3E **62**
BOLSOVER HOSPITAL. 4A **6**
Bolsover Rd. *Glap* 6K **15**
Bolsover St. *Mans* 3D **40**
Bolsover Woodhouse. 1G **5**
Bolton St. *Swanw* 4D **54**
Bonington Rd. *Mans* 3H **39**
Bonnington Dri. *Som* 3K **55**
Bonsal Ct. *Mans* 3H **41**
Bonsall Dri. *Som* 3J **55**
Bonsall La. *Alf* 6F **45**
Bonser Cres. *Huth* 6G **37**
Bonser Gdns. *Sut A* 7B **38**
Booth Av. *Ple* 3E **28**
Booth Cres. *Mans* 6H **29**
Boothgate. 1J **67**
Boothgate. *Belp* 1J **67**
Booth St. *Mans W* 5B **30**
Booth St. *Rip* 2E **62**
Boots Yd. *Huth* 6H **37**
Border Bank. *Rip* 6D **62**
Borders Av. *Kirk A* 2C **48**
Borrowdale Clo. *Mans* 6D **40**
Bosley M. *Belp* 2D **66**
Boswell Clo. *Mans* 6C **40**
Bosworth St. *Mans* 2H **39**
Botany Av. *Mans* 3K **39**
Botany Commercial Pk.
  Mans 3K **39**
Bottom Row Cotts. *Oll* 5F **23**
        (off Wellow Rd.)
Boughton. 1K **23**
Boughton Clo. *Sut A* 4D **38**
Boughton Dri. *Swanw* 3F **55**
Bould St. *Mans* 1K **39**
Boundary Clo. *Lang J* 1J **17**
Boundary Cres. *Blid* 5D **52**
Boundary Gdns. *Tib* 4B **36**
Boundary Wlk. *Lang* 5K **7**
Bourne Av. *Kirk A* 7F **49**
Bourne Av. *Sels* 4J **57**
Bourne Dri. *R'hd* 1G **61**
Bowler Dri. *Klbrn* 7K **67**
Bowler St. *Rip* 5D **62**
Bowling St. *Mans* 3D **40**
Bowne St. *Sut A* 6D **38**
Bowns Yd. *Som* 3K **55**
Box Cres. *Kirk A* 4D **48**
Boy La. *Edwin* 6K **21**
Bracken Av. *Heath* 5B **14**
Bracken Av. *New O* 1J **23**
Bracken Clo. *Kirk A* 4D **48**
Bracken Clo. *Wars* 4J **19**
Brackendale Clo. *Dane* 6E **24**
Brackendale Rd. *Swanw* 3F **55**
Brackenfield Av. *Mans W* 4E **30**
Brackenfield Dri. *R'hd* 7G **51**
Bracken Hill. *Mans* 4G **41**
Bracken Rd. *Shire* 4G **17**
Brackenwood Clo. *For T* 7G **31**
Brackley. *Klbrn* 6K **67**
Brackmills Clo. *For T* 7E **30**
Bradder Way. *Mans* 4A **40**
Bradforth Av. *Mans* 2G **41**
Bradgate Cft. *Ches* 1C **12**
Bradgate Dri. *Rip* 3B **62**
        (Heage Rd.)
Bradgate Dri. *Rip* 4F **63**
        (Peasehill)
Bradley Dri. *Belp* 3F **67**

Bradley's Yd. *Wars* 3H 19
Bradmore Ct. *Mans* 6G 41
Bradshaw Av. *Ridd* 5K 55
Bradshaw Cft. *Belp* 1C 66
Bradwell Gro. *Dane* 7D 24
Bradwell Way. *Belp* 2F 67
Braemar Rd. *For T* 5K 31
Brafield Clo. *Belp* 3H 67
Brailsford Clo. *Mans* 3H 41
Brake La. *Boug* 1J 23
Brake Vw. *New O* 1J 23
Bramble Clo. *B'thpe* 1H 23
Bramble Clo. *Heath* 6B 14
Bramble Clo. *Shire* 1J 17
Bramble Cft. *Sut A* 1A 48
Bramble La. *Mans* 4G 41
Bramble Way. *Klbrn* 5K 67
Bramble Way. *Som* 7B 46
Brambling Clo. *Mans* 2E 40
Bramcote Ct. *Mans* 6G 41
Bramley Ct. *Sut A* 6D 38
Bramley Rd. *Doe L* 6G 15
Bramley St. *Som* 4A 56
Bramley-Vale. 6G 15
Bramley Wlk. *Mans* 2H 39
Brampton Ct. *Belp* 3H 67
Branch La. *Pils* 3A 26
Brand Ct. *Stan H* 3A 38
Brand La. *Stan H* 4A 38
Brandon Wlk. *Sut A* 2B 48
Brandreth Av. *Sut A* 5B 38
Bransdale Av. *For T* 7E 30
Brassington Ct. *Mans W* 4E 30
Brassington La. *Old T* 1C 24
(in two parts)
Brassington St. *Clay C* 4D 24
Braybrook Clo. *Swanw* 3F 55
Break La. *Pap* 6E 60
Brechin Ct. *Mans W* 2B 30
Breckbank. *For T* 7E 30
Breck Bank. *New O* 2G 23
Breck Bank Cres. *New O* 2G 23
Brecon Clo. *Rain* 1F 53
Brenden Av. *Som* 4J 55
Brenden Clo. *Som* 3J 55
Bretby Ct. *Mans* 3H 41
Bretton Av. *Bsvr* 4A 6
Bretton Rd. *Belp* 2J 67
Bretton Rd. *R'hd* 7H 51
Brewers Way. *Mans* 4F 41
Briar Briggs Rd. *Bsvr* 3H 5
Briar Clo. *Alf* 7J 45
Briar Clo. *Rain* 1D 52
Briar Clo. *Shire* 5J 17
Briar Clo. *Stan H* 3A 38
Briar Ct. *New O* 2G 23
Briar La. *Mans* 5G 41
Briar Rd. *New O* 2G 23
Briars Way. *Rip* 3D 62
Briarwood Clo. *For T* 7H 31
Brick Kiln La. *Mans* 2G 39
Brickyard La. *Cuc* 1F 9
Brickyard La. *Klbrn* 5K 67
Brickyard La. *Rip* 3F 63
Brickyard La. *S Norm* 4C 46
Bri. End Av. *Sels* 3H 57
Bridge Foot. *Belp* 2C 66
Bridgehill. 2C 66
Bridge Hill. *Belp* 2C 66
Bridge St. *Belp* 3D 66
Bridge St. *Clay C* 4C 24
Bridge St. *Mans* 2C 40
Bridge St. *New T* 6D 12
Bridge St. *Pils* 6J 25
Bridge St. Ind. Est. *Clay C* 4C 24
Bridge Vw. *Milf* 7E 66
Bridgewater St. *New T* 6C 12
Bridgford St. *Mans* 4F 41
Bridle Clo. *Stan H* 3K 37
Bridle La. *Heage & Lwr H* 2A 62
Bridle La. *Lea* 4H 55
Bridle La. *Rip* 1D 62
(in two parts)
Bridleway, The. *For T* 6F 31
Brierley Forest Golf Course.
. . . . .5J 37
Brierley Forest Pk. Vis. Cen.
. . . . .5J 37
Brierley Pk. Clo. *Sut A* 4A 38

Brierley Pk. Ind. Est. *Sut A* 4A 38
Brierley Rd. *Ston* 6F 35
Brierly Cotts. *Sut A* 6C 38
Brierly Rd. *Sut A* 5B 38
Bright Sq. *Mans* 6H 29
Bright St. *N Wing* 1F 25
Bright St. *Norm* 5B 46
Brimington Ct. *Mans W* 4E 30
(off Brackenfield Av.)
Brinsley. 6G 65
Brinsley Hill. *Jack* 2E 64
Brisbane Clo. *Mans W* 2C 30
Britannia Av. *Wain* 5G 63
Britannia Rd. *Ches* 1B 12
Brittain Dri. *Rip* 3G 63
Brittain Pit Farm Pk. 7G 55
Broad Dri. *Edwin* 3F 21
(in two parts)
Broadholm. 1E 66
Broadlands. *S Norm* 6C 46
Broadlands Clo. *Sut A* 5F 39
Broad La. *Brins* 3G 65
Bradleys. *Clay C* 5C 24
Broadmeadows. 6C 46
Broad Oak Dri. *Brins* 3F 65
Broadoak Pk. *Kirk A* 2D 58
Broadway. *Rip* 2A 62
Broadway. *Swanw* 4F 55
Broadway Av. *Rip* 3E 62
Broadway Ct. *Rip* 2E 62
Broadway, The. *Mans* 3C 40
Brockenhurst Rd. *Mans* 3H 39
Brocklehurst Dri. *Edwin* 7K 21
Brockley Wood. *Bsvr* 1A 6
Brockway Clo. *Dane* 6D 24
Brockwell, The. *S Norm* 6D 46
Bronte St. *Stre* 4C 34
Brook Av. *Alf* 7H 45
Brook Av. *Alf* 7H 45
Brookdale Rd. *Sut A* 6E 38
Brooke St. *Tib* 3C 36
Brookfield Av. *Sut A* 5B 38
Brookfield Clo. *Cod* 3H 63
Brookfield Cres. *Shire* 2J 17
Brookfield Rd. *Bsvr* 6J 5
Brookhill Av. *Pinx* 6F 47
Brookhill Ct. *Sut A* 7C 38
(off Langton Rd.)
Brookhill Ind. Est. *Pinx* 1G 57
Brookhill La. *Pinx* 6F 47
Brookhill Rd. *Pinx* 1F 57
Brookhouse Ct. *Neth L* 5A 8
Brookland Av. *Mans* 2K 39
Brook La. *Alf* 7H 45
Brook La. *Rip* 5D 62
Brook Side. *Belp* 4D 66
Brookside Av. *Mans W* 3C 30
Brookside Way. *Huth* 1G 47
Brook St. *Clay C* 4A 24
Brook St. *Los* 7H 63
Brook St. *Sut A* 7C 38
Brookvale Av. *Cod* 4H 63
Brookvale Clo. *Mans* 3G 41
Broom Av. *Pils* 6J 25
Broom Av. *Swanw* 4F 55
Broom Clo. *Belp* 2C 66
Broom Dri. *Gras* 5E 12
Broome Acre. *S Norm* 6E 46
Broomfield Av. *Has* 1D 12
Broomhill La. *Chur W* 1K 19
(in two parts)
Broomhill La. *Mans* 1K 39
Brougham Av. *Mans* 6H 29
Broughton Clo. *Ridd* 4J 55
Brown Av. *Mans* 4A 30
Brown Cres. *Sut A* 5E 38
Browning St. *Mans* 2A 40
Brownlow Rd. *Mans* 7K 29
Brown St. *Mans* 1K 39
Broxtowe Dri. *Mans* 3C 40
Brunnen, The. *S Norm* 6D 46
Brunner Av. *Shire* 4K 17
Brunswick St. *Pils* 7J 25
Brunts Bus. Cen. *Mans* 1C 40
(off Samuel Brunts Way)
Brunt St. *Mans* 2C 40
Bryant La. *S Norm* 5C 46
Brynsmoor Rd. *Brins* 5G 65
Bryony Way. *Mans W* 4F 31

Buckfast Clo. *Swanw* 3E 54
Buckingham Clo. *Kirk A* 4D 48
Buckingham Clo. *Mans W* 3E 30
Buckingham Clo. *Swanw* 4G 55
Budby. 5H 11
Budby Av. *Mans* 3F 41
Budby Cres. *Med V* 5A 10
Budby Dri. *Bud* 3D 10
Budby Rd. *Cuc* 3H 9
Budget La. *Scarc* 1C 16
Builder's Yd. *Cod* 4H 63
Bullace Ct. *For T* 7E 30
Bull Farm. 6H 29
Bullock Clo. *Mans W* 3B 30
Bullock La. *Ridd & Iron* 6A 56
Bullsmoor. 4G 67
Bullsmoor. *Belp* 3G 67
Bully La. *Wars V* 4D 18
Bulwer Rd. *Kirk A* 5D 48
Bumpmill La. *Shirl* 1B 44
Bungalows, The. *Ston* 6E 34
Buntingbank Clo. *S Norm*
. . . . .6B 46
Bunyan Cres. *Ston* 6F 35
Bunyan Grn. Rd. *Sels* 5F 57
Burbage Clo. *Belp* 3H 67
Burbage Ct. *Mans* 3H 41
Burgess Clo. *Has* 1D 12
Burke Dri. *Som* 3K 55
Burleigh Cres. *Swanw* 3F 55
Burley Clo. *Ches* 1A 12
Burlington Av. *Lang J* 1K 17
Burlington Dri. *Mans* 6J 29
Burma Rd. *Blid* 4C 52
Burnaston Ct. *Mans W* 4E 30
Burnaston Rd. *Mans* 3H 41
Burnham Ct. *Mans* 5C 40
Burns Av. *Mans W* 6C 30
Burns Dri. *Gras* 4E 12
Burnshaw St. *Stre* 4C 34
Burnside Av. *Shirl* 1C 44
Burnside Clo. *Kirk A* 3D 48
Burnside Dri. *Mans* 6J 29
Burns La. *Chur W* 2H 19
Burns St. *Mans* 2A 40
Burns, The. *Wars* 2J 19
Burn St. *Sut A* 6E 38
Burnt Oaks Clo. *Mans W* 5D 30
Burnwood Av. *Mans* 2G 41
Burrow Wlk. *Kirk A* 6C 48
Burton Clo. *Sut A* 6A 38
Burton Ri. *Kirk A* 3E 58
Burton Rd. *Sut A* 6A 38
Burwell Ct. *Mans W* 4E 30
Buskeyfield La. *Cuc* 2E 8
Butler Cres. *Mans* 6B 52
Butler Dri. *Blid* 4C 52
Butterfield Cres. *Swanw* 4F 55
Butterley. 1F 63
Butterley Ct. *Iron* 7B 56
(off Old Stone Bri.)
Butterley Cft. Bus. Cen.
Rip 4F 63
Butterley Hill. *Rip* 2D 62
Butterley La. *Rip* 7D 54
Butterley Lodge. *Iron* 7B 56
(off Parkside Dri.)
Butterley Park. 1G 63
Butterley Pk. Miniature Railway.
. . . . .7F 55
Butterley Pk. Railway Mus.
. . . . .7G 55
Butterley Row. *Rip* 7D 54
Buttermilk La. *Bsvr* 3E 4
Butterwick Clo. *For T* 7F 31
Buttery La. *Sut A* 1A 38
Butt La. *Mans W* 6C 30
Butts, The. *Belp* 4E 66
Buxton Rd. *Mans* 7H 29
Byron Av. *Alf* 6H 45
Byron Av. *Kirk A* 3F 49
Byron Av. *Mans W* 6C 30
Byron Av. *Sut A* 5F 39
Byron Clo. *Gras* 4E 12
Byron Cres. *R'hd* 7E 50
Byron Gro. *Ston* 6F 35
Byron Rd. *Ann* 5J 59
Byron St. *Blid* 5D 52
Byron St. *Mans* 2A 40

Byron St. *News V* 5H 59
Byron St. *Shire* 3J 17
Byron St. *Shirl* 1C 44
Bythorn Clo. *Skeg* 4F 39
Bywell La. *Klbrn* 6K 67

C

Cabot Clo. *Belp* 2J 67
Cadeby Ct. *Ridd* 5J 55
Caernarfon Clo. *Swanw* 4G 55
Calke Av. *Huth* 7G 37
Calke Ri. *Rip* 3F 63
Calladine Clo. *Sut A* 1B 48
Calladine Gro. *Sut A* 1B 48
Calladine La. *Sut A* 2A 48
Calver Av. *N Wing* 1G 25
Calver Clo. *Belp* 1F 67
Calver St. *Mans W* 5E 30
Cambourne Gdns. *R'hd* 1F 61
Cambria Rd. *Ple* 4G 29
Cambridge Clo. *Rain* 2D 52
Cambridge Cres. *Doe L* 6G 15
(in two parts)
Cambridge Rd. *Rain* 2C 52
Cambridge St. *B'wll* 1A 46
Cambridge St. *Mans* 4A 40
Camerons, The. *Mans* 4H 39
Campbell St. *Belp* 4D 66
Campion Clo. *Shire* 6H 17
Canada St. *Belp* 5E 66
Candlemass Ct. *Mans W* 6D 30
Cannell Clo. *Clay C* 4B 24
Cannon St. *Mans* 7K 29
Canterbury Clo. *Mans W* 3C 30
Cantley Rd. *Ridd* 5J 55
Cape St. *Mans* 2K 39
Carburton Av. *Med V* 6K 9
Carburton Way. *Kirk A* 4H 49
Cardale Rd. *Ple* 4G 29
Cardinal Ct. *Sut A* 1G 49
Cardle Clo. *For T* 6G 31
Carisbrook Av. *Mans* 2G 41
Carisbrooke Clo. *Kirk A* 6G 49
Carlton Clo. *Dane* 6D 24
Carlton Clo. *For T* 5K 31
Carlton Rd. *Ches* 1A 12
Carlton St. *Mans* 7C 30
Carlyle Rd. *Ston* 6F 35
Carnarvon Gro. *Sut A* 6K 37
Carnarvon Rd. *Huth* 7H 37
Carnarvon St. *Tev* 2K 37
Carnation Rd. *Shire* 4G 17
Carnfield Hall. 5K 45
Carnfield Hill. *S Norm* 5J 45
Carnoustie Clo. *Kirk A* 3C 48
Caroline Clo. *R'hd* 7H 51
Carpenter Av. *Mans* 6H 29
Carr Clo. *S Norm* 3C 46
Carr Farm Rd. *Kirk A* 2D 58
Carrfield Clo. *Sut A* 6B 38
Carr Gro. *Kirk A* 5C 48
Carr La. *Brac* 3C 46
Carr La. *Pal* 7G 5
Carr La. *Wars* 3G 19
Carr Vale. 6H 5
Carr Va. Rd. *Bsvr* 5H 5
Carsic La. *Sut A* 6C 38
Carsic Rd. *Sut A* 4B 38
Carsington Ct. *Mans W* 5E 30
Carter La. *Chur W* 3B 18
Carter La. *Mans* 3D 40
Carter La. *Shire* 3H 17
Carter La. E. *S Norm* 4E 46
Carter La. W. *Shire* 3H 17
Carter La. W. *S Norm* 5D 46
Cartwright La. *S Norm* 3G 47
Carver Clo. *Edwin* 6K 21
Casson St. *Iron* 7A 56
Castle Dri. *Cod* 4K 63
Castle Dri. *Som* 3K 55
Castlefields. *Iron* 1B 64
Castle Grn. *Bsvr* 6K 5
Castle Hill. 6B 48
Castlehill. *Iron* 2A 64
Castle Hill Clo. *Kirk A* 5C 48
Castle La. *Bsvr* 5H 5
Castle La. *Iron* 2A 64

Castle Leisure Pk. 5H 5
Castle M. *Mans W* 5B 30
Castle St. *Bsvr* 4J 5
Castle St. *Mans* 2A 40
Castle St. *Mans W* 5B 30
Castleton Av. *Ridd* 5H 55
Castleton Clo. *Mans W* 4C 30
Castleton Clo. *R'hd* 7G 51
Castleton Way. *Sels* 4J 57
Castle Vw. *Pal* 1J 15
Castlewood Gro. *Sut A* 1B 48
Catherine Av. *Mans W* 5C 30
Catherine Clo. *Kirk A* 3D 48
Catherine St. *Alf* 6J 45
Caton Clo. *Sut A* 6B 38
Cator Rd. *Ple* 5G 29
Caudwell Clo. *New T* 7D 12
Caudwell Rd.
    Sut A & Mans 7H 39
     (in two parts)
Caunton Clo. *Mans* 3K 39
Caunton Clo. *Med V* 7K 9
Caunt's Cres. *Sut A* 6B 38
Cavell Dri. *Dane* 6E 24
Cavendish Av. *Edwin* 5H 21
Cavendish Av. *Sut A* 6C 38
Cavendish Clo. *Hlmwd* 6A 14
Cavendish Cres. *Kirk A* 2E 58
Cavendish Dri. *Rip* 3C 62
Cavendish Rd. *Bsvr* 6K 5
Cavendish St. *Lang* 6K 7
Cavendish St. *Mans* 4C 40
Cavendish St. *Mans W* 5A 30
Cavendish St. *Sut A* 5E 38
Cavendish Wlk. *Bsvr* 4J 5
Cawthorne Way. *Mans* 2F 41
Caythorpe Ct. Mans W 5E *30*
    (off Sedgebrook St.)
Cedar Av. *Alf* 5G 45
Cedar Av. *Kirk A* 6D 48
Cedar Av. *Mans W* 3B 30
Cedar Av. *Rip* 3D 62
Cedar Clo. *Glap* 6K 15
Cedar Clo. *Shire* 1J 17
Cedar Clo. *Sut A* 2B 38
Cedar Dri. *Sels* 4H 57
Cedar Gro. *Belp* 5F 67
Cedar Gro. *S Norm* 6C 46
Cedar La. *New O* 1G 23
Cedar Pk. Dri. *Bsvr* 4A 6
Cedar St. *Mans* 4C 40
Cedar St. *Stre* 4C 34
Cemetery La. *Rip* 3D 62
Cemetery Rd. *Belp* 1E 66
Cemetery Rd. *Dane* 6D 24
Cemetery Rd. *Lea* 4H 55
Central Av. *Blid* 5D 52
Central Av. *Kirk A* 7F 49
Central Av. *Mans* 4C 40
Central Av. *S Norm* 5D 46
Central Clo. *Shire* 4J 17
Central Dri. *B'wll* 1A 46
Central Dri. *Clip V* 6B 32
Central Dri. *Shire* 4J 17
Central Dri. *Wing* 4A 12
Central Rd. *Alf* 6G 45
Central St. *Hlmwd* 7K 13
Central St. *Sut A* 5F 39
Centre St. *Doe L* 6F 15
Century Av. *Mans* 4K 39
Chadburn Rd. *Mans* 1E 40
Chadwick Gro. *Rip* 3B 62
Chaffinch Clo. *Mans* 2F 41
Champion Cres. *Mans* 1K 39
Chancery Clo. *Sut A* 3E 38
Chantry, The. *Mans* 4F 41
Chapel Clo. *Edwin* 6K 21
Chapel Hill. 6C 14
Chapel La. *R'hd* 3H 61
Chapel Rd. *Bsvr* 5H 5
Chapel Rd. *Gras* 4E 12
Chapel Rd. *Sels* 5G 57
Chapel St. *Alf* 6G 45
Chapel St. *Belp* 4D 66
Chapel St. *Holb* 7G 67
Chapel St. *Klbrn* 7K 67
Chapel St. *Kirk A* 2E 58
    (Nuncargate Rd.)

Chapel St. *Kirk A* 5C 48
    (Sutton Rd.)
Chapel St. *Lang* 3A 8
Chapel St. *Lea* 4J 55
Chapel St. *N Hou* 1E 28
Chapel St. *Rip* 2D 62
Chapel St. *Sels* 4J 57
Chapel St. *Ston* 5G 35
Chapel St. *Swanw* 4E 54
Chapel Ter. *News V* 5H 59
Chapel Wlk. *Bsvr* 4J 5
Chapel Way. *New T* 6D 12
Chapman La. *Gras* 4F 13
Charity Rd. *Ridd* 6H 55
Charles St. *Alf* 5F 45
Charles St. *Lea* 4J 55
Charles St. *Mans* 7A 30
Charles St. *Mans W* 4C 30
Charles St. *Sut A* 6E 38
Charlesworth Ct. Mans W . . .5E *30*
    (off Sedgebrook St.)
Charlesworth Gdns. Bsvr 6G *5*
    (off Charlesworth St.)
Charlesworth St. *Bsvr* 6G 5
Charnwood Av. *Belp* 3E 66
Charnwood Clo. *R'hd* 3G 61
Charnwood Clo. *Swanw* 4F 55
Charnwood Cres. *Nwtn* 6D 36
Charnwood Dri. *Rip* 3C 62
Charnwood Gro. *Mans* 2G 41
Charnwood Gro. *Mans W* . . .3B 30
Charnwood St. *Sut A* 7K 37
Charters Clo. *Kirk A* 3D 48
Chartwell Rd. *Kirk A* 5G 49
Chatham Av. *Alf* 7J 45
Chatham Ct. *Belp* 3H 67
Chatsworth Av. *Lang J* 1J 17
Chatsworth Av. *Sels* 4J 57
Chatsworth Clo. *Alf* 7F 45
Chatsworth Clo. *Bsvr* 4A 6
Chatsworth Clo. *Mans* 7E 40
Chatsworth Clo. *R'hd* 7G 51
Chatsworth Dri. *Sut A* 4D 38
Chatsworth Dri. *N Wing* 2F 25
Chatsworth St. *Sut A* 6D 38
Chatsworth St. *Tib* 3C 36
Chatsworth Ter. *News V* 4H 59
Chaucer Cres. *Sut A* 5F 39
Chaucer St. *Mans* 2A 40
Chavery Rd. *Clay C* 4E 24
Chaworth St. *Blid* 5D 52
Cheapside. *Belp* 4D 66
Cheddar Clo. *Rain* 1E 52
Chelmorton Clo. *Mans W* . . .5E 30
Cheltenham Ct. *Mans* 2F 41
Chepstow Wlk. *Mans* 2F 41
Cheriton Clo. *Mans* 7J 29
Cheriton Dri. *R'hd* 1H 61
Chermside Clo. *R'hd* 2H 61
Chernside. *R'hd* 7G 51
Cherry Av. *Kirk A* 3B 48
Cherry Clo. *Shire* 1J 17
Cherry Gro. *S Norm* 3D 46
Cherry Gro. *Mans* 3J 39
Cherry Gro. *Wars* 3J 39
Cherry La. *Mans* 6B 40
Cherry Tree Av. *Belp* 1E 66
Cherry Tree Av. *Lea* 4G 55
Cherry Tree Av. *Rip* 4D 62
Cherry Tree Clo. *Bsvr* 5K 5
Cherrytree Clo. *Brins* 4G 65
Cherry Tree Clo. *Mans W* . . .4B 30
Cherry Tree Dri. *Duck* 2C 4
Cherry Tree Gro. *N Wing* 3F 25
Cheshire Way. *W'wd* 7E 56
Chess Burrow. *Mans W* 6D 30
Chesterfield Rd. *Belp* 3E 66
    (Belper)
Chesterfield Rd. *Belp* 1G 67
    (Far Laund)
Chesterfield Rd. *Bsvr* 1G 5
Chesterfield Rd. *Cal & Duck* . . .4A 4
Chesterfield Rd. *Gras* 6F 13
Chesterfield Rd. *Hghm* 6C 34
Chesterfield Rd. *Huth* 3F 37
Chesterfield Rd. *N Hou* 7C 16
    (in two parts)
Chesterfield Rd. *Pils* 5B 26

Chesterfield Rd. *Shirl* 2E 44
Chesterfield Rd. *Temp N* 4J 13
Chesterfield Rd. N. *Mans* 3F 29
Chesterfield Rd. S. *Mans* 7K 29
Chester St. *Mans* 7J 29
Chestnut Av. *Belp* 5E 66
Chestnut Av. *Glap* 7K 15
Chestnut Av. *Holb* 7G 67
Chestnut Av. *Kirk A* 6D 48
Chestnut Av. *Oll* 1B 22
Chestnut Av. *R'hd* 2G 61
Chestnut Av. *Ridd* 6K 55
Chestnut Av. *Rip* 4D 62
Chestnut Clo. *New O* 1H 23
Chestnut Ct. *Har W* 3E 50
Chestnut Ct. *Pinx* 7G 47
Chestnut Dri. *Mans* 7E 40
Chestnut Dri. *New O* 1G 23
Chestnut Dri. *Sels* 4H 57
Chestnut Dri. *Shire* 3H 17
Chestnut Dri. *S Norm* 6D 46
Chestnut Gdns. *Sut A* 1B 48
Chestnut Gro. *Kirk A* 5D 48
Chestnut Gro. *Mans W* 3B 30
Chestnut Gro. *Tib* 4B 36
Chestnut Hill. *Mans* 7E 40
Chestnut M. *Mans* 7E 40
Chestnut Way. *Swanw* 3F 55
Chevinend. 7C 66
Chevin Golf Course. 7B 66
Chevin Rd. *Belp & Milf* 3B 66
Chevinside. 5C 66
Chevin Vw. *Belp* 3D 66
Cheviot Av. *Iron* 1B 64
Chichester Clo. *Mans* 3G 39
Chiltern Clo. *Gras* 4F 13
Chiltern Wlk. *Gras* 4F 13
Chilton Cres. *Mans W* 2C 30
Chine, The. *S Norm* 7C 46
Chirnside. *Mans* 4H 39
Chisworth Ct. *Mans W* 5E 30
Church Av. *Dane* 5E 24
Church Av. *Sut A* 7B 38
Church Circ. *New O* 2G 23
Church Clo. *Chur W* 1H 19
Church Clo. *N Wing* 3A 12
Church Clo. *Westh* 1J 45
Church Ct. *Shire* 4J 17
Church Cft. *Rip* 2D 62
Church Dri. *R'hd* 1F 61
Church Dri. *Shire* 4J 17
Chu. Farm Gdns. *W'low* 6J 23
Churchfield Dri. *Rain* 7B 42
Church Gdns. *Mans W* 5C 30
Church Gdns. *Sut A* 7B 38
Church Hill. 7C 36
    (Blackwell)
Church Hill. 3F 25
    (North Wingfield)
Church Hill. *B'wll* 1C 46
Church Hill. *Jack* 1D 64
Church Hill. *Kirk A* 6B 48
Church Hill. *Mans W* 5C 30
Church Hill. *Sut A* 7C 38
Chu. Hill Av. *Mans W* 5C 30
Churchland Av. *Hlmwd* 7K 13
Church La. *Askh* 2K 23
Church La. *Belp* 3D 66
Church La. *Brins* 6G 65
Church La. *Heath* 4D 14
    (in two parts)
Church La. *Mans* 3C 40
Church La. *Mort* 5F 35
Church La. *N Wing* 3F 25
Church La. *Ple* 3E 28
    (in two parts)
Church La. *Sels* 4F 57
Church La. *S Wing* 6A 44
Church La. *Sut A* 7C 38
Church La. *Temp N* 4H 13
Church La. *Tib* 2B 36
Church La. *Und* 1J 65
Church Mead. *Huth* 6H 37
Church Meadows.
    N Wing 3F 25
Church M. *Kirk A* 6C 48
Church M. *Sut A* 7C 38
Church Paddock. *N Wing* 3F 25
Church Ri. *Stre* 5C 34

Church Rd. *Boug* 1K 23
Church Rd. *Chur W* 1H 19
Church Rd. *Clip V* 5A 32
Church Rd. *Stanf* 1J 5
    (in two parts)
Church Side. *Has* 1D 12
Church Side. *Huth* 6H 37
Church Side. *Mans* 2C 40
Churchside La. *Has* 1D 12
Church St. *Alf* 6F 45
Church St. *Belp* 3E 66
Church St. *Bsvr* 5J 5
Church St. *Edwin* 4K 21
Church St. *Klbrn* 7K 67
Church St. *Kirk A* 5B 48
Church St. *Lang* 4A 8
Church St. *Mans* 2B 40
Church St. *Mans W* 5C 30
Church St. *Oll* 4E 22
Church St. *Pils* 7J 25
Church St. *Ple* 3F 29
Church St. *Ridd* 5K 55
Church St. *Rip* 2D 62
Church St. *Shirl* 7D 34
Church St. *S Norm* 4C 46
Church St. *Sut A* 7B 38
Church St. *Wain* 5G 63
Church St. *Wars* 3H 19
Church St. E. *Pinx* 7F 47
Church St. W. *Pinx* 7E 46
Church Vw. *B'wll* 1B 46
Church Vw. *Glap* 7K 15
Church Vw. *N Hou* 1D 28
Church Vw. *Oll* 4E 22
Church Vw. *Stan H* 3B 38
Church Vw. Gdns. *Kirk A* 3C 58
Church Wlk. *Brins* 6G 65
Church Wlk. *Ridd* 5A 56
Church Warsop. 7G 9
Cinder Bank. *Iron* 7B 56
Cinderhill. 5J 67
Cinder La. *Oll* 5F 23
Cinder Rd. *Som* 4K 55
Circle, The. *Clip V* 5C 32
Circle, The. *Mans* 4B 30
Clare Hill. *Blid* 6C 52
Claremont Clo. *Mans W* 4E 30
Clarence St. *Mans* 3A 40
Clarence St. *Ple* 5G 29
Clarence St. *Ston* 5H 35
Clarendon Rd. *Mans* 1J 39
Clare Rd. *Sut A* 2D 48
Clarkwoods Clo. *Boug* 3H 23
Claverton Ct. *Mans* 6G 41
Clay Cross. 4C 24
CLAY CROSS COMMUNITY
    HOSPITAL. 4D 24
Clay Cross Countryside Cen.
    . . . . .5C 24
Clay La. *Clay C* 6B 24
Clay St. *Shirl* 1E 44
Clayton Gro. *Los* 7J 63
Clayworth Ct. *Mans* 6G 41
Clegg Hill Dri. *Huth* 5G 37
Clerkson's All. Mans 2B *40*
    (off Leeming St.)
Clerkson St. *Mans* 3B 40
Cleveland Rd. *Ston* 6F 35
Cliff La. *Pinx* 7H 47
Cliff Nook. *S Norm* 6D 46
Clifford St. *Mans* 5B 40
Cliff St. *Mans* 2C 40
Clifton Gro. *Mans* 5F 41
Clifton Pl. *Mans* 2B 40
Clinton Av. *Brins* 6F 65
Clipstone. 6B 12
Clipstone Av. *Mans* 1C 40
Clipstone Av. *Sut A* 5E 38
Clipstone Dri. *For T* 6J 31
Clipstone Dri. *Old C* 6B 20
Clipstone Rd. *Edwin* 2F 33
Clipstone Rd. E. *For T* 6J 31
Clipstone Rd. W. *For T* 1F 41
Close, The. *Lang J* 2K 17
Close, The. *Rain* 7A 42
Clover Ct. *Tib* 2D 36
Clover Nook Ind. Est. *Som* . . .1A 56
Clover Nook Pk. *Som* 2J 55
Clover Nook Rd. *Som* 1K 55

Clover St. *Kirk A* 4E 48
Clover Way. *Mans W* 4F 31
Clumber Av. *Brins* 3G 65
(in two parts)
Clumber Av. *Edwin* 4H 21
Clumber Av. *Rain* 1B 52
Clumber Clo. *Rip* 3E 62
Clumber Ct. *Mans* 6J 29
Clumber Ct. *Wars* 3H 19
Clumber Cres. *Stan H* 3A 38
Clumber Dri. *Mans* 6J 29
Clumber Pk. Country Pk. 1J 11
Clumber St. *Kirk A* 5G 49
Clumber St. *Mans* 2B 40
Clumber St. *Sut A* 7B 38
Clumber St. *Wars* 3H 19
Clun Ct. *Mans W* 6D 30
Cluster Rd. *Belp* 3D 66
Clusters Ct. *Belp* 3D 66
Coach La. *Wars* 5J 19
Coach Rd. *But* 2F 63
Coach Rd. *Ridd* 1H 63
(in two parts)
Coach Rd. *Wars* 5J 19
(in two parts)
Coalfield Clo. *Sut A* 1A 48
Cobden Pl. *Mans* 6J 29
Cobden St. *Kirk A* 6E 48
Cobden St. *Rip* 2D 62
Coburn St. *Sut A* 1D 48
Cochrane Ter. *Stan H* 3B 38
Cockerhouse Rd. *E'wd* 7G 65
Cocking Moor La. *W'low* 7K 23
Cockle Clo. *Mans* 4E 40
Cockshut La. *Lang* 2A 8
Cockshutt La. *Som* 4B 56
Codnor. 4H 63
Codnor Breach. 7G 63
Codnor Castle. 4A 64
(Remains of)
Codnor Gate. 3H 63
Codnor Ga. *Cod* 3H 63
Codnor Ga. Ind. Est. *Rip* 2H 63
Codnor La. *Ridd* 1J 63
Codnor Park. 7B 56
Coggins La. *Chur W* 1J 19
Cokefield Ter. *Hilc* 1E 46
Colby Clo. *For T* 6H 31
Colin Av. *Cod* 4H 63
Colin St. *Alf* 6G 45
Colledge St. *Ridd* 5J 55
College Ho. *Mans* 2A 40
(off Connexion, The)
Collier Av. *Mans W* 3B 30
Colliers Way. *Clay C* 4B 24
Colliery Rd. *Alf* 7F 45
Colliery Rd. *B'wll* 1B 46
Colliery Row. *Alf* 5H 45
Colliery Row. *Pinx* 1F 57
Colliery Vs. *Edwin* 5A 22
Collingham Rd. *Mans* 7H 29
Collins Av. *S Norm* 3C 46
Collins Av. *Sut A* 1C 48
Colne Clo. *Mans W* 6D 30
Colonade. *Shire* 5J 17
Colston Rd. *Mans* 6G 41
Columbia Av. *Mans* 4F 41
Columbia Av. *Sut A* 7K 37
Columbia Clo. *Sels* 4J 57
Columbia St. *Huth* 6H 37
Colwick Clo. *Mans* 7J 29
Commercial Ga. *Mans* 3B 40
Commercial St. *Mans* 3B 40
Common La. *Ple & Shire* 2E 28
(Chesterfield Rd.)
Common La. *Ple V & Mans W*
. . . . .2K 29
(Pleasley Va.)
Common La. *Shirl* 6C 34
Commonpiece Rd. *Clay C* 5D 24
Common Rd. *Huth* 6H 37
Commonside. 7H 37
(Huthwaite)
Commonside. 3H 57
(Selston)
Common Side. *Sels* 3G 57
Common, The. *S Norm* 5C 46
Compton St. *Hlmwd* 6A 14

Compton St. *Lang* 6K 7
Concorde Way. *Mans* 5J 29
Conduit Rd. *Bsvr* 6K 5
Coney Grn. Rd. *Clay C* 4E 24
Coniston Clo. *Mans W* 4E 30
Coniston Dri. *Clay C* 6B 24
Coniston Rd. *Kirk A* 4G 49
Connaught Ct. *Alf* 7H 45
Connexion, The. *Mans* 2A 40
Conway Clo. *Mans* 1H 39
Cook Clo. *Belp* 2J 67
Cooke Clo. *Old T* 2B 24
Cookson St. *Kirk A* 5C 48
Co-operative St. *Stan H* 3A 38
Coopers Ri. *Rain* 1C 52
Cooper St. *Rip* 3D 62
Coopers Yd. *Wars* 3H 19
Copeland Av. *Kirk A* 4C 48
Copeland Rd. *Kirk A* 4C 48
Copenhagen Rd. *Clay C* 4E 24
Copper Beeches. *Rip* 2C 62
Coppice Clo. *Has* 1D 12
Coppice Cft. *Sut A* 1A 48
Coppice Rd. *For T* 5K 31
Coppice, The. *Shire* 4H 17
Coppice Vw. *S Norm* 6C 46
Copse Clo. *R'hd* 7C 50
Copse, The. *Mans* 7C 40
Copse, The. *Sut A* 4A 38
Copse Wood. *S Norm* 6B 46
Coral Way. *Clay C* 4D 24
Corbriggs. 2F 13
Cordy La. *Brins* 5G 65
Corene Av. *Sut A* 1C 48
Corn Clo. *S Norm* 4D 46
Corn Cft. *S Norm* 7E 30
(off Alder Clo.)
Corner Cft. *Huth* 6J 37
Corner Pin Dri. *Kirk A* 4F 49
Cornfield Av. *S Norm* 6C 46
Cornhill Ct. *Alf* 6H 45
Cornhill Dri. *Alf* 6H 45
Cornhill Clo. *Bsvr* 4K 5
Cornwall Av. *Mans* 7F 41
Cornwall Clo. *W'wd* 7E 56
Cornwall Dri. *Gras* 4F 13
Cornwall Dri. *Oll* 4F 23
Coronation Av. *Belp* 2E 66
Coronation Av. *N Hou* 1D 28
Coronation Dri. *For T* 1F 41
Coronation Dri. *Shire* 5K 17
Coronation Dri. *S Norm* 5D 46
Coronation St. *Mans* 3D 40
Coronation St. *Sut A* 1C 48
Corporation St. *Mans* 2A 40
Cosgrove Av. *Sut A* 4E 38
Cotes Park. 1K 55
Cotes Pk. Ind. Est. *Som* 1K 55
(Cotes Pk. La.)
Cotes Pk. Ind. Est. *Som* 2J 55
(Wheatley Av.)
Cotes Pk. La. *Som* 1J 55
Cotgrave Rd. *Mans* 6K 29
Coton Clo. *Mans W* 4E 30
Cotswold Dri. *Gras* 4E 12
Cotswold Gro. *Mans* 3G 41
Cottage Clo. *Blid* 6B 52
Cottage Clo. *Stan H* 3A 38
Cottage La. *Cuc* 6H 19
(in two parts)
Cottam Gro. *Mans* 3H 39
Cotterdale Clo. *For T* 7E 30
Cotton St. *Bsvr* 5J 5
Coulton's Av. *Sut A* 6A 38
Coulton's Clo. *Sut A* 6A 38
County Est., The. *Huth* 7G 37
(Little La.)
County Est., The. *Huth* 7G 37
(Nunn Brook Rd.)
County Est., The. *Huth* 1H 47
(Nunn Clo.)
Coupe La. *Clay C & Old T* 3A 24
Coupe La. *Rip* 4F 63
Coupland Pl. *Som* 2J 55
Court-Field Rd. *Sut A* 3E 38
Courtney Way. *Belp* 2H 67
Cowham Clo. *Alf* 7J 45
Cowhill. 5E 66
Cowpasture La. *Kirk A* 1C 48

Cow Pasture La. *Kirk A* 5B 48
Cowpes Clo. *Sut A* 5B 38
Cowsell Dri. *Dane* 6E 24
Cox Moor. 5G 49
Coxmoor Golf Course. 3K 49
Coxmoor Rd. *Sut A & R'hd* . . .6F 39
(in two parts)
Cox's La. *Mans W* 3A 30
Cracroft La. *Scarc* 1D 16
Cragg La. *B'wll* 6C 36
Craggs Rd. *Bsvr* 4J 5
Craigs Grn. *Mans* 4J 39
Crampton Clo. *Sut A* 6K 37
Crampton Rd. *Mans* 1E 40
Cranborne Clo. *Mans* 2G 39
Cranbrook Ct. *Mans W* 2C 30
Cranmer Gro. *Mans* 5H 29
Cranswick Clo. *Mans W* 6G 31
Craster St. *Sut A* 1C 48
Cray's Hill. *Lea* 4G 55
Crescent Rd. *Sels* 5F 57
Crescent, The. *Alf* 7H 45
Crescent, The. *Blid* 5D 52
Crescent, The. *Lang J* 1J 17
Crescent, The. *Mans* 6C 40
Crescent, The. *Sut A* 2B 38
Cressbrook Av. *N Wing* 1H 25
Cressy Rd. *Alf* 6G 45
Creswell Ct. *Mans W* 4E 30
Creswell Rd. *Cuc* 2E 8
Crewe Clo. *Blid* 5C 52
Crich La. *Belp & Ambgt* 2E 66
Crich Pl. *N Wing* 2F 25
Crich Vw. *Bsvr* 6K 5
Crich Vw. *Nwtn* 5C 36
Cricket Clo. *Kirk A* 2D 58
Crocus St. *Kirk A* 6F 49
Croft Av. *Mans* 7D 40
Croft Clo. *Pinx* 7E 46
Croft Ct. *Huth* 5H 37
Croft, The. *Belp* 6G 67
Croft, The. *Lea* 4J 55
Croft, The. *S Norm* 4C 46
Croft, The. *Stan H* 3A 38
Cromarty Clo. *Mans* 4H 39
Cromer Clo. *Mans* 5C 40
Cromford Av. *Mans* 4A 40
Cromford Clo. *Lan M* 7D 64
Cromford Clo. *N Wing* 1H 25
Cromford Ct. *R'hd* 7G 51
Cromford Rd. *Clay C* 3A 24
Cromford Rd. *Kirk A* 2E 58
Cromford Rd. *Lan M* 6A 64
(in two parts)
Cromford Rd. *Rip* 2D 62
Crompton Rd. *Ple* 5H 29
Crompton St. *N Hou* 1D 28
Crompton St. *Tev* 2K 37
Cromwell Av. *B'wll* 1A 46
Cromwell Dri. *Swanw* 4D 54
Cromwell Rd. *Bsvr* 6K 5
Cromwell St. *Mans* 4C 40
Cromwell St. *Mans* 4C 40
Crook Dale Dri. *Edwin* 5E 20
Crookes Av. *Ple* 3E 28
Crook's Av. *Mans W* 5C 30
Cropston Clo. *Ches* 1C 12
Cropwell Ct. *Mans* 2D 40
Crosby Clo. *For T* 6G 31
Cross Dri. *Kirk A* 3F 49
Cross Dri. *Rain* 1D 52
Cross Hill. 6H 63
Crosshill. *Cod* 6H 63
Cross Keys La. *Swanw* 3E 54
(off Derby Rd.)
Cross La. *Blid* 5J 51
Cross La. *Cod* 5H 63
Cross La. *Huth* 7H 37
(in two parts)
Cross La. *Shirl* 2E 44
Crossley Av. *Huth* 6J 37
Crossley St. *Rip* 3D 62
Cross Rd. *Ann* 4G 59
Cross St. *Bsvr* 6A 6
Cross St. *Clay C* 5C 24
Cross St. *Doe L* 6F 15
Cross St. *Gras* 4E 12
Cross St. *Kirk A* 3G 49

Cross St. *Mans W* 6B 30
Cross St. *N Wing* 2E 24
Crow Cft. Rd. *Pils* 6J 25
Crow Hill. *Pal* 2J 15
Crow Hill. *Ple* 3F 29
Crow Hill Ct. *Mans* 1B 40
Crow Hill Dri. *Mans* 1B 40
Crow Hill La. *Mans W* 6B 30
Crow Hill Ri. *Mans* 1B 40
Crow La. *Hghm* 4A 34
Crown Av. *For T* 1G 41
Crown Clo. *Rain* 2E 52
Crown Farm Ind. Pk.
. . . . .2H 41
Crown Farm La. *Mans* 2H 41
Crown Farm Way. *For T* 2G 41
Crown St. *Mans* 3F 41
Crown Ter. *Belp* 3D 66
Crown Wlk. *Mans* 2B 40
(off Quaker Way)
Crowtrees Dri. *Sut A* 1A 48
Croxton Ct. *Mans W* 5E 30
Cuckney. 3G 9
Cuckney Hill. *Chur W* 6H 9
Cuckney Rd. *Lang* 5C 8
Culworth Clo. *Belp* 3H 67
Cumberland Av. *Wars* 2F 19
Cumberland Clo. *W'wd* 7E 56
Cumberland Dri. *Mans* 2H 39
Cundy Rd. *Bsvr* 3J 5
Cupar Clo. *Chur W* 2J 19
Curbar Clo. *N Wing* 1G 25
Cursham St. *Sut A* 7D 38
Curzon Clo. *Rain* 1C 52
Cuttings Av. *Sut A* 2K 47
Cutts Row. *Kirk A* 3D 58

D

Dabek Ri. *Kirk A* 2E 58
Dahlia Av. *S Norm* 3D 46
Dale Av. *Nwtn* 6C 36
Dale Av. *Ridd* 5J 55
Dale Clo. *Blid* 5C 52
Dale Clo. *Lang* 6J 7
Dale Clo. *Mans* 1A 40
Dale Clo. *Ston* 5H 35
Dale Clo. *Sut A* 4E 38
Dale Ct. *Klbrn* 7K 67
Dale Cres. *New T* 6C 12
Dale La. *Blid* 5C 52
Dale La. *Glap* 1A 28
Dale Pk. Av. *Klbrn* 7K 67
Dale Rd. *New T* 6C 12
Dales Av. *Sut A* 4D 38
Dalestorth Av. *Mans* 7H 29
Dalestorth Clo. *Sut A* 4E 38
Dalestorth Gdns. *Skeg* 4E 38
Dalestorth Rd. *Sut A* 4E 38
Dalestorth St. *Sut A* 5E 38
Dale St. *Mans* 7B 30
Daleswood. *S Norm* 7C 46
Dale Vw. *Stre* 5C 34
Dale Vw. Clo. *Lwr P* 5H 25
Dale Vw. Gdns. *Klbrn* 7K 67
Dale Vw. Rd. *Lwr P* 4H 25
Dallas St. *Mans* 3A 40
Dalley La. *Belp* 1A 66
Daltons Clo. *Lan M* 7C 64
Dame Flogan St. *Mans* 3B 40
Dam La. *Shirl* 1F 45
Dam Side. *Belp* 4E 66
Damon Clo. *Pils* 7J 25
Danbury Clo. *Gras* 4E 12
Danesby Cres. *Den* 6K 67
Danesby Ri. *Den* 6K 67
Danesmoor. 5E 24
Danesmoor Ind. Est.
Dane 5F 25
Daniel Cres. *Mans* 2K 39
Dannah Cres. *Rip* 3F 63
Dannah St. *Rip* 2E 62
Danners Hill. *Pap* 7D 60
Dark La. *Asvr* 6J 25
Dark La. *Mak* 7F 67
Dark La. *N Wing* 1G 25

Darley Av. *Kirk A* 4G **49**
Darley Av. *N Wing* 1G **25**
Darley Dale Clo. *Mans* 6C **40**
Darley Dri. *Rip* 1C **62**
Darley Way. *N Wing* 1G **25**
(in two parts)
Darlton St. *Mans* 3H **39**
Darricott Clo. *Rain* 2D **52**
Darwin Clo. *Mans* 6C **40**
Darwood La. *Bsvr* 6J **5**
Davenport Rd. *New T* 7C **12**
Davey Ct. *Bsvr* 3H **5**
Davey Rd. *Mans* 2K **39**
David St. *Kirk A* 3F **49**
Davies Av. *Sut A* 5C **38**
Davies Clo. *Sut A* 6C **38**
Davis Clo. *Clip V* 4D **32**
Dawgates La. *Ple* 6D **28**
Daykins Row. *Cod* 5J **63**
Days La. *Belp* 4D **66**
Day St. *Wars* 3H **19**
Deacon Clo. *Swanw* 4E **54**
Deamon St. *B'will* 1A **46**
Dean Clo. *Mans* 5C **40**
Deansgate. *Ple* 3E **28**
Debdale Ga. *Mans W* 6A **30**
(in two parts)
Debdale La. *Mans* 6K **29**
Deben Down. *Mans W* 5D **30**
Deepdale. *Iron* 7B **56**
Deepdale Ct. *Sut A* 5D **38**
(off Slater St.)
Deepdale Gdns. *Sut A* 5D **38**
Deepdale Pk. *Sut A* 5D **38**
Deepdale Rd. *Belp* 2F **67**
Deepdale Rd. *Bsvr* 3H **5**
Deepdale Rd. *For T* 7D **30**
Deepdale St. *Sut A* 5D **38**
Deep La. *Pils* 5B **26**
Deerlands Rd. *Wing* 4A **12**
Deerpark Cres. *Wing* 4A **12**
Deincourt Cres. *N Wing* 7F **13**
De Lacy Ct. *New O* 3F **23**
Delamere Clo. *Mans* 5C **40**
Delamere Clo. *Swanw* 4F **55**
Delamere Rd. *Mans* 4C **40**
Dell Lea. *Mans* 6G **41**
Dell, The. *Kirk A* 3D **58**
Delves Bank Rd. *Swanw* 4G **55**
Delves, The. *Swanw* 4F **55**
De Morgan Clo. *Und* 2J **65**
Denbigh Clo. *Rain* 1E **52**
Denbury Rd. *R'hd* 1G **61**
Denby Dri. *Mans* 7D **40**
Denham St. *Clay C* 5D **24**
Dennor Dri. *Mans W* 3E **30**
Denton Clo. *For T* 7E **30**
Denton Way. *Swanw* 4F **55**
Derby Rd. *Alf* 1F **55**
Derby Rd. *Ann & Kirk A* 4F **59**
Derby Rd. *Belp & Milf* 5D **66**
Derby Rd. *Ches & Wing* 1A **12**
Derby Rd. *Lwr K & Klbrn* 7J **67**
Derby Rd. *Old T & Clay C* 1B **24**
Derby Rd. *Rip* 3D **62**
Derby Rd. *Swanw* 4E **54**
(Green, The)
Derby Rd. *Swanw & Rip* 5E **54**
(Swanwick Hill)
Derbyshire Dri. *W'wd* 7E **56**
Derby St. *Mans* 3C **40**
Derwent Av. *Mans* 3G **41**
Derwent Av. *Milf* 6D **66**
Derwent Clo. *Mans* 4G **41**
Derwent Clo. *Rain* 2D **52**
Derwent Clo. *Wars* 2J **19**
Derwent Dri. *Kirk A* 3E **58**
Derwent Dri. *Sels* 4J **57**
Derwent Dri. *Tib* 3B **36**
Derwent Gro. *Alf* 1F **55**
Derwent Pl. *Clay C* 3A **24**
Derwent Rd. *Rip* 3C **62**
Derwentside Ind. Pk. *Belp* 6D **66**
Derwent St. *Belp* 4C **66**
Derwent Av. *Belp* 5D **66**
Derwent Valley Vis. Cen. 2D **66**
Derwent Vw. *Belp* 2D **66**
Desborough Rd. *Sels* 4F **57**
Desmond Ct. *Und* 2J **65**

Dethick Way. *N Wing* 1H **25**
Devon Clo. *Gras* 5F **13**
Devon Dri. *Mans* 1K **39**
Devonshire Av. *Rip* 2C **62**
Devonshire Clo. *Huth* 7J **37**
Devonshire Cotts. *Scarc* 1C **16**
Devonshire Dri. *Lang* 6K **7**
Devonshire Dri. *Lea* 4H **55**
Devonshire Dri. *Oll* 4E **22**
Devonshire Sq. *Sut A* 7C **38**
(off Manor St.)
Devonshire St. *N Hou* 1D **28**
Devonshire Ter. *Hlmwd* 6A **14**
Devonshire Vs. *Hlmwd* 7A **14**
(off Heath Rd.)
Diamond Av. *Kirk A* 6F **49**
Diamond Av. *Rain* 1E **52**
Dickens Dri. *Hlmwd* 6K **13**
Dingley Clo. *Mans W* 3E **30**
Division Rd. *Shire* 3J **17**
Dixie St. *Jack* 7D **56**
Doe Hill La. *Ston* 4J **35**
Dog and Bear La. *Ann* 6E **58**
Dog La. *Shirl* 7E **34**
Doles La. *Kirk A* 4K **47**
Dorchester Clo. *Mans* 7D **40**
Dorchester Dri. *Mans* 7D **40**
Dorchester Rd. *Kirk A* 2F **59**
Doreen Dri. *Sut A* 7B **38**
Dormy Clo. *Mans W* 3E **30**
Dorothy Av. *Mans W* 7C **30**
Dorothy Dri. *For T* 7F **31**
Dorset Way. *Mans* 5G **41**
Douglas Rd. *For T* 6H **31**
Douglas Rd. *Som* 3K **55**
Douglas Rd. *Sut A* 7B **38**
Dove Clo. *Klbrn* 7K **67**
Dove Clo. *New O* 3F **23**
Dove Cft. *New O* 3F **23**
Dovedale Av. *Sut A* 1B **48**
Dovedale Clo. *Edwin* 5H **21**
Dovedale Clo. *Mans* 6D **40**
Dovedale Clo. *Rip* 6D **62**
Dovedale Ct. *Belp* 3F **67**
Dovedale Cres. *Belp* 3F **67**
Dove Dri. *Sels* 4J **57**
Dove Green. 5G **57**
Dover Beck Clo. *R'hd* 1F **61**
Doveridge Ct. *R'hd* 7G **51**
Dove Rd. *Rip* 3C **62**
Downham Gdns. *R'hd* 1H **61**
Downing St. *S Norm* 4C **46**
Downing St. *Sut A* 5D **38**
Downs, The. *For T* 7F **31**
Draycott Rd. *N Wing* 1F **25**
Drayton Av. *Mans* 7H **29**
Drive, The. *Clip V* 5C **32**
Dronley Dri. *Chur W* 7J **9**
Duckmanton. 1C **4**
Duckmanton Moor. 5A **4**
Duckmanton Rd. *Duck* 1C **4**
Duesbury, The. *S Norm* 6D **46**
Dukes Clo. *Hlmwd* 6A **14**
Dukes Clo. *Sut A* 7G **39**
Duke's Dri. *Glap* 2J **27**
Duke St. *Huth* 6J **37**
Duke St. *S Norm* 4C **46**
Duke St. *Sut A* 7C **38**
(off King St.)
Dumbles Rd. *Bsvr* 5H **5**
Dumbles, The. *Sut A* 1A **48**
Dunbar Dri. *Mans* 4H **39**
Duncan Av. *R'hd* 2G **61**
Duncan Clo. *Belp* 1F **67**
Dundee Dri. *Mans W* 5D **30**
Dunelm Clo. *Sut A* 6A **38**
Dunmore Dri. *Mans* 4H **39**
Dunn Brigg. *Mans W* 6D **30**
Dunnett Rd. *Mans* 4J **39**
Dunoon Rd. *Mans* 4J **39**
Dunsford Rd. *Alf* 5H **45**
Dunstil Wlk. *Clay C* 4E **24**
Dunsil Rd. *Newt* 7K **65**
Dunsil Rd. *Pinx* 1F **57**
Dunvegan Av. *Dane* 6E **24**
Dunwoody Clo. *Mans* 2F **41**
Durham Av. *Gras* 5F **13**
Durham Av. *Mans* 4D **30**

Dykes Clo. *Bsvr* 4J **5**
Dymond Clo. *Gras* 4F **13**

E

Each Well La. *Alf* 7F **45**
Eakring Clo. *Mans* 2F **41**
Eakring Ct. *Mans* 3E **40**
Eakring Rd. *B'thpe* 1J **43**
Eakring Rd. *Mans* 3E **40**
(in three parts)
Eakring Rd. *W'low* 7H **23**
Earlswood Dri. *Mans* 4F **41**
East Cres. *Duck* 1C **4**
East Cres. *Holb* 7G **67**
Eastern Av. *Bsvr* 6K **5**
Eastfield Clo. *Clip V* 6B **32**
Eastfield Dri. *S Norm* 5C **46**
Eastfield Rd. *Rip* 3G **63**
Eastfield Side. *Sut A* 5E **38**
Eastlands La. *Chur W* 1H **19**
Eastland Ter. *Med V* 6A **10**
East La. *Edwin* 5K **21**
Eastleigh Dri. *Mans W* 2B **30**
East St. *Clay C* 4D **24**
East St. *Doe L* 6F **15**
East St. *Scarc* 1C **16**
East St. *Sut A* 6E **38**
East Vw. *Bsvr* 7K **5**
East Vw. *Lang* 3A **8**
East Vw. *Lang J* 1K **17**
E. View Clo. *Kirk A* 2G **59**
Eastwood Av. *Wars* 2H **19**
Eather Av. *Mans W* 4C **30**
Eaton Clo. *Rain* 2C **52**
Eaton Ct. *Mans* 6G **41**
Eckford Ct. *Mans* 7G **41**
(off Bellamy Rd.)
Eckington Wlk. *Mans* 3H **41**
(in two parts)
Eclipse Yd. Mans 2B **40**
(off Clumber St.)
Edale Clo. *Mans* 6G **41**
Edale Ct. *Sut A* 5C **38**
Edale Dri. *S Norm* 3D **46**
Edale Rd. *Mans* 3H **41**
Edale Way. *Belp* 2D **66**
Eddery Av. *Mans* 5D **30**
Edensor Clo. *N Wing* 2F **25**
Edensor Dri. *Belp* 1G **67**
Edgar Av. *Mans* 1C **40**
Edgehill Gro. *Mans W* 6C **30**
Edinburgh Ct. *Swanw* 4F **55**
Edingley Av. *Mans* 2H **39**
Edison St. *Kirk A* 2D **58**
Edmonton Rd. *Clip V* 6A **32**
Edwalton Ct. *Mans* 6G **41**
Edward Av. *Jack* 7D **56**
Edward Av. *Sut A* 5D **38**
Edward St. *Belp* 2E **66**
Edward St. *Kirk A* 4F **49**
Edward St. *Wars* 2G **19**
Edward Wlk. *New T* 6D **12**
(off Ivanhoe Clo.)
Edwinstowe. 5K **21**
Edwin Stowe Dri. *Sels* 4K **57**
Edwin St. *Sut A* 6C **38**
Egerton Clo. *Mans* 2G **41**
Egham Clo. *Rain* 1E **52**
Egmanton Rd. *Mans* 6G **41**
Egmanton Rd. *Med V* 6K **9**
Egstow. 4D **24**
Egstow Pl. *Clay C* 4D **24**
Egstow St. *Clay C* 4D **24**
Eider Clo. *Shire* 4H **17**
Eighth Av. *For T* 1G **41**
Eland Rd. *Lang J* 2K **17**
Elder Clo. *Swanw* 3G **55**
Elder St. *Kirk A* 4C **48**
Elder St. *Sut A* 2B **38**
Eldon St. *Clay C* 4C **24**
Elizabeth Pk. *Iron* 6B **56**
Elkesley Pl. *Med V* 5A **10**
Elkesley Rd. *Med V* 5A **10**
Ellesmere Av. *Alf* 6H **45**
Ellesmere Rd. *For T* 1F **41**
Ellis St. *Kirk A* 5F **49**

Elma La. *Cuc* 1D **8**
Elm Av. *Belp* 5F **67**
Elm Clo. *Bsvr* 5A **6**
Elm Clo. *Pinx* 7F **47**
Elmfield. *Wars* 4G **19**
Elm Gro. *Chur W* 1G **19**
Elm Gro. *Clay C* 5D **24**
Elmhirst Av. *S Norm* 5B **46**
Elmhurst Clo. *S Norm* 6B **46**
Elmhurst Dri. *Huth* 6J **37**
Elmhurst Rd. *For T* 7F **31**
Elm Rd. *Pils* 7J **25**
Elms Av. *Alf* 6G **45**
Elms Av. *Rip* 4D **62**
Elms Clo. *Alf* 6G **45**
Elms, The. 4D **62**
Elm St. *Temp N* 3H **13**
Elmton La. *Bsvr* 4K **5**
Elm Tree Av. *Mans W* 4A **30**
Elm Tree Av. *Sels* 4H **57**
Elm Tree Av. *Shire* 3H **17**
Elm Tree Av. *Shirl* 1C **44**
Elm Tree Rd. *Kirk A* 4D **48**
Elm Tree Row. *Tib* 4B **36**
Elm Tree St. *Mans* 2C **40**
Elm Wlk. *Pils* 7J **25**
Elmwood Dri. *Alf* 7J **45**
Elsecar Clo. *Belp* 2H **67**
Elston Clo. *Mans* 7H **29**
Elton Clo. *Mans* 3H **41**
Elton Clo. *N Wing* 3G **25**
Elton Rd. *Mans* 3F **41**
Elvaston Ct. *Mans* 3H **41**
Elvaston Rd. *N Wing* 2F **25**
Elvin Way. *New T* 7C **12**
Ely Clo. *Mans W* 4D **30**
Elyn Av. *N Wing* 1H **25**
Emerald Clo. *Mans* 7K **29**
Emerald Clo. *Sut A* 1G **49**
Emerald Gro. *Kirk A* 6G **49**
Emerald Gro. *Rain* 1E **52**
Emma Bates Way. *Blid* 4D **52**
Emmas Williams Ct. *Rip* 3D **62**
Emmerson Rd. *Ridd* 4J **55**
Empire St. *Mans* 3D **40**
Enderby Cres. *Mans* 3F **41**
Engine La. *Newt* 7K **65**
Enterprise Clo. *Mans* 5J **29**
Enterprise Dri. *Hlmwd* 6K **13**
Enterprise Way. *Mans* 6H **29**
Epperstone Ct. *Mans* 7G **41**
Epping Way. *For T* 1H **41**
Epsom St. *Mans* 3F **41**
Erewash Rd. *Pinx* 1G **57**
Erewash St. *Kirk A* 5E **48**
Erewash St. *Pye B* 5C **56**
Erica Dri. *S Norm* 3D **46**
Erin Rd. *Pool & Duck* 1D **4**
Eskdale Clo. *Bsvr* 5H **5**
Eskdale Clo. *Mans* 4F **41**
Ethelbert Av. *Kirk A* 2G **59**
Evans Av. *Sut A* 6A **38**
Evelyn Devonshire Cotts.
Pils .6C **26**
Everest Dri. *Som* 3K **55**
Evershill Clo. *Mort* 4F **35**
Evershill La. *Mort* 4F **35**
(in two parts)
Everton St. *Mans* 7J **29**
Ewart La. *Alf* 7F **45**
Exchange Row. Mans 2B **40**
(off Queen St.)
Exe Fold. *Mans W* 6D **30**
Exford Clo. *Mans W* 2C **30**
Export Dri. *Huth* 2H **47**
Eyam Clo. *Mans* 3H **41**
Eyam Clo. *N Wing* 7G **13**
Eyam Wlk. *Belp* 2E **66**
Eyre St. *Clay C* 4C **24**

F

Fabric Vw. *Hlmwd* 7K **13**
Fackley. 2K **37**
Fackley Rd. *Tev* 2K **37**
Fackley Way. *Stan H* 3K **37**
Factory Yd. *Sut A* 5E **38**
Fairfield Av. *Hilc* 1E **46**

Fairfield Av. *Ston*	.5H 35
Fairfield Clo. *Neth L*	.4A 8
Fairfield Dri. *Mans*	.2G 41
Fairfield Dri. *N Wing*	.2G 25
Fairfield Rd. *Bsvr*	.6J 5
Fairfield Rd. *Sut A*	.6F 39
Fairfields Dri. *R'hd*	.7C 50
Fairhaven. *Kirk A*	.7F 49
Fairholme Cvn. Pk. *Oll*	.4F 23
Fairholme Clo. *Clip V*	.6B 32
Fairholme Dri. *Mans*	.7J 29
Fairlawns. *Mans*	.2H 41
Fairlie Av. *Mans*	.4H 39
Fairview Av. *Und*	.2H 65
Fairways Dri. *Kirk A*	.3D 48
Fairways, The. *Dane*	.5E 24
Fairways, The. *Mans W*	.2D 30
Fairweather Clo. *Boug*	.1K 23
Falcons Ri. *Belp*	.2G 67
Fal Paddock. *Mans W*	.6D 30
Faraday Rd. *Mans*	.4E 40
Far Cft. Av. *Sut A*	.6A 38
Farfield La. *Glap*	.3A 28
Far Laund.	.1G 67
Farm Clo. *Belp*	.3G 67
Farm Clo. *Rip*	.5B 54
Farm Clo. *Som*	.3J 55
Farm Cft. Rd. *Mans W*	.2C 30
Farmfields Clo. *Bsvr*	.3G 5
Farmilo Cres. *Mans*	.7J 29
Farm Vw. *New T*	.7D 12
Farm Vw. Rd. *Kirk A*	.5G 49
Farmway. *Mans W*	.6C 30
Farnah Green.	.4B 66
Farnah Grn. Rd. *Belp*	.5B 66
Farndale Clo. *Sut A*	.4D 38
Farndale Rd. *Sut A*	.4D 38
Farndon Rd. *Sut A*	.1F 49
Farndon Way. *Mans*	.2J 39
Farnsfield Ct. *Mans*	.7G 41
Farnsworth Av. *Rain*	.7A 42
Farnsworth Gro. *Huth*	.6H 37
Farrendale Clo. *For T*	.7D 30
Farr Way. *Blid*	.6C 52
Fearn Av. *Rip*	.3E 62
Featherbed La. *Bsvr*	.1J 5
Featherstone Clo. *Mans*	.5H 39
Felley Av. *Kirk A*	.2C 58
Felley Mill La. (North) *Und*	.1K 65
Felley Mill La. (South) *Und*	.3J 65
Fellside. *Belp*	.3E 66
Fell Wilson Gro. *Wars*	.3J 19
Fell Wilson St. *Wars*	.3J 19
Felton Av. *Mans W*	.2C 30
Fen Clo. *Nwtn*	.6C 36
Fenwick St. *Wars*	.3H 19
Ferguson Av. *Mans W*	.4B 30
Fern Bank Av. *B'wll*	.1A 46
Fern Clo. *Heath*	.6B 14
Fern Clo. *R'hd*	.3H 61
Fern Clo. *Shire*	.1J 17
Ferndale Clo. *New O*	.1J 23
Fern Lea. *Shirl*	.6D 34
Fernleigh Ri. *For T*	.6D 30
Fern St. *Sut A*	.5C 38
Fernwood Clo. *For T*	.7G 31
Fernwood Clo. *Shirl*	.6D 34
Ferrers Way. *Rip*	.1C 62
Festus St. *Kirk A*	.6E 48
Field Clo. *Mans W*	.3D 30
Field Dri. *Shire*	.5J 17
Fielden Av. *Mans*	.6H 29
Field Ind. Est. *Kirk A*	.4E 48
Field La. *Belp*	.3D 66
Field La. *Blid*	.6B 52
Field La. *Glap*	.2K 27
Field La. *S Norm*	.3B 46
Field Pl. *Kirk A*	.2B 48
Field Row. *Belp*	.3D 66
Field St. *Cod*	.5H 63
Field Ter. *Rip*	.3D 62
Field Vw. *Ches*	.1A 12
Field Vw. *S Norm*	.3C 46
Field Vw. *Sut A*	.1A 48
Fifth Av. *Clip V*	.5B 32
Fifth Av. *Edwin*	.5H 21
Fifth Av. *For T*	.1G 41

Findern Clo. *Belp*	.1F 67
Findern Clo. *Mans*	.3H 41
Finley Way. *S Norm*	.6D 46
Finningley Rd. *Mans*	.7G 41
Firbeck Av. *Mans*	.4F 41
Fir Clo. *Shire*	.1J 17
Fireman's Row. *Sut A*	.7C 38
Firestone. *Haz*	.7B 66
Firs Av. *Alf*	.5G 45
Firs Av. *Rip*	.3D 62
Firs Gdns. *Alf*	.6G 45
First Av. *Clip V*	.5C 32
First Av. *Edwin*	.5J 21
First Av. *For T*	.7G 31
First Av. *Rain*	.7B 42
Fir Tree Av. *Stre*	.5C 34
Fir Tree Clo. *For T*	.6K 31
Fir Vw. *New O*	.2H 23
Fisher Clo. *Sut A*	.4B 38
Fisher La. *Mans*	.4C 40
Fishers St. *Kirk A*	.2E 58
Fishpond Hill.	.2H 39
Fishponds Clo. *Wing*	.4A 12
Fishpool Rd. *Blid*	.7K 51
Fiskerton Ct. *Mans*	.6G 41
Fitzherbert St. *Wars*	.3J 19
Fitzwilliam Dri. *For T*	.6F 31
Five Pits Trail. *Hlmwd*	.1A 26
Five Pits Trail. *N Wing*	.6G 13
Five Pits Trail. *Tib*	.7A 26
Flatts La. *W'wd*	.1F 65
Flaxpiece Rd. *Clay C*	.5C 24
Fleet Cres. *Belp*	.4D 66
Fleet Pk. *Belp*	.4E 66
Fleet, The. *Belp*	.5D 66
Fletcher's Row. *Rip*	.2F 63
Fletcher St. *Rip*	.2E 62
Fletchers Way. *For T*	.1H 41
Flint Av. *For T*	.7F 31
Flintham Ct. *Mans*	.6H 41
Florence Clo. *Ple*	.4D 28
Florence Rd. *Clay C*	.4D 24
Flowery Leys La. *Alf*	.7H 45
Fonton Hall Dri. *Sut A*	.2K 47
Ford Av. *Los*	.7J 63
Fordbridge La. *B'wll*	.1B 46
Ford Clo. *Rip*	.4C 62
Ford St. *Belp*	.3D 66
Ford St. *New T*	.1D 24
Forest Av. *Mans*	.4C 40
Forest Clo. *Belp*	.2F 67
Forest Clo. *Kirk A*	.3E 58
Forest Clo. *Rain*	.1E 52
Forest Clo. *Sels*	.4K 57
Forest Corner. *Mans*	.4K 21
Forest Dri. *Mans*	.2H 41
Forest Dri. *Pils*	.6J 25
Foresters Rd. *Rip*	.2C 62
Forest Gdns. *Kirk A*	.3F 59
Forest Hill. *Mans*	.7C 40
Forest Ho. Mobile Home Pk. *Oll*	.4E 22
Forest Pk. Mobile Homes. *For T*	.6E 30
Forest Ri. *Wars*	.5J 19
Forest Rd. *Blid*	.5D 52
Forest Rd. *Clip V*	.5A 32
Forest Rd. *Kirk A*	.3E 58
Forest Rd. *Mans*	.5B 40
Forest Rd. *New O*	.3F 23
Forest Rd. *Sut A*	.3D 38
Forest Rd. *Wars*	.5K 19
Forest St. *Kirk A*	.3E 58
	(Forest Rd.)
Forest St. *Kirk A*	.6F 49
	(Kingsway)
Forest St. *Sut A*	.6C 38
Forest Town.	.7G 31
Forest Vw. *New O*	.3F 23
Forge La. *Mans*	.5F 17
	(in two parts)
Forge Row. *Iron*	.1B 64
Forster St. *Kirk A*	.5D 48
Forty Horse Clo. *Rip*	.3G 63
Fossetts Av. *Sels*	.4H 57
Foster St. *Mans*	.3C 40
Foston Clo. *Mans*	.3H 41
Foundry La. *Milf*	.7D 66

Foundry Ter. *News V*	.4J 59
Fountains Clo. *Mans*	.5G 49
Fountains Clo. *Kirk A*	.6B 44
Fourlane Ends.	.6B 44
Four Seasons Shop. Cen. *Mans*	.2B 40
Fourth Av. *Clip V*	.5B 32
Fourth Av. *Edwin*	.5H 21
Fourth Av. *For T*	.1G 41
Fourth Av. *Rain*	.7B 42
Fox Covert Clo. *Sut A*	.1A 48
Fox Covert Way. *For T*	.2H 41
Fox Cft. *Tib*	.4B 36
Fox Hill.	.7D 6
Fox Hill. *Scarc*	.1D 16
Foxhill Clo. *Sut A*	.6K 37
Foxpark Vw. *Tib*	.4A 36
Fox St. *Kirk A*	.3E 58
Fox St. *Sut A*	.6D 38
Foxwood Clo. *Has*	.1D 12
Frances St. *Brins*	.3F 65
Francis St. *Mans*	.2E 40
Francis Way. *Mans*	.5J 39
Franderground Dri. *Kirk A*	.5C 48
Frank Av. *Mans*	.4K 39
Franklin Rd. *Jack*	.7C 56
Fraser St. *News V*	.5H 59
Frederick Av. *Kirk A*	.4B 48
Frederick St. *Alf*	.5G 45
Frederick St. *Gras*	.4E 12
Frederick St. *Mans*	.3C 40
Frederick St. *Ridd*	.6J 55
Frederick St. *Ridd*	.1K 47
Freeby Av. *Mans W*	.3D 30
French Ter. *Lang*	.4A 8
Friar La. *Wars*	.5J 19
Friars Clo. *Sels*	.4K 57
Friend La. *Edwin*	.6K 21
Friezeland.	.2K 65
Fritchley Clo. *Mans*	.3H 41
Frith Gro. *Mans*	.2J 39
Froggett Clo. *Som*	.4K 55
Fuller Clo. *Mans*	.5B 40
Fulwood.	.2K 47
Fulwood Clo. *Sut A*	.2J 47
Fulwood Ind. Est. *Sut A*	.2H 47
Fulwood Ri. *Sut A*	.2J 47
Fulwood Rd. N. *Sut A*	.2H 47
Fulwood Rd. S. *Sut A*	.2H 47
Furnace Clo. *Gras*	.5E 12
Furnace Hill. *Clay C*	.3D 24
Furnace Hillock Way. *Gras*	.2E 12
Furnace La. *Los*	.7J 63
Furnace Row. *Som*	.4A 56

Gables Clo. *Hlmwd*	.7K 13
Gaitskell Cres. *Edwin*	.6A 22
Gamston Rd. *Mans*	.6H 41
Gang La. *Scarc*	.1C 16
Garden Av. *N Hou*	.1D 28
Garden Av. *Rain*	.1C 52
Garden Av. *Shire*	.3J 17
Garden Cres. *S Norm*	.6B 46
Gardeners Ct. *Bsvr*	.4K 5
Garden La. *Sut A*	.6E 38
	(in two parts)
Garden Rd. *Mans*	.3B 40
Garden Row. *Doe L*	.6F 15
Gardens, The. *Rip*	.5D 62
Garden Ter. *News V*	.4H 59
Gardiner Ter. *Stan H*	.3B 38
Garibaldi Rd. *For T*	.6K 31
Garnham Clo. *Som*	.1K 55
Garnon St. *Mans*	.4J 39
Garratt Av. *Mans*	.2C 40
Garret Grn. *Dane*	.6E 24
Garret La. *Dane*	.5D 24
Garside Av. *Sut A*	.7B 38
Garth Av. *Kirk A*	.2C 48
Garth Rd. *Mans*	.5A 40
Garwick Clo. *For T*	.6H 31
Gate Brook Clo. *Cod*	.3H 63
Gattlys La. *New O*	.2F 23
Gedling St. *Mans*	.4B 40
Gentshill.	.6E 24
Gentshill Av. *Dane*	.6E 24
George Cres. *Ridd*	.5J 55

George Dere Clo. *New O*	.1H 23
George Percival Pl. *Clay C*	.4A 24
George Shooter Ct. *Wars*	.2J 19
George St. *Alf*	.6G 45
George St. *Belp*	.3D 66
George St. *For T*	.7G 31
George St. *Kirk A*	.5B 48
George St. *Lang*	.4A 8
George St. *Mans*	.1K 39
George St. *Mans W*	.5D 30
George St. *N Wing*	.1E 24
George St. *Pinx*	.6E 46
George St. *Ridd*	.5K 55
George St. *Som*	.3K 55
George St. *S Norm*	.5B 46
George St. *Sut A*	.6K 37
George St. *Wars*	.3H 19
	(Appleton St.)
George St. *Wars*	.6F 19
	(Mansfield Rd.)
Gibbons Rd. *Mans*	.4K 39
Gibfield La. *Belp*	.5D 66
Gilcroft St. *Mans*	.3B 40
Gilcroft St. *Sut A*	.3C 38
Gillies, The. *Mans*	.4J 39
Gill's La. *Gras*	.5E 12
Gill St. *Sels*	.5J 57
Gill St. *Sut A*	.7A 38
Gipsy La. *Chur W*	.1F 19
Girton Ct. *Mans*	.7H 41
Gisburn Gro. *For T*	.1H 41
Gladstone Av. *B'wll*	.1A 46
Gladstone Dri. *Brins*	.5G 65
Gladstone Rd. *Alf*	.7F 45
Gladstone St. *Kirk A*	.5F 49
Gladstone St. *Mans*	.2D 40
	(in two parts)
Gladstone St. *Mans W*	.6C 30
Gladstone St. *S Norm*	.4D 46
Gladstone Ter. *Kirk A*	.5D 48
Gladstone Ter. *Mans W*	.6C 30
Glannis Sq. *Chur W*	.1J 19
Glapwell.	.7K 15
Glapwell La. *Glap*	.6K 15
Glasby Clo. *Oll*	.3F 23
Glasby Ct. *Oll*	.3F 23
	(off Glasby Clo.)
Glasshouse Hill. *Cod*	.3H 63
Glastonbury Clo. *Mans W*	.4D 30
Glaven Clo. *Mans W*	.6D 30
Glebe Av. *Pinx*	.7F 47
Glebe Av. *Rip*	.2C 62
Glebe Av. *Wars*	.3J 19
Glebe Clo. *Hlmwd*	.7K 13
Glebe Clo. *S Norm*	.5C 46
Glebe Gdns. *N Wing*	.3F 25
Glebe St. *Kirk A*	.3D 58
Glebe Vw. *For T*	.1D 40
Glen Clo. *Nwtn*	.6C 36
Gleneagles Dri. *Kirk A*	.3C 48
Glen Mooar Clo. *For T*	.6G 31
Glenside. *Kirk A*	.5G 49
Glen St. *Sut A*	.5C 38
Glen Vw. *Belp*	.5D 66
Glen Vine. *Rip*	.3G 63
Glinton Av. *B'wll*	.1A 46
Glossop Av. *Mans*	.3H 41
Glove Gro. *Mans W*	.4F 31
Glovers Clo. *Cuc*	.3G 9
Glove's La. *B'wll*	.7K 35
	(in two parts)
Golden Valley.	.1J 63
Golden Valley. *Ridd*	.1J 63
Golden Valley Country Pk.	.7H 55
Golden Valley Light Railway.	.7H 55
Goldfinch Clo. *Mans*	.2E 40
Goldies Dri. *Mans*	.1D 40
Goldsmith Ho. *Mans*	.2A 40
	(off Connexion, The)
Goldsmith St. *Mans*	.2A 40
Goodacre St. *Mans*	.2C 40
Goodhand Cres. *Mans*	.3J 39
Goods Rd. *Belp*	.5D 66
Goods Rd. Ind. Est. *Belp*	.5D 66
Goods Yd. *Belp*	.6D 66
Goodwin's La. *Haz*	.6A 66
Goodwood Way. *Mans*	.2F 41

Gooker La. *Alf* 7F **45**
Goosegreen. 6D **34**
Goose Grn. La. *Shirl* 7D **34**
Goose La. *Cod* 4J **63**
Gordon Av. *Mans* 3E **40**
Gordon Brae. *Mans* 6C **40**
Gordon Cres. *S Norm* 6D **46**
Gordondale Rd. *Mans* 7B **30**
Gordon Rd. *Swanw* 3F **55**
Gorse Av. *Mans* 4G **41**
Gorse Bank. *Heath* 5B **14**
Gorse Hill. *R'hd* 2G **61**
Gorsethorpe La. *Old C* 6B **20**
Gorse Valley Rd. *Has* 1E **12**
Gorseway. *Clip V* 5C **32**
Gorsey Clo. *Belp* 1C **66**
Grafton Clo. *Sut A* 4F **39**
Grainger Av. *Kirk A* 2F **59**
Granby Av. *Mans* 1B **40**
Granby Clo. *Pils* 6J **25**
Grange Av. *Mans* 4K **39**
Grange Av. *Oll* 4F **23**
Grange Clo. *Som* 1B **56**
Grange Clo. *Sut A* 1A **38**
Grange Ct. *Kirk A* 5H **49**
Grange Ct. *Som* 2J **55**
Grange Farm Clo. *Sut A* . . .2A **48**
Grange Rd. *Blid* 5D **52**
Grange Rd. *Pils* 6J **25**
Grange St. *Alf* 7G **45**
Grange, The. *S Norm* 6C **46**
Grange Wlk. *Gras* 5E **12**
Grangewood Dri. *Milf* 7E **66**
Grangewood Rd. *Ches* 1A **12**
Grangewood Rd. *Kirk A* 3D **48**
Granton Ri. *Mans* 4H **39**
Grasmere Av. *Clay C* 5B **24**
Grasmere Ct. *Mans* 2A **40**
     (off Layton Av.)
Grasshill. 3E **12**
Grassmoor. 4E **12**
Grassmoor Country Pk. .3F **13**
Grassmoor Golf Course. .3E **12**
Grass Rd. *Shirl* 6D **34**
Gratton Ct. *Kirk A* 3C **48**
Gray Fallow. *S Norm* 6D **46**
Grays Dri. *R'hd* 5H **61**
Grayswood Clo. *Swanw* . . .4G **55**
Greasley Ct. *Mans* 6H **41**
Gt. Central Rd. *Mans* 3C **40**
Gt. Northern Cotts. *Ple* 3E **28**
     (off Pit Hill)
Gt. Northern Cotts. *Shire* . . .4J **17**
     (off Peak, The)
Greaves St. *Rip* 2E **62**
Greaves St. *Shirl* 1E **44**
Greenacre. *Mans* 4F **41**
Greenacre. *Stan H* 4A **38**
Greenacres. *Kirk A* 1F **59**
Greenacres Dri. *S Norm* . . .4D **46**
Greenaway Dri. *Bsvr* 6H **5**
Green Bank. *Rain* 2E **52**
Greenbank Dri. *Sut A* 5C **38**
Green Clo. *Blid* 6C **52**
Green Clo. *Nwtn* 6C **36**
Green Cres. *Sels* 5G **57**
Greendale Av. *Edwin* 4H **21**
Greendale Clo. *Stan H* 3A **38**
Greendale Clo. *Wars* 3G **19**
Greendale Cres. *Clip V* 4D **32**
Green Dri. *Old C* 4D **20**
Grn. Farm Rd. *Sels* 5F **57**
Greenfield Clo. *For T* 7H **31**
Greenfield Clo. *Edwin* 7K **21**
Greenfields Cres. *New O* . . .3G **23**
Greenhill Av. *Rip* 4E **62**
Greenhill La. *Kirk A* 3D **58**
Greenhill La. *Lea & Ridd* . . .4J **55**
Greenhillocks. 4E **62**
Greenholme Clo. *Kirk A* 6E **48**
Greenholme Pk. *Mans W* . . .2E **30**
Greenland Clo. *N Wing* 1G **25**
Greenland Rd. *Sut A* 2C **38**
Green La. *Belp* 3D **66**
Green La. *Mans* 6C **40**
Green La. *Mans W* 3F **31**
Green La. *N Hou* 7B **16**
Green La. *New T* 6D **12**
Green La. *Pils* 5J **25**

Green La. *Ple* 7D **28**
Green La. *Shire* 5G **17**
Greensfields. *Sut A* 4E **38**
Green Side. *Sels* 5F **57**
Greensquare Rd. *Pinx* 1G **57**
Green, The. *Alf* 7H **45**
Green, The. Belp 2E **66**
     (off Cemetery Rd.)
Green, The. *Glap* 7K **15**
Green, The. *Has* 1D **12**
Green, The. *Huth* 7J **37**
Green, The. *Mans W* 3A **30**
Green, The. *Nwtn* 6C **36**
Green, The. *N Wing* 1G **25**
Green, The. *Pils* 5C **26**
Green, The. *Swanw* 4E **54**
Greentrees Ct. *Sut A* 1B **48**
Greenview Clo. *For T* 7H **31**
Greenway. *For T* 5K **31**
Green Way. *Wing* 5C **12**
Greenwich. 2E **62**
Greenwood Av. *Edwin* 5K **21**
Greenwood Av. *Huth* 7H **37**
Greenwood Av. *Mans W* . . .4B **30**
Greenwood Cotts. *Mans* . . .1F **41**
Greenwood Cres. *Boug* . . .2J **23**
Greenwood Dri. *Kirk A* 5C **48**
Greer La. *N Hou* 7B **16**
Gregorys Way. *Belp* 2G **67**
Grendon Clo. *Belp* 1F **67**
Grendon Way. *Sut A* 2F **39**
     (Beck La.)
Grendon Way. *Sut A* 4F **39**
     (Cosgrove La.)
Grenvoir Dri. *Rip* 3G **63**
Grey St. *Kirk A* 5B **48**
Griceson Clo. *Oll* 5F **23**
Grives La. *Kirk A* 1F **59**
Grizedale Clo. *For T* 1H **41**
Grizedale Ri. *For T* 1G **41**
Grosvenor Av. *Sut A* 7B **38**
Grosvenor Pl. Sut A 7B **38**
     (off Grosvenor Av.)
Grosvenor Rd. *Rip* 3D **62**
Grove Cotts. *Ple* 3F **29**
Grove Ct. *Rip* 4F **63**
Grove Rd. *Chur W* 1G **19**
Grove Rd. *Sut A* 6F **39**
Grove St. *Mans* 3B **40**
Grove St. *Mans W* 5B **30**
Grove, The. *Ann* 3F **59**
Grove Way. *Mans W* 5B **30**
Grundy Av. *Sels* 4F **57**
Grundy Rd. *Clay C* 5C **24**
Guildford Av. *Mans W* 2C **30**
Guildford Clo. *Dane* 5E **24**
Guildford La. *Dane* 5E **24**
Guildhall Dri. *Sels* 1G **57**
Gunthorpe Ct. *Mans* 6H **41**
Gutter, The. 3F **67**

H

Hack La. *Sut A* 7C **38**
Haddon Clo. *Alf* 7F **45**
Haddon Clo. *Sels* 4J **57**
Haddon Pl. *Lang J* 1J **17**
Haddon Rd. *Mans* 1B **40**
Haddon Rd. *N Wing* 7G **13**
Haddon Rd. *R'hd* 7G **51**
Haddon St. *Sut A* 5C **38**
Haddon St. *Tib* 3C **36**
Hadfield Wlk. Mans 3H **41**
     (off Edale Rd.)
Hagg Hill. *New T* 6E **12**
Haggnook Wood. *R'hd* 7D **50**
Halam Clo. *Mans* 2H **39**
Halcyon App. *Wing* 5C **12**
Haldane Cres. *Bsvr* 4H **5**
Halfmoon Dri. *Kirk A* 7E **48**
Hallam Rd. *New O* 1H **23**
Hallam Way. *Mans* 7C **30**
Hardy St. *Alf* 7E **45**
Hall Barn La. *Mans* 1H **39**
     (in two parts)
Hall Bungalows. *Wing* 4A **12**
Hall Clo. *Rain* 2D **52**
Hall Dri. *Sut S* 1C **14**
Hall Farm La. *Has* 1D **12**

Hall Farm Cotts. *Sut S* 1C **14**
Hallfield Clo. *Wing* 3B **12**
Hallfield Gate. 1C **44**
Hallfieldgate La. *Shirl* 1C **44**
Hallfield Rd. *Nwtn* 6C **36**
Hallfields Ri. *Shirl* 1C **44**
Hallgate La. *Pils* 6H **25**
Hall Green. 3G **57**
Hallifax Av. *Chur W* 7H **9**
Hall La. *Brins* 5E **64**
Hall La. *Nwtn* 6C **36**
Hall La. *Pap* 6D **60**
Hall Rd. *Lan M* 7E **64**
Hall St. *Alf* 6F **45**
Hall St. *Mans* 3E **40**
Hall St. *Sut A* 3C **38**
Hall Ter. *Clay C* 5D **24**
Hall Wlk. *New T* 6D **12**
Hamble Clo. *Mans W* 5D **30**
Hambleton Av. *N Wing* 2F **25**
Hambleton Ri. *For T* 7F **31**
Hamill Clo. *N Wing* 1F **25**
Hamilton Dri. *Wars* 3G **19**
Hamilton Rd. *Sut A* 7G **39**
Hamilton St. *Mans* 3E **40**
Hamilton Way. *Mans* 6J **39**
Hamlet La. *S Norm* 5C **46**
Hamlet, The. *S Norm* 5C **46**
Hammer Leys. *S Norm* 6E **46**
Hammersmith. 7D **54**
Hammersmith. *Rip* 1D **62**
Hammerwater Dri. *Wars* . . .4G **19**
Hammond Gro. *Kirk A* 1F **59**
Hampden St. *Kirk A* 5D **48**
Hampshire Ct. *Jack* 7D **56**
Hanbury Ct. *Mans* 3H **41**
Handley Arc. *Mans* 2C **40**
Handley La. *Clay C* 1A **34**
Handstubbing. 5H **57**
Hanger Hill Dri. *Med V* 5D **10**
Hankin Av. *Und* 2J **65**
Hanstubbin Rd. *Sels* 5H **57**
Harby Av. *Mans W* 3D **30**
Harby Av. *Sut A* 1G **49**
Harcourt Clo. *Ches* 1C **12**
Harcourt St. *Kirk A* 5E **48**
Harcourt St. *Mans* 6F **39**
Hardie Av. *S Norm* 4C **46**
Hardstaff Clo. *Kirk A* 2C **58**
Hardstaff Homes, The.
   Mans W 5B **30**
Hardstoft. 5C **26**
Hardstoft Common. 5A **26**
Hardstoft Rd. *Pils* 6A **26**
Hardwick Av. *Glap* 7K **15**
Hardwick Av. *Rain* 1B **52**
Hardwick Av. *Shire* 3J **17**
Hardwick Av. *Sut A* 3E **38**
Hardwick Clo. *Hlmwd* 7A **14**
Hardwick Clo. *Rip* 1C **62**
Hardwick Clo. *Sut A* 3E **38**
Hardwick Dri. *Ark T* 3A **4**
Hardwick Dri. *B'wll* 1K **45**
Hardwick Dri. *Oll* 4E **22**
Hardwick Dri. *Sels* 4K **57**
Hardwick Hall. 4G **27**
Hardwick Hall Country Pk.
     . . . . .4H **27**
Hardwick Hall Country Pk.
   Info. Cen. 4E **26**
Hardwick La. *Sut A* 7D **38**
Hardwick Old Hall. 4G **27**
Hardwick Pk. 3G **27**
Hardwick St. *Lang* 6K **7**
Hardwick St. *Mans* 2D **40**
Hardwick St. *Shire* 3A **18**
Hardwick St. *Sut A* 7D **38**
Hardwick St. *Tib* 2C **36**
Hardwick Vw. *Sut A* 3E **38**
Hardwick Vw. Rd. *Hlmwd* . . .6B **14**
Hardy Cres. *Cod* 4H **63**
Hardy Pl. *Mans* 3K **39**
Hareholme St. *Mans* 1A **40**
Harewood Av. *Swanw* 3F **55**
Harewood Clo. *Belp* 2H **67**
Harewood Cres. *Old T* 2A **24**
Harlow Av. *Mans* 6C **40**
Harlow Clo. *Mans W* 2C **30**

Harlow Clo. *Sut A* 3D **38**
Harlow St. *Blid* 5D **52**
Harpole Clo. *Swanw* 3F **55**
Harport Dri. *Dane* 6E **24**
Harrier Rd. *Belp* 2G **67**
Harriers Gro. *Sut A* 5K **39**
Harris Av. *Rip* 2C **62**
Harris Clo. *Rip* 3C **62**
Harrison La. *Tib* 3B **36**
Harrison Rd. *Mans* 3J **39**
Harrop White Rd. *Mans* 1K **39**
Harrow La. *Rain* 2C **52**
Harrow La. *Boug* 2K **23**
Harthill Dri. *Mans* 4K **39**
Hartington Ct. *Mans* 3H **41**
Hartington Dri. *Sels* 4J **57**
Hartington Dri. *Sut A* 5F **39**
Hartington St. *Lang* 6K **7**
Hartshay Hill. *Rip* 1B **62**
     (in two parts)
Harvester Clo. *Rip* 2C **62**
Harvey Ct. *Bsvr* 4H **5**
Harvey Rd. *Mans* 4E **40**
Harwood Clo. *Sut A* 5E **38**
Harwood Pl. *Sut A* 5E **38**
Harworth Clo. *Mans* 3H **39**
Haslam Ct. *Bsvr* 4H **5**
Hasland. 1D **12**
Hasland By-Pass. *Has* 1E **12**
Haslemere Gdns. *R'hd* 1F **61**
Hassocky La.
   Temp N & Cal 2H **13**
Hassop Wlk. Mans 3H **41**
     (off Hindlow Ct.)
Haston Clo. *Mans* 3K **55**
Hatfield Av. *Med V* 6B **10**
Hatfield Clo. *Rain* 1D **52**
Hathaway Clo. *For T* 2B **24**
Hathersage Dri. *Lea* 4H **55**
Hathersage Ri. *R'hd* 7G **51**
Hathersage Wlk. Mans 3H **41**
     (off Edale Rd.)
Hathersage Way. *Sut A* 5C **38**
Hatton Ct. *Mans* 3H **41**
Havelock St. *Rip* 2E **62**
Haven Clo. *Clip V* 5B **32**
Haven Clo. *Sut A* 6B **38**
Hawkesworth Av. *For T* 7H **31**
Hawkhill Clo. *Oll* 5E **22**
Hawking La. *Heath* 1B **26**
Hawthorn Av. *Rip* 4D **62**
Hawthorn Clo. *Mans W* 3E **30**
Hawthorn Cres. *Kirk A* 4E **48**
Hawthorn Dri. *New O* 2H **23**
Hawthorne Av. *Glap* 7K **15**
Hawthorne Av. *Shire* 3H **17**
Hawthorne Av. *Stre* 4C **34**
Hawthorne Av. *Tib* 1D **36**
Hawthorne Clo. *Klbrn* 5K **67**
Hawthorne Clo. *Stan H* 3A **38**
Hawthorne Rd. *Pinx* 7F **47**
Hawthornes Av. *S Norm* 5B **46**
Hawthorne Way. *Edwin* 7K **21**
Hawthorns, The. *Belp* 2H **67**
Hawthorns, The. *Kirk A* 4D **48**
Hawthorns, The. *Wars* 3G **19**
Hawton Clo. *Mans* 7K **29**
Haycroft Clo. *Mans W* 3D **30**
Hayes Clo. *Pinx* 7E **46**
Hayes Cres. *Swanw* 4F **55**
Hayes La. *Swanw* 4F **55**
Hayfield Clo. *Belp* 2F **67**
Hayfield Clo. *Wing* 4A **12**
Haywood Av. *Blid* 5C **52**
Haywood Oaks Forest Walks.
     . . . . .7F **53**
Haywood Oaks La. *Blid* 6C **52**
Hazel Av. *Lwr P* 5H **25**
Hazel Cres. *Shire* 3H **17**
Hazel Dri. *Wing* 4B **12**
Hazelford Way. *News V* 4H **59**
Hazel Gro. *Kirk A* 5G **49**
Hazel Gro. *Mans W* 3B **30**
Hazel Gro. *S Norm* 5D **46**
Hazelhurst. *Has* 1D **12**

Hazel Rd. *New O* 2H 23
Hazel St. *Sut A* ...2B 38
Hazeltree Clo. *Rip* 4C 62
Hazelwood. 7A 66
Hazelwood Clo. *For T* ...6H 31
Hazelwood Hill. *Haz* 7A 66
Hazelwood Rd. *Duf* 7A 66
Headstocks, The. *Huth* ...7J 37
Heage Rd. *Rip* 3B 62
Heage Rd. Ind. Est. *Rip* ...3B 62
Healdswood St. *Sut A* ...2B 38
Heanor Rd. *Cod* 5H 63
Heanor Wlk. *Mans* 3H 41
  (off Edale Rd.)
Heath. 5D 14
Heath Av. *Mans* 2H 41
Heath Comn. *Heath* 4D 14
Heathcote St. *Sut A* ...1C 48
Heathcote Pl. *Sut A* ...7E 38
Heather Av. *Heath* 5B 14
Heather Clo. *Kirk A* ...3D 48
Heather Clo. *Mans* 3A 40
Heather Clo. *S Norm* ...7C 46
Heather Clo. *Swanw* ...3G 55
Heather La. *R'hd* 3H 61
Heatherley Dri. *For T* ...7E 30
Heathers, The. *Boug* 2J 23
Heather Way. *Mans* 3G 41
Heathfield Clo. *Wing* ...3B 12
Heathfield Ct. *Kirk A* ...3C 48
Heathfield Gdns. *Tib* ...2C 36
Heathland Clo. *Mans* ...3G 41
Heath Rd. *Hlmwd & Heath* ...7K 13
  (in two parts)
Heath Rd. *Rip* 3D 62
Heavytrees Av. *R'hd* ...2G 61
Heddon Bar. *Mans W* ...5E 30
Hedgerow Clo. *Sut A* ...1A 48
Hedley Clo. *Som* 3K 55
Helmsdale Clo. *Mans* ...4J 39
Helmsley Rd. *Rain* 7A 42
Helpston Clo. *Westh* ...1J 45
Heming Av. *Pils* 6J 25
Henmoor. 4A 24
Henning La. *Sut A* 1K 47
Henry Av. *Mans W* 3B 30
Henry Cres. *Alf* 7J 45
Henry St. *Gras* 4E 12
Henry St. *Rip* 2D 62
Henry St. *Sut A* 1D 48
Henton Rd. *Edwin* 6K 21
Hepthorne Lane. 2E 24
Herbert Rd. *Kirk A* 2F 59
Herbert St. *Mans* 3A 40
Herb Garden. 5B 26
Hereford Av. *Mans W* ...3C 30
Hereford Av. *Oll* 3F 23
Hereford Rd. *R'hd* 7G 51
Hereward Clo. *Shire* ...3K 17
Hermitage Av. *Mans* ...4K 39
Hermitage Av. *Ridd* ...6J 55
Hermitage La. *Mans* ...5J 39
Hermitage, The. *Mans* ...5J 39
Hermitage Way. *Mans* ...5J 39
Herne St. *Sut A* 5E 38
Herrods Vw. *Stan H* ...3A 38
Hett's La. *Wars* 2H 19
Hewett St. *Wars V* 2D 18
Hexham Clo. *Mans* 4F 41
Heydon Clo. *Belp* 1F 67
Heyes, The. *R'hd* 2F 61
Heywood St. *Mans* 2D 40
Hibbert Cres. *Sut A* ...6E 38
Hibbert Rd. *Mans* 2D 40
Hickleton Clo. *Rip* ...3C 62
Hickling Ct. *Mans* 2D 40
Hickory Clo. *Kirk A* ...3D 48
Hickton Rd. *Swanw* ...5F 55
Hides Grn. *Bsvr* 4J 5
Higham. 6B 34
Higham La. *Shirl & Mort* ...6C 34
Highcliffe Av. *Shire* ...3H 17
High Clo. *Kirk A* 2F 59
High Cres. *Kirk A* 2F 59
High Edge M. *Belp* 2D 66
Highfield Av. *Kirk A* ...4C 48
Highfield Av. *Lang J* ...1H 17
Highfield Av. *Mans* ...7B 30
Highfield Clo. *Los* 7H 63

Highfield Clo. *Mans* ...7B 30
Highfield Clo. *R'hd* ...1G 61
Highfield Dri. *S Norm* ...5D 46
Highfield Rd. *Belp* 5D 66
Highfield Rd. *Bsvr* 5J 5
Highfield Rd. *Klbrn* ...7K 67
Highfield Rd. *Sut A* ...6A 38
Highfield Rd. *Swanw* ...5D 54
Highfields. 1J 25
Highfields. *Cod* 4G 63
Highfields Dri. *Hlmwd* ...7K 13
Highfields Way. *Hlmwd* ...7K 13
Highfield Way. *Rip* ...4C 62
High Gro. *Belp* 3H 67
High Hazel Clo. *Clay C* ...4E 24
High Hazel Wlk. *Clay C* ...4E 24
  (off High Hazel Clo.)
High Hazles Dri. *Huth* ...7J 37
High Holborn Rd. *Rip* ...3G 63
Highland Clo. *Mans W* ...5D 30
Highland Dri. *Sut A* ...1B 48
Highland Rd. *Mans* 7E 40
High Leys Dri. *R'hd* ...7C 50
High Mdw. Clo. *Rip* ...4D 62
High Oakham Clo. *Sut A* ...5F 39
High Oakham Dri. *Mans* ...6B 40
High Oakham Hill. *Mans* ...5A 40
High Oakham Rd. *Mans* ...6B 40
High Pavement. *Belp* ...4E 66
High Pavement. *Sut A* ...7C 38
High Ridge. *For T* 6F 31
Highstairs La. *Stre* ...2B 34
High St. *Alf* 6G 45
High St. *Belp* 3E 66
High St. *Bsvr* 5J 5
High St. *Brins* 3F 65
High St. *Clay C* 4C 24
High St. *Cod* 4H 63
High St. *Edwin* 5K 21
High St. *Huth* 6J 37
High St. *Los* 7J 63
High St. *Mans W* 5C 30
High St. *Ple* 3F 29
High St. *Ridd* 6K 55
High St. *Rip* 2D 62
High St. *Som* 3J 55
High St. *S Norm* 4C 46
High St. *Stan H* 3A 38
High St. *Sut A* 7C 38
High St. *Swanw* 4B 36
High St. *Tib* 4E 54
High St. *Wars* 3H 19
High Tor. *Sut A* 2C 38
High Vw. Rd. *S Norm* ...3E 46
Highwood Av. *Belp* ...6F 67
High Wood Bank. *Belp* ...6G 67
Hilary Clo. *Belp* 2J 67
Hilcote. 1E 46
Hilcote La. *Hilc* 1B 46
Hilcote St. *S Norm* ...3C 46
Hill Cres. *Sut A* 5E 38
Hill Crest Av. *Wess* ...6C 46
Hillcrest Dri. *Cod* ...4H 63
Hillcrest Rd. *Has* 1D 12
Hill Fields. *S Norm* ...7B 46
Hillmoor St. *Ple* 4F 29
Hillocks, The. *Sut A* ...6F 39
Hillsborough Av. *Sut A* ...2B 48
Hillsborough Way. *Sut A* ...2B 48
Hillside Pk. *Oake* 6B 44
Hillside Ri. *Belp* 5D 66
Hillside Rd. *Blid* 6C 52
Hillside Wlk. *Blid* ...6C 52
Hillstown. 6A 6
Hill St. *Clay C* 5C 24
Hill St. *Ple* 3F 29
Hill St. *Rip* 1D 62
Hill Top. *Bsvr* 3J 5
Hilltop Av. *Shire* 3H 17
Hilltop Clo. *Glap* ...7K 15
Hilltop La. *Klbrn* ...5J 67
Hilltop Rd. *Pinx* 6E 46

Hill Top Rd. *Ridd* 6J 55
Hill Top Vw. *Sut A* ...1A 48
Hillview Ct. *Mans W* ...4D 30
Hill Vw. Rd. *Kirk A* ...5G 49
Hillyfields. 1G 25
Hilton Pk. *Blid* 5B 52
Hilton Pk. Dri. *Lea* ...3J 55
Hindlow Ct. *Mans* 3H 41
Hoades St. *New T* 7C 12
Hobhouse Rd. *Mans* ...6H 29
Hob La. *Haz* 6A 66
Hobsic. 4F 65
Hobsic Clo. *Brins* 4F 65
Hobsic La. *Sels* 3F 57
Hockley. 5A 12
Hockley La. *Wing* 4A 12
Hockley Pl. *Kirk A* ...6C 48
Hockley Way. *Nix H* ...1H 55
Hodgkinson Rd. *Kirk A* ...6F 49
Hodmire La. *Heath* ...1F 27
Hoggbarn La. *Los* 7K 63
Holbeck Av. *Bsvr* 4A 6
Holbeck Way. *Rain* ...1D 52
Holbrook Vw. *Cod* 4G 63
Holborn Av. *N Wing* ...1G 25
Holbrook Clo. *Ple* ...3E 28
Holbrook Ct. *Mans* ...3H 41
Holbrook Cres. *Old C* ...2D 32
Holbrook Moor. 7G 67
Holbrook Rd. *Belp* ...5D 66
Holbrook Vw. *Klbrn* ...7K 67
Holbrook Way. *N Wing* ...1G 25
  (off Holbrook Av.)
Holden St. *Mans* 3A 40
Holland Clo. *Mort* ...4F 35
Holland Cres. *Sels* ...4K 57
Holles Ct. *Boug* 2J 23
Hollies, The. *Rain* ...1D 52
Hollies, The. *R'hd* ...2F 61
Hollington Way. *Mans* ...3H 41
Hollingwell Dri. *Mans* ...2H 41
Hollinwell Clo. *Kirk A* ...3C 48
Hollinwell Golf Course. ...2J 59
Holly Av. *Rip* 4D 62
Hollybank Clo. *Oake* ...7B 44
Holly Bank Clo. *Ple* ...2E 28
Holly Ct. *For T* 7E 30
Holly Dri. *For T* 7G 31
Holly Gro. *Kirk A* ...4D 48
Holly Gro. *Swanw* ...3F 55
Holly Hill Rd. *Sels* ...5H 57
Hollyhouse Dri. *S Norm* ...4D 46
Hollyhurst Row. *Ridd* ...5B 56
Hollyhurst Ter. *Ridd* ...5B 56
Holly Ri. *New O* 2H 23
Holly Rd. *For T* 6F 31
Hollywell Av. *Cod* ...5H 63
Holmewood. 7A 14
Holmewood Ind. Est. *Hlmwd* ...7B 14
Holmewood Ind. Pk. *Hlmwd* ...5K 13
Holmgate Rd. *Clay C* ...4A 24
Holm La. *Oake* 6A 44
Holmwood Rd. *Rain* ...1C 12
Homecroft Av. *Sut A* ...3D 38
Homecroft Dri. *Sels* ...4G 57
Home Farm Ct. *Sels* ...5E 56
Homelands, The. *Sut A* ...7D 38
Homesteads, The. *Kirk A* ...4D 48
Homesteads, The. *Wars* ...3H 19
Homewood Dri. *Kirk A* ...3C 48
Honeycroft Clo. *Belp* ...4F 67
Honey Cft. Ct. *S Norm* ...6D 46
Honeyfield Dri. *Rip* ...4F 63
Honeysuckle Dri. *S Norm* ...3D 46
Honister Clo. *Mans* ...5C 40
Honister Ct. *Mans* ...5C 40
  (off Honister Clo.)
Hooley St. *Sels* 5H 57
Hope St. *Mans* 3D 40
Hopping Hill. *Milf* ...7D 66
Hopping Hill Ter. E. *Milf* ...7E 66
Hopping Hill Ter. W. *Milf* ...7E 66
Hopton Clo. *Rip* 3F 63
Hornscroft Rd. *Bsvr* ...5J 5
Horsehead La. *Bsvr* ...4K 5

Horsley Cres. *Holb* ...7G 67
Horsley Rd. *Hors & Klbrn* ...7K 67
Horton Clo. *Swanw* ...3F 55
Hosiery St. *Kirk A* ...5E 48
Houfton Cres. *Bsvr* ...3H 5
Houfton Rd. *Bsvr* ...3H 5
Houfton Rd. *Mans* ...1E 40
Houghton Bassett. ...5C 16
Houghton Felley. ...6C 16
Houldsworth Cres. *Bsvr* ...3H 5
Howard Dri. *N Wing* ...3F 25
Howard Rd. *Mans* ...1K 39
Howard St. *Kirk A* ...5D 38
Hoylake Clo. *Mans W* ...2E 30
Hoyland Ct. *Belp* ...2J 67
Hucklow Av. *N Wing* ...7G 13
Hucklow St. *Mans* ...3H 41
Hucknall Rd. *News V* ...4H 59
Hudson Mt. *Bsvr* ...6K 5
Hunloke Estate. ...5C 12
Hunloke Rd. *Hlmwd* ...6A 14
Hunloke Vw. *Wing* ...3B 12
Hunt Clo. *Kirk A* ...3G 49
Hunter Dri. *Klbrn* ...7K 67
Hunter Rd. *Belp* ...2H 67
Hunters Chase. *Mans W* ...6B 30
Hunters Ct. *Kirk A* ...5C 48
Huntingdon Av. *Bsvr* ...5K 5
Huntly Clo. *Mans* ...4H 39
Hurst Clo. *Rain* ...1B 52
Hurst La. *Hghm* ...4A 34
Huthwaite. ...6J 37
Huthwaite La. *B'will* ...7D 36
Huthwaite Leisure Cen. ...5H 37
Huthwaite Rd. *Sut A* ...6K 37
Hutt Farm Ct. *R'hd* ...2F 61
Hyndley Rd. *Bsvr* ...4H 5

I

Idlewells Shop. Cen. *Sut A* ...7C 38
Ilion St. *Mans* ...6K 29
Independent Hill. *Alf* ...7F 45
Infield La. *Cuc* ...1G 9
Ingles Channel. *Belp* ...3D 66
Ingleton Rd. *Has* ...1B 12
Inkerman Rd. *Sels* ...6H 57
Inkerman St. *Sels* ...6H 57
Inkersall. ...1A 4
Inkersall Rd. *Stav* ...1A 4
Institute La. *Alf* ...6G 45
Institute St. *Stan H* ...3A 38
Intake Av. *Mans* ...4K 39
Intake Rd. *Bsvr* ...4G 5
Intake Rd. *Clip V* ...4C 32
Iona Clo. *Tib* ...4B 36
Ireton Houses. *Belp* ...4J 67
Iron Cliff Rd. *Bsvr* ...3H 5
Ironville. ...7A 56
Ivanhoe Clo. *New T* ...6D 12
Iveagh Clo. *Wars* ...2J 19
Iveagh Wlk. *Ridd* ...5A 56
Ivy Gro. *Kirk A* ...4D 48
Ivy Gro. *Rip* ...3D 62
Ivy Spring Clo. *Wing* ...3B 12

J

Jacklin Ct. *Kirk A* ...4D 48
Jacksdale. ...7D 56
Jackson Av. *New T* ...7C 12
Jackson Rd. *Dane* ...5E 24
Jackson Rd. *Doe L* ...6G 15
Jackson's La. *Heage* ...1H 67
Jacksons La. *Heage* ...7C 66
Jackson's La. *S Wing* ...3A 54
Jackson Ter. *Med V* ...6A 10
James Av. *Som* ...4K 55
James Murray M. *Mans* ...
  (off Rock Valley)
James St. *Kirk A* ...2E 58
James St. *Lea* ...4J 55
James William Turner Av.
  Sut A ...1C 48
James' Yd. *Mans* ...2C 40
  (off Rock Ct.)
Jasmin Clo. *Shire* ...1H 17

Jasmine Clo. *Swanw* 4F **55**
Jasmine Dri. *Tib* 2D **36**
Jeacock Dri. *Rain* 2E **52**
Jellicoe St. *Lang* 4A **8**
Jenford St. *Mans* 3J **39**
Jenkins Av. *Mans* 2H **39**
Jennison St. *Mans* 7A **30**
Jenny Beckett's La. *Mans* 4E **40**
Jenny's Ct. *Belp* 2G **67**
Jephson Bldgs. *Sut A* 2D **48**
Jephson Rd. *Sut A* 2D **48**
Jessop Av. *Iron* 7B **56**
Jessop's Monument. 1A **64**
Jessop St. *Cod* 5H **63**
Jessop St. *Wain* 5G **63**
Jodrell Av. *Belp* 3H **67**
John Barrow Clo. *Rain* 2E **52**
John Davis Workshops.
 Huth 5H **37**
JOHN EASTWOOD HOSPICE.
 .5G **39**
John O'Gaunts Way. *Belp* 3G **67**
Johnson Dri. *Mans* 6C **40**
John St. *Alf* 6G **45**
John St. *Clay C* 4D **24**
John St. *N Wing* 1E **24**
John St. *Som* 3J **55**
John St. *Sut A* 5D **38**
John Woodhead Ct. *Mans*
 .1K **39**
Joseph St. *Belp* 3D **66**
Jubilee Av. *Rip* 3C **62**
Jubilee Ct. *Belp* 5E **66**
Jubilee Ct. *Pinx* 7F **47**
Jubilee Gdns. *Sut A* 7A **38**
Jubilee Rd. *Sut A* 6B **38**
Jubilee Way N. *Mans* 2H **41**
Jubilee Way S. *Mans* 4H **41**
Julia Cres. *Ston* 6F **35**
Julias Way. *Kirk A* 2F **49**
Junction Rd. *Sut A* 7F **39**
Jura Av. *Rip* 2D **62**

K

Kaye Rd. *Mans* 2H **39**
Keane Clo. *Blid* 5B **52**
Keats Av. *Sut A* 6K **37**
Keats Rd. *Ston* 6F **35**
Keats Wlk. *Ston* 6F **35**
Keats Way. *Gras* 3E **12**
Kedleston Clo. *Huth* 7H **37**
Kedleston Clo. *Rip* 1C **62**
Kedleston Ct. *Tib* 3D **36**
Kedleston Wlk. *Mans* 3G **41**
 (off Oak Tree La.)
Kelham Rd. *Mans* 2J **39**
Kelstedge Dri. *Mans* 3H **41**
Kelstern Clo. *Mans* 2G **41**
Kelvin Clo. *For T* 5K **31**
Kempton Rd. *Mans* 2F **41**
Kendal Clo. *Kirk A* 3D **58**
Kendray Clo. *Belp* 2H **67**
Kenilworth Av. *Sut A* 5F **39**
Kenilworth Rd. *Rip* 3C **62**
Kenmere Clo. *Dane* 6D **24**
Kenmore Clo. *Mans* 4J **39**
Kennack Clo. *S Norm* 4E **46**
Kennedy Av. *Mans W* 4D **30**
Kennel La. *Ann* 7D **58**
Kennet Paddock. *Mans W* 5D **30**
Kenning St. *Clay C* 5C **24**
Kensington Clo. *Mans W* 3E **30**
Kensington Clo. *Sut A* 7C **38**
Kent Av. *Jack* 7D **56**
Kepple Ga. *Rip* 4F **63**
Kerry's Yd. *Klbrn* 7K **67**
Kestral Rd. *Mans* 5J **39**
Kestrel Clo. *Bsvr* 3H **5**
Kestrel Heights. *Iron* 1B **64**
Keswick Clo. *Bsvr* 5H **5**
Keys Rd. *Nix H* 1H **55**
Keyworth Clo. *Mans* 2J **39**
Keyworth Dri. *For T* 7H **31**
Kibworth Clo. *Ches* 1C **12**
Kighill La. *R'hd* 4G **61**
Kilbourne Rd. *Belp* 3G **67**
Kilburn La. *Belp* 4H **67**

Kilburn Toll Bar. *Klbrn* 6K **67**
Killis La. *Klbrn* 7H **67**
Kilton Av. *Mans* 2H **41**
King Edward Av. *Mans* 5A **40**
King Edward St. *Shire* 3K **17**
King Edwins Clo. *Edwin* 6J **21**
Kingfield Clo. *Rain* 2D **52**
Kingfisher Ct. *Bsvr* 3H **5**
King George V Av. *Mans* 4D **40**
King George IV M. *Mans* 6J **29**
King John's Palace. 2E **32**
 (Remains of)
King John's Rd. *Clip V* 4C **32**
King John's Workshop Mus., The.
 .7F **47**
King Rd. *Wars* 3G **19**
Kings Ct. *Kirk A* 3F **59**
Kings Dri. *Brins* 5G **65**
Kingsley Av. *Mans W* 3D **30**
Kingsley Clo. *Mans W* 4D **30**
Kingsley Ct. *Mans W* 3D **30**
Kingsley Cres. *Ston* 6F **35**
Kingsley St. *Kirk A* 6F **49**
Kings Lodge Dri. *Mans* 5J **39**
Kingsmeadow. *Rain* 2E **52**
KING'S MILL CENTRE FOR
 HEALTH CARE SERVICES.
 .4G **39**
Kings Mill La. *Mans* 5H **39**
 (in two parts)
Kings Mill Rd. E. *Sut A* 4F **39**
Kings Mill Way. *Mans* 5J **39**
Kingsthorpe Clo. *For T* 7E **30**
Kingston Dri. *Oll* 4E **22**
Kingston Rd. *Mans* 2D **40**
King St. *Alf* 7F **45**
King St. *Belp* 4D **66**
King St. *Clay C* 5C **24**
King St. *Huth* 6K **37**
King St. *Kirk A* 6E **48**
King St. *Mans* 2D **40**
King St. *Mans W* 6C **30**
King St. *Pinx* 6F **47**
King St. *S Norm* 5B **46**
King St. *Sut A* 7C **38**
King St. *Tib* 2C **36**
King St. *Wars V* 2D **18**
Kingsway. *For T* 7G **31**
Kingsway. *Kirk A* 6F **49**
Kingsway Av. *New O* 1H **23**
Kingswood Av. *Belp* 1G **67**
Kingswood Dri. *Kirk A* 3D **48**
King William Cen. *Iron* 7B **56**
King William St. *Iron* 7B **56**
Kipling St. *Mans* 2A **40**
Kirby Clo. *Blid* 6C **52**
Kirby Hardwick. 2F **49**
Kirkby Folly Rd. *Sut A* 1F **49**
Kirkby Ho. Dri. *Kirk A* 5C **48**
Kirkby in Ashfield. 5F **49**
Kirkby La. *Pinx* 7H **47**
Kirkby Mill Vw. *Kirk A* 5C **48**
Kirkby Rd. *R'hd* 6C **50**
Kirkby Rd. *Sut A* 2C **48**
 (in two parts)
Kirkby Woodhouse. 2C **58**
Kirk Clo. *Rip* 4C **62**
Kirk Dri. *Boug* 1J **23**
Kirkland Av. *Mans* 3K **39**
Kirkland Clo. *Sut A* 1F **49**
Kirklington Rd. *Rain* 1C **52**
Kirkman Rd. *Los* 7J **63**
Kirk Pl. *Pinx* 7G **47**
Kirks Cft. *Blid* 6B **52**
Kirk's La. *Belp* 4F **67**
Kirkstead. 7F **47**
Kirkstead Clo. *Pinx* 7F **47**
Kirkstead Rd. *Pinx* 7F **47**
Kirton Clo. *Mans* 2H **39**
Kirton Clo. *Med V* 6A **10**
Kissingate Leisure Cen. 3K **17**
Kitchener Dri. *Mans* 3C **40**
Kitchener Ter. *Lang* 4A **8**
Kitson Av. *Jack* 7E **56**
Kneesall Clo. *Wars* 7K **9**
Knighton Ct. *N Wing* 2E **24**
Knighton St. *N Wing* 2E **24**
Knoll, The. *Mans* 3J **39**
Knoll, The. *Shire* 4H **17**

Knowl Av. *Belp* 1C **66**
Kynance Clo. *S Norm* 4E **46**

L

Laburnum Av. *Kirk A* 7B **48**
Laburnum Av. *Shire* 2J **17**
Laburnum Clo. *Bsvr* 5K **5**
Laburnum Clo. *S Norm* 3D **46**
Laburnum Cres. *Swanw* 3G **55**
Laburnum Gro. *Mans W* 4A **30**
Laceby Ct. *Mans W* 4E **30**
Ladybrook. 2J **39**
Ladybrook La. *Mans* 3H **39**
Ladybrook Pl. *Mans* 2J **39**
Lady Margarets Cres. *Nor* 1J **9**
Lady Well Ct. *Belp* 4E **66**
Ladywood Av. *Belp* 2F **67**
Lake Av. *Los* 7J **63**
Lake Av. *Mans* 2H **39**
Lake Farm Rd. *Rain* 1B **52**
Lakeside Ct. *Ann* 5E **58**
Lakeside Vw. *Sut A* 5F **39**
Lake Vw. Dri. *Ann* 5D **58**
Lamb Clo. *E'wd* 6K **65**
Lamb Clo. Dri. *Newt* 7K **65**
Lamb Cres. *Rip* 3F **63**
Lambcroft Rd. *Pinx* 6F **47**
Lambley Av. *Mans* 4F **41**
Lammas Clo. *Sut A* 7C **38**
Lammas Rd. *Sut A* 7B **38**
Lamond Clo. *Mans* 4J **39**
Lancaster Ri. *Belp* 1E **66**
Lancaster St. *Doe L* 6G **15**
Lander La. *Belp* 3E **66**
Lane End. 2C **36**
Lane End. *Kirk A* 5E **48**
Lane, The. *Rip* 2C **62**
Langar Pl. *For T* 1H **41**
Langer Fld. Av. *Ches* 1A **12**
Langer La. *Wing & Ches* 1A **12**
Langford Rd. *Mans* 3H **39**
Langford St. *Sut A* 6C **38**
Langham Pl. *Mans* 2K **39**
Langley Av. *Som* 3J **55**
Langley Clo. *Mans* 7J **29**
Langley Mill By-Pass.
 Lan M 7C **64**
Langstone Av. *Bsvr* 5A **6**
Langton Av. *Kirk A* 4B **48**
Langton Ct. *Sut A* 7C **38**
 (off Langton Rd.)
Langton Hollow. *Sels* 5F **57**
Langton Rd. *Sut A* 7C **38**
Langwell Dri. *For T* 6J **31**
Langwith. 6K **7**
Langwith Dri. *Lang* 5K **7**
Langwith Junction. 2J **17**
Langwith Lodge Dri. *Neth L* . . .4B **8**
Langwith Maltings. *Lang* 6K **7**
Langwith Rd. *Bsvr* 5K **5**
Langwith Rd. *Cuc* 4F **9**
Langwith Rd. *Lang J* 1K **17**
Lansbury Av. *New O* 1G **23**
Lansbury Av. *Pils* 7J **25**
Lansbury Dri. *S Norm* 4C **46**
Lansbury Gdns. *Mans* 1E **40**
Lansbury Rd. *Edwin* 5K **21**
Lansbury Rd. *Sut A* 1D **48**
Lansdowne Av. *Mans* 7D **40**
Larch Av. *Mans W* 3B **30**
Larch Av. *Rip* 3D **62**
Larch Av. *Shire* 3H **17**
Larch Clo. *Und* 1K **65**
Larchdale Clo. *S Norm* 6C **46**
Larch Rd. *New O* 2H **23**
Lark Ct. *Swanw* 3F **55**
Larkfield Av. *Kirk A* 2C **58**
Larkfields Cres. *Swanw* 3F **55**
Larkhall Pl. *Mans* 4J **39**
Larkhill. *Swanw* 3F **55**
Larkhill Clo. *Swanw* 3F **55**
Larkspur Clo. *For T* 6D **30**
Larkspur Clo. *S Norm* 6C **46**
Larwood Cres. *Kirk A* 2D **58**
Lathkil Dri. *S Norm* 5B **46**
Lathkil Gro. *Tib* 3B **36**
Lathkill Dri. *Rip* 6D **62**

Lathkill Dri. *Sels* 4H **57**
Lathkill Gro. *Dane* 7D **24**
Laund Av. *Belp* 1F **67**
Laund Clo. *Belp* 1F **67**
Laund Hill. *Belp* 2E **66**
Laund Nook. *Belp* 2E **66**
Launds Av. *Sels* 4F **57**
Laurel Av. *Ark T* 3A **4**
Laurel Av. *Chur W* 7G **9**
Laurel Av. *For T* 7F **31**
Laurel Av. *Mans* 4C **40**
Laurel Av. *Rip* 3D **62**
Laurel Clo. *Shire* 1H **17**
Laurel Clo. *Swanw* 3G **55**
Laurel Gro. *Kirk A* 5G **49**
Laurel Gro. *S Norm* 6C **46**
Lavender Clo. *Shire* 4H **17**
Lavender Clo. *Tib* 2D **36**
Lavender Rd. *Swanw* 3G **55**
Lavender Wlk. *S Wing* 5A **44**
Laverick Rd. *Jack* 7C **56**
Lawman Gdns. *Alf* 6F **45**
Lawn Av. *Sut A* 7D **38**
Lawn La. *Sut A* 7D **38**
Lawn Rd. *Sut A* 6F **39**
Lawns Rd. *Kirk A* 3D **58**
Lawrence Av. *Hlmwd* 6K **13**
Lawrence Av. *Kirk A* 5C **48**
Lawrence Av. *Mans W* 4A **30**
Lawrence Av. *Rip* 4C **62**
Lawrence Cres. *Sut A* 5F **39**
Lawrence Dri. *Brins* 5G **65**
Lawrence Pk. *Und* 1K **65**
Laxton Av. *Sut A* 1G **49**
Laxton Dri. *Med V* 6K **9**
Laybrook. *Mans* 2J **39**
Layton Av. *Mans* 2A **40**
Layton Burroughs. *Mans* 2A **40**
Lea Bank. *S Norm* 6C **46**
Leabrooks. 4H **55**
Leabrooks Av. *Mans W* 3D **30**
Leabrooks Av. *Sut A* 2G **48**
Leabrooks Rd. *Som* 3J **55**
Lea Clo. *R'hd* 1H **61**
Lea Cres. *Ridd* 5J **55**
Leadale Av. *Lea* 4G **55**
Leadale Cres. *Mans W* 3E **30**
Lea La. *Sels* 5H **57**
Leam Glen. *Mans W* 6D **30**
Leamington Dri. *S Norm* 5D **46**
Leamington Dri. *Sut A* 2C **48**
Leamington Hall Bungalows.
 Sut A 1C **48**
Leamington Hall Flats.
 Sut A 1C **48**
 (off Leamington Hall Bungalows)
Leamington St. *Rip* 2E **62**
Leamoor Av. *Som* 3H **55**
Lea Rd. *R'hd* 2H **61**
Lea Rd. *Wars* 4J **19**
Leas Av. *Ple* 3E **28**
Leas Rd. *Mans W* 4D **30**
Leaway. The. *Shire* 4H **17**
Leche Cft. *Belp* 3H **67**
Ledo Av. *Rip* 2D **62**
Leeming Clo. *Wars* 2J **19**
Leeming La. *Mans W* 2E **30**
Leeming La. N. *Mans W* 5D **30**
Leeming La. S. *Mans W* 7C **30**
Leeming Pk. *Mans W* 5C **30**
Leeming St. *Mans* 2B **40**
Leen Valley Dri. *Shire* 5H **17**
Lees Av. *Mans* 3H **39**
Lees La. *S Norm* 4B **46**
Lees Rd. *Mans* 2H **39**
Leeway Clo. *Rain* 7A **42**
Leeway Rd. *Rain* 7A **42**
Legion Dri. *Sut A* 3B **38**
Leigh Way. *N Wing* 1F **25**
Lemont Rd. *Mans W* 6G **31**
Leopold St. *Sut A* 1C **48**
Leverton Rd. *Mans* 2J **39**
Ley Av. *Alf* 7H **45**
Leycote Way. *Belp* 2D **66**
Ley Gdns. *Alf* 7H **45**
Ley La. *Mans W* 4C **30**
Leys Ct. *Belp* 2H **67**
Leyton Av. *Sut A* 4D **38**

Liber Clo.—Mansfield St.

Liber Clo. *For T* 1G **41**
Lichfield Av. *Mans* 7C **40**
Lichfield Clo. *Mans* 7C **40**
Lichfield La. *Mans* 6D **40**
Lidget La. *Scarc* 7C **6**
Lidgett. 7A 22
Lilac Clo. *Heath* 5B **14**
Lilac Gro. *Bsvr* 5A **6**
Lilac Gro. *Chur W* 7F **9**
Lilac Gro. *For T* 6K **31**
Lilac Gro. *Glap* 7K **15**
Lilac Gro. *Kirk A* 6B **48**
Lilac Gro. *Shire* 2J **17**
Lilac Gro. *S Norm* 6C **46**
Lilac Way. *Shirl* 1D **44**
Limb Cres. *Sut A* 1D **48**
(in two parts)
Lime Av. *Huth* 6J **37**
Lime Av. *Rip* 3D **62**
Lime Av. *Sut A* 5D **38**
Lime Clo. *Pinx* 7F **47**
Lime Cres. *Belp* 5F **67**
Lime Cres. *Chur W* 1F **19**
Limecroft Vw. *Wing* 4A **12**
Lime Gro. *For T* 6J **31**
Lime Gro. *S Norm* 5C **46**
Limekiln Field. 3K 5
Limekiln Fields Rd. *Bsvr* 4J **5**
Lime Kiln Pl. *Mans* 3A **40**
Limes Av. *Alf* 5G **45**
Limes Av. *Neth L* 4A **8**
Limes Ct. *Sut A* 7G **39**
Limes Cres. *Shire* 2H **17**
Limes Pk. *Rip* 3C **62**
Limestone Ter. *Mans W* 4B **30**
Lime St. *Kirk A* 6E **48**
Lime St. Mans . . . . *.2C 40*
(off Toothill La.)
Lime St. *Sut A* 5E **38**
Lime Tree Av. *Glap* 7K **15**
Lime Tree Av. *Kirk A* 5D **48**
Lime Tree Av. *Mans W* 4A **30**
Lime Tree Av. *Sut A* 3B **38**
Lime Tree Clo. *New O* 2H **23**
Lime Tree Dri. *Har W* 3E **50**
Lime Tree Gro. *Dane* 6E **24**
Lime Tree Pl. *Mans* 3C **40**
Lime Tree Pl. *Rain* 1E **52**
Lime Tree Rd. *New O* 2G **23**
Linacre Av. *Dane* 6D **24**
Linberry Clo. *Oake* 6B **44**
Linby Av. *Mans* 3H **39**
Lincoln Clo. *Tib* 3C **36**
Lincoln Dri. *Mans W* 4D **30**
Lincoln St. *Alf* 7F **45**
Lincoln St. *Tib* 3C **36**
Lincoln Way. *N Wing* 2F **25**
Lind Clo. *Rain* 1B **52**
Linden Av. *Clay C* 6D **24**
Linden Ct. *Clay C* 6D **24**
Linden Dri. *Has* 1D **12**
Linden Gro. *Kirk A* 4B **48**
Linden Gro. *Shire* 2K **17**
Linden Rd. *For T* 1F **41**
Linden St. *Mans* 7A **30**
Linden St. *Shire* 2K **17**
Lindholme Way. *Sut A* 4D **38**
Lindhurst La. *Mans* 7G **41**
(Bellamy Rd., in two parts)
Lindhurst La. *Mans* 5F **41**
(Woodland Dri.)
Lindleys Ct. *Kirk A* 6E **48**
Lindley's La. *Kirk A* 7E **48**
(in two parts)
Lindley St. *Mans* 2A **40**
Lindley St. *Sels* 5F **57**
Lindrick Clo. *Mans W* 2D **30**
Lindrick Rd. *Kirk A* 3D **48**
Lindsay Av. *Kirk A* 2F **59**
Lindsay Clo. *Mans* 3A **40**
Lindsey Dri. *Mans* 6G **41**
Lingfield Clo. *Mans* 4F **41**
Lingforest Clo. *Mans* 4G **41**
Lingforest Ct. *Mans* 4G **41**
Lingforest Rd. *Mans* 3G **41**
Ling La. *Pal* 3K **15**
Ling La. *Wars* 4A **20**
Lings Cres. *N Wing* 7G **13**
Lings Vw. *Wars* 4J **19**
Lingwood Gro. *Mans* 2F **41**
Links, The. *Mans* 3G **41**
Links, The. *Sels* 5F **57**
Linnet Dri. *Mans* 2E **40**
Linton Av. *Edwin* 5H **21**
Linton Clo. *Mans* 3H **41**
Linton Dri. *Boug* 2J **23**
Linwood Ct. *Mans W* 4E **30**
Linwood Cres. *R'hd* 7F **51**
Lismore Ct. *Mans* 4H **39**
Little Acre. *Mans W* 3E **30**
Lit. Barn Ct. *Mans* 3F **41**
Lit. Barn Gdns. *Mans* 4F **41**
Lit. Barn La. *Mans* 4F **41**
Little Breck. *S Norm* 6C **46**
Lit. Carter La. *Mans* 2E **40**
Lit. Debdale La. *Mans* 6K **29**
Little Fen. *Tib* 4B **36**
Little Hollies. *For T* 6G **31**
Lit. John Av. *Wars* 5H **19**
Lit. John Clo. *New O* 1H **23**
Lit. John Dri. *Rain* 1C **52**
Little La. *Huth* 7G **37**
Little La. *Ple* 3F **29**
Little La. *Shire* 4H **17**
Littlemoor. 5D 36
Littlemoor La. *Nwtn* 6D **36**
Lit. Morton Rd. *N Wing* 2F **25**
Lit. Oak Av. *Kirk A* 3F **59**
Lit. Oak Dri. *Ann* 4D **58**
Littleover Av. *Mans* 3H **41**
Lit. Ricket La. *R'hd* 7D **50**
Lit. Robins Ct. *Mans* 4J **39**
Littlewood La. *Mans W* 1E **30**
(Leeming La.)
Littlewood La. *Mans W* 1A **30**
(Northfield La.)
Littleworth. *Mans* 3C **40**
Litton Av. *Sut A* 4E **38**
Litton Clo. *Belp* 2F **67**
Litton Clo. *R'hd* 7G **51**
Litton Rd. *Mans W* 4E **30**
Livingstone St. *News V* 5J **59**
L.N.E.R. Cotts. *Ple* 3D **28**
Locko La. *Pils* 5K **25**
Locko Rd. *Lwr P* 4H **25**
Loco Ter. *Has* 1C **12**
Lodge Dri. *Belp* 2C **66**
Lodge Dri. *Wing* 3A **12**
Lodge La. *Kirk A* 6H **49**
Lodge La. *Lan M* 6A **64**
Lonan Clo. *For T* 6G **31**
Longbourne Ct. *For T* 6F **31**
Longcourse La. *Duck* 4C **4**
Longcroft Clo. *New T* 7D **12**
Long Dale. 5J 61
Longdale. *For T* 7E **30**
Longdale Av. *R'hd* 2G **61**
Longdale Craft Cen. Village Mus.
. . . . .5K 61
Longdale La. *R'hd* 2F **61**
Longden Ter. *Stan H* 3B **38**
Longden Ter. *Wars* 3H **19**
Long Duckmanton. 3C 4
Longedge Gro. *Wing* 3A **12**
Longedge La. *Wing* 4A **12**
Longedge Ri. *Wing* 3B **12**
Longford Wlk. *Mans* 3H **41**
Longhedge La. *N Hou* 1B **28**
(in two parts)
Longhill Ri. *Kirk A* 2D **58**
Longland La. *Farn* 6K **53**
Longlands. *Bsvr* 4K **5**
Long La. *Iron* 2K **63**
Long La. *Shire* 4J **17**
(Central Dri.)
Long La. *Shire* 4J **17**
(Prospect Dri., in three parts)
Long Mdw. *Mans W* 3D **30**
Long Mdw. Rd. *Alf* 7F **45**
Longnor Wlk. *Mans* 3H **41**
Long Row. *Belp* 3D **66**
Longshaw Clo. *N Wing* 2F **25**
Longshaw Rd. *Mans* 3H **41**
Long Sleets. *S Norm* 6D **46**
Longster La.
Wars V & Sook 3C **18**
Longstone Ri. *Belp* 1F **67**
Longstone Way. *Mans* 3H **39**
Long Stoop Way. *For T* 2G **41**
Longwalls La. *Black* 1A **66**
Longwood Dri. *Sut A* 2B **48**
Longwood Rd. *Pinx* 1G **57**
Lonsdale Rd. *Pils* 6H **25**
Loom Clo. *Belp* 2G **67**
Lords Clo. *Bsvr* 5J **5**
Lord St. *Mans* 4B **40**
Loscoe. 7J 63
Loscoe-Denby La.
Den V & Los 7J **63**
Losk La. *Pal* 3K **15**
Lound Ho. Clo. *Sut A* 4D **38**
Lound Ho. Rd. *Sut A* 4D **38**
Louwil Av. *Mans W* 3E **30**
Love La. *Ston* 5H **35**
Lower Bagthorpe. *Bagt* 7H **57**
Lower Birchwood. 3A 56
Lwr. Chapel St. *Ston* 5H **35**
Lower Dri. *Swanw* 4D **54**
Lower Hartsay. 1A 62
Lwr. Mantle Clo. *Clay C* 4D **24**
Lwr. Oakham Way. *Mans* 6J **39**
Lower Pilsley. 5H 25
Lower Somercotes. 4A 56
Lower Somercotes. *Som* 4K **55**
Lowes Hill. *Rip* 1D **62**
(in two parts)
Lowlands Rd. *Belp* 2F **67**
Lowmoor Bus. Pk. *Kirk A* 3G **49**
Lowmoor Ct. *Kirk A* 4G **49**
Low Moor Rd. *Kirk A* 4F **49**
Low Rd. *Sut A* 2D **38**
Low St. *Sut A* 7D **38**
Loxley Dri. *Mans* 6G **41**
Lucknow Dri. *Mans* 4J **39**
Lucknow Dri. *Sut A* 6F **39**
Ludborough Wlk.
Mans W 4E **30**
Lumb La. *Haz* 4A **66**
(in three parts)
Lune Mdw. *Mans W* 5D **30**
Lupin Clo. *Shire* 4G **17**
Luther Av. *Sut A* 7C **38**
Lydford Rd. *Alf* 5G **45**
Lymington Rd. *Mans* 3H **39**
Lyncroft Av. *Rip* 2E **62**
Lyndale Dri. *Cod* 4H **63**
Lynd Clo. *Sels* 4K **57**
Lyndhurst Av. *Blid* 5D **52**
Lynds Clo. *Edwin* 5K **21**
Lynham Clo. *Dane* 5E **24**
Lynnes Clo. *Blid* 6C **52**
Lynton Clo. *Rip* 1D **62**
Lynton Dri. *Sut A* 2B **48**
Lytham Rd. *Kirk A* 3C **48**

M

Mabel Av. *Sut A* 1E **48**
McArthurglen Designer Outlet.
S Norm 3G **47**
Macdonald Clo. *Gras* 4F **13**
Mackworth Ct. *Mans* 4H **41**
Madin St. *New T* 7D **12**
Mag La. *Lang* 1G **7**
Magnolia Way. *Swanw* 3G **55**
Maida La. *Oll* 3F **23**
Maid Marian Av. *Sels* 4K **57**
Maid Marion Dri. *Edwin* 5A **22**
Maid Marion Ri. *Wars* 3H **19**
Maid Marion Way. *New O* 1H **23**
Maidwell Clo. *Belp* 1F **67**
Main Av. *For T* 7G **31**
Main Rd. *Boug* 2J **23**
Main Rd. *Heath* 5D **14**
Main Rd. *Jack* 1D **64**
Main Rd. *Kirk A* 2C **58**
Main Rd. *Lang* 5K **7**
Main Rd. *Lea* 4J **55**
Main Rd. *Lwr H* 7A **54**
Main Rd. *Mort* 4F **35**
Main Rd. *Pent* 6B **54**
Main Rd. *Pye B* 4B **56**
Main Rd. *R'hd* 7E **50**
Main Rd. *Shirl* 7D **34**
Main Rd. *Stre* 2C **34**
Main Rd. *Und* 1G **65**
Mainside Cres. *Und* 3J **65**
Main St. *Blid* 6B **52**
Main St. *Bsvr* 6H **5**
Main St. *Brins* 3F **65**
Main St. *Huth* 6H **37**
Main St. *Kirk A* 3D **58**
(in two parts)
Main St. *Lang* 4A **8**
Main St. *Nwtn* 5C **36**
Main St. *Oll* 4E **22**
Main St. *Pal* 2J **15**
Main St. *Pap* 6E **60**
(Blidworth Waye)
Main St. *Pap* 7D **60**
(Danners Hill)
Main St. *Scarc* 1C **16**
Main St. *Shire* 4G **17**
Main St. *S Norm* 4D **46**
Major Oak, The. 3J 21
Makeney Rd. *Holb* 7G **67**
Mallard Clo. *Shire* 4H **17**
Mallatratt Pl. *Mans W* 4B **30**
Maltby Av. *Mort* 4E **34**
Maltby Rd. *Mans* 4E **40**
Malthouse Yd. *Rip* 3D **62**
Malthouse Yd. *Scarc* 1C **16**
Maltkiln Clo. *Oll* 5F **23**
Maltkin Row. *Cuc* 3G **9**
Manby Ct. *Med V* 6K **9**
Mandeen Gro. *Mans* 5G **41**
Manifold Dri. *Sels* 4J **57**
Manitoba Way. *Sels* 4H **57**
Manor Clo. *Boug* 1K **23**
Manor Clo. *Nwtn* 6C **36**
Manor Clo. *Pils* 7K **25**
Manor Clo. *Sut A* 1A **38**
Manor Ct. *Chur W* 1J **19**
Manor Ct. *Ridd* 5A **56**
Manor Ct. Rd. *Bsvr* 3H **5**
Manor Cres. *Kirk A* 7F **49**
Manor Cft. *Rip* 7D **54**
Mnr. Farm M. *Duck* 3C **4**
Mnr. Farm Ri. W'low . . . . *.6J 23*
(off Newark Rd.)
Manor Ho. *Mans W* 5B **30**
Manor Ho. Ct. *Kirk A* 6B **48**
Manor Pk. Sports Complex.
. . . . .3D 30
Manor Rd. *Belp* 4D **66**
Manor Rd. *Chur W* 1J **19**
Manor Rd. *Mans W* 4A **30**
Manor Rd. *Sut A* 2C **38**
Manor St. *Sut A* 7C **38**
Mansfield. 3B 40
Mansfield & District Crematorium.
Mans 7B **40**
MANSFIELD COMMUNITY
HOSPITAL. 3A 40
Mansfield La. *Sut A* 3E **38**
Mansfield Leisure Cen. 1A 40
Mansfield Mus. & Art Gallery.
. . . . .2B 40
Mansfield Rd. *Alf* 6G **45**
Mansfield Rd. *Blid* 4B **52**
Mansfield Rd. *Brins* 7G **65**
Mansfield Rd. *Clip V* 6B **32**
Mansfield Rd. *Cuc* 3H **9**
Mansfield Rd. *Doe L* 6F **15**
Mansfield Rd. *E'ly* 4D **22**
Mansfield Rd. *Edwin* 6F **21**
Mansfield Rd. *Glap* 6A **16**
Mansfield Rd.
Has & Temp N 1E **12**
Mansfield Rd. *Mans W* 6C **30**
Mansfield Rd. *Pal* 2K **15**
Mansfield Rd. *Rain & Farn* 2E **52**
Mansfield Rd. *R'hd* 3F **61**
(Blidworth Waye)
Mansfield Rd. *R'hd* 7E **50**
(Nottingham Rd.)
Mansfield Rd. *Scarc* 3B **16**
Mansfield Rd. *Sels* 5H **57**
Mansfield Rd. *Skeg* 3B **38**
Mansfield Rd. *S Norm* 5D **46**
Mansfield Rd. *Sut A* 5D **38**
Mansfield Rd. *Tib* 2D **36**
Mansfield Rd. *Und & Ann* 2K **65**
Mansfield Rd. *Wars* 6F **19**
Mansfield St. *Som* 3J **55**

A-Z Mansfield 79

Mansfield Woodhouse—Mount Pleasant

Mansfield Woodhouse. 5C 30
Mansfield Woodhouse Golf Course. 2E 30
Manton Clo. *Rain* 2D **52**
Manvers Av. *Rip* 3E **62**
Manvers Ct. *Shire* 3A **18**
Manvers Cres. *Edwin* 5H **21**
Manvers St. *Mans* 2A **40**
Manvers St. *Mans W* 5B **30**
Manvers St. *Rip* 3E **62**
Manvers St. *Shire* 3A **18**
Manvers St. *Wars* 4H **19**
Manvers Vw. *Boug* 2J **23**
Maple Av. *Rip* 3C **62**
Maplebeck Av. *Med V* 6K **9**
Maple Clo. *For T* 7E **30**
Maple Cres. *Kirk A* 4D **48**
Maple Cft. *Mans* 4F **41**
Maple Dri. *Belp* 5F **67**
Maple Dri. *S Norm* 6D **46**
Maple Gro. *Glap* 7K **15**
Mapletoft Av. *Mans W* 3A **30**
Mapleton Way. *Sut A* 5E **38**
Mappleton Dri. *Mans* 4H **41**
Mapplewells Cres. *Sut A* 1K **47**
Mapplewells Rd. *Sut A* 1K **47**
Marehay. 6D 62
Marion Av. *Kirk A* 1F **59**
Market Clo. *Shire* 3K **17**
Market Clo. *S Norm* 4C **46**
Market Head. *Belp* 3E **66**
Mkt. House Pl. Mans *2B* **40**
(off Queen St.)
Market Pl. *Belp* 4E **66**
Market Pl. *Bsvr* 5J **5**
Market Pl. *Cod* 4J **63**
Market Pl. *Huth* 6H **37**
Market Pl. *Iron* 7B **56**
Market Pl. *Mans* 2B **40**
Market Pl. *Mans W* 5C **30**
Market Pl. *Oll* 4E **22**
Market Pl. *Ridd* 5A **56**
Market Pl. *Rip* 3D **62**
Market Pl. *Shire* 3K **17**
Market Pl. *Som* 3J **55**
Market Pl. *S Norm* 4C **46**
Market Pl. *Sut A* 7C **38**
Market St. *Clay C* 5C **24**
Market St. *Huth* 6H **37**
Market St. *Iron* 7A **56**
Market St. *Mans* 3B **40**
Market St. *Shire* 3K **17**
Market St. *S Norm* 5C **46**
Market St. *Sut A* 7C **38**
Market Warsop. 3H 19
Market Warsop (Bradmer Hill) Towermill. 6A 20
Markham Clo. *New O* 3F **23**
Markham Ct. *Duck* 1C **4**
(Duckmanton Rd.)
Markham Ct. *Duck* 1D **4**
(Markham Rd.)
Markham La. *Duck* 2D **4**
Markham Pl. *Mans* 2H **39**
Markham Ri. *Clay C* 4B **24**
Markham Rd. *Duck* 1C **4**
Markhams, The. *New O* 3F **23**
Markham St. *News V* 5H **59**
Markham Vs. Duck *1C* **4**
(off Markham Rd.)
Marklew Clo. *Blid* 5C **52**
Marlborough Dri. *Belp* 2G **67**
Marlborough Rd. *Kirk A* 5F **49**
Marlborough Rd. *Mans* 7K **29**
Marlpit La. *Bsvr* 4A **6**
Marly Bank. *Mans* 4E **40**
Marples Av. *Mans W* 3E **30**
Marriott Av. *Mans* 3K **39**
Marriotts La. *Blid* 6B **52**
Marshall Av. *Kirk A* 6G **49**
Marshall St. *Alf* 6G **45**
Marshall Ter. *Stan H* 3B **38**
Marsh La. *Belp* 2E **66**
Marsh La. Cres. *Belp* 3F **67**
Marston Av. *Med V* 6K **9**
Marston Clo. *Belp* 1G **67**
Martindale Ct. *Belp* 2H **67**
Martins La. *Old T* 7A **12**
Martyn Av. *Sut A* 1D **48**
Marx Ct. *Clay C* 5C **24**
Mary St. *Kirk A* 3F **49**
Mary St. *Lang* 4A **8**
Masefield Av. *Hlmwd* 7K **13**
Mason St. *Sut A* 5F **39**
Mather's Way. *New T* 6D **12**
Matlock Av. *Mans* 5A **40**
Matlock Rd. *Belp* 2D **66**
Matlock Rd. *Brac* 3A **44**
Mattersey Ct. Mans *7B* **30**
(off W. Bank Lea)
Mattley Av. *Kirk A* 2E **58**
Matt Orchard. *S Norm* 6D **46**
Maun Av. *Kirk A* 3F **49**
Maun Clo. *Mans* 5K **39**
Maun Cres. *New O* 2G **23**
Maundale Av. *Sut A* 5F **39**
Maunleigh. *For T* 7E **30**
Maunside. *Grn L* 5K **39**
Maunside Av. *Sut A* 1F **49**
Maun Valley Ind. Pk. *Sut A* 7F **39**
Maun Way. *Mans* 5K **39**
Mavis Av. *R'hd* 2G **61**
Mawkin La. *Pinx* 5H **47**
Maycroft Gdns. *Huth* 6K **37**
Mayfair Av. *Mans* 3D **40**
Mayfield Clo. *Mans* 4H **41**
Mayfield Dri. *N Wing* 2F **25**
Mayfield Pl. *Sut A* 7B **38**
Mayfield St. *Kirk A* 7B **48**
Mayfield Ter. *Wars* 4H **19**
Mayflower Ct. *Shire* 3J **17**
Mayhall Av. *Mans W* 4A **30**
Maypole Ct. *W'low* 7H **23**
Maypole Rd. *W'low* 7J **23**
Maythorne Gro. *Edwin* 4K **21**
Meadow Av. *Cod* 4H **63**
Meadow Av. *Mans* 4C **40**
Meadow Bank. *Mans W* 2E **30**
Meadow Bank. *S Norm* 3C **46**
Meadow Clo. *Bsvr* 6J **5**
Meadow Clo. *Kirk A* 4C **48**
Meadow Clo. *Tib* 2D **36**
Meadow Cotts. *Mans W* 5C **30**
Meadow Ct. *Belp* 3D **66**
Meadow Ct. *S Norm* 6B **46**
Meadow Cft. *Hlmwd* 7K **13**
Meadow Dri. *Sut A* 6A **38**
Mdw. Farm Vw. *Kirk A* 5C **48**
Meadow Gro. *Nwtn* 6C **36**
Meadowlands. *Bsvr* 4A **6**
Meadow La. *Alf* 6H **45**
Meadow La. *S Norm* 3A **46**
(in two parts)
Meadow La. Ind. Est. *Alf* 5H **45**
(Lydford Rd.)
Meadow La. Ind. Est. *Alf* 5J **45**
(Salcombe Rd.)
Meadow Lark Clo. *Sut A* 1B **48**
Meadow Pl. *Wars* 3G **19**
Meadow Rd. *Blid* 5C **52**
Meadow Rd. *Clay C* 4A **24**
Meadow Rd. *Rip* 3D **62**
Meadowside Clo. *Wing* 3A **12**
Meadows, The. *Blid* 6B **52**
Meadows, The. *Swanw* 4E **54**
Meadow St. *Iron* 6B **56**
(in two parts)
Meadow Vw. *Belp* 4D **66**
Meadow Vw. *Hlmwd* 7J **13**
Meadow Vw. *S Wing* 5A **44**
Meadow Way. *N Hou* 1E **28**
Meden Av. *N Hou* 1D **28**
Meden Av. *Wars* 3J **19**
Meden Bank. 3K 37
Meden Bank. *Ple* 3F **29**
Meden Bank. *Stan H* 3A **38**
Meden Clo. *Ple* 3F **29**
Meden Cres. *Sut A* 5A **38**
Meden Glen. *Chur W* 7J **9**
Meden La. *Ple V* 2K **29**
Meden Pl. *Wars* 2H **19**
Meden Rd. *Mans W* 4D **30**
Medenside. *Med V* 7K **9**
Meden Sq. *Ple* 3F **29**
Meden Trail. 2F 29
Meden Vale. 6A 10
Melbourne Clo. *Belp* 5E **66**
Melbourne Ct. *Mans* 3H **41**
Melbourne St. *Mans W* 3C **30**
Melbourne St. *Sels* 5K **57**
Mellors Rd. *Mans* 1H **39**
Melrose Av. *Mans* 4D **40**
Melton Ct. *Ridd* 5J **55**
Melton Way. *Mans* 6J **39**
Melville Ct. *Med V* 6K **9**
Mendip Clo. *Mans* 5E **40**
Mentmore Clo. *Swanw* 4G **55**
Mercer Cres. *Alf* 7J **45**
Merchant St. *Shire* 3A **18**
Merlin Av. *Bsvr* 3H **5**
Merlin Clo. *Belp* 2G **67**
Merryvale Dri. *Mans* 3H **39**
Merryweather Clo. *Edwin* 7A **22**
Methuen Av. *Mans* 3E **40**
Metro Av. *Nwtn* 6C **36**
Michael Clo. *Wing* 2A **12**
Micklebring Clo. *Rip* 3C **62**
Mickley Estate. 5C 34
Mickley La. *Stre* 4C **34**
Middlebrook Rd. *Und* 7J **57**
Middlefield La. *Oll* 4F **23**
Middle La. *Dane* 5E **24**
Middle St. *Bsvr* 6A **6**
Middleton Av. *Cod* 7H **63**
Middleton Clo. *Sels* 4K **57**
Middleton Ct. *Mans* 3H **41**
Middleton Ct. *New O* 2G **23**
Middleton Rd. *Mans W* 3C **30**
Middleton Way. *Ridd* 4J **55**
Midfield Rd. *Kirk A* 2F **59**
Midland Ct. *Has* 1B **12**
Midland Railway Mus. 7F 55
Midland Rd. *Sut A* 7F **39**
Midland Ter. *Has* 1B **12**
(in two parts)
Midland Ter. *Westh* 1J **45**
Midland Vw. *N Wing* 1F **25**
Midway Cen. *Clay C* 4D **24**
Midworth St. *Mans* 3B **40**
Milehill. 2F 13
Milford. 7E 66
Milford Cres. *Mans* 2H **39**
Millbank Av. *Belp* 5F **67**
Mill Clo. *Huth* 6J **37**
Mill Clo. *Swanw* 4F **55**
Mill Ct. *Mans* 4J **39**
Mill Cres. *Wing* 4C **12**
Mill Cft. *Sut A* 1C **48**
Milldale Clo. *Rip* 6D **62**
Milldale Ct. *Belp* 4F **67**
Milldale Ct. *Mans* 4G **41**
Milldale Wlk. *Sut A* 5C **38**
Millenium Bus. Pk. *Mans* 6H **29**
Millersdale Av. *Mans* 5H **39**
Millersdale Clo. *Belp* 2F **67**
Millersdale Dri. *S Norm* 3C **46**
Millers Way. *Mans* 4H **39**
Millfield Pk. (Cvn. Site) *Old T* 3A **24**
Mill Hill. *Sut S* 1D **14**
Mill Hill Clo. *Rip* 3F **63**
Mill Holme. *S Norm* 6D **46**
Mill La. *Belp* 4E **66**
Mill La. *Bsvr* 3J **5**
Mill La. *Cod* 4G **63**
Mill La. *Edwin* 6J **21**
Mill La. *Heath* 5D **14**
(in three parts)
Mill La. *Huth* 6J **37**
(in two parts)
Mill La. *Kirk A* 6B **48**
(in two parts)
Mill La. *Old T & Clay C* 3A **24**
Mill La. *Pinx* 1F **57**
Mill La. *Wing* 4C **12**
(in three parts)
Millside. *Mans* 1D **40**
Millstone Clo. *Mans* 4E **40**
Millstone La. *Oake & Pent* 1C **54**
Mill St. *Belp* 3D **66**
Mill St. *Mans* 3D **40**
Mill St. *Som* 2J **55**
Mill St. *Sut A* 7C **38**
Mill Vw. *Belp* 2D **66**
Mill Wlk. *Bsvr* 3J **5**
Mill Wlk. Mans *2B* **40**
(off Quaker Way)
Millway. *Mans W* 7D **30**
Mill Yd. *Som* 3J **55**
Milner Av. *Cod* 4H **63**
Milner St. *Sut A* 3E **38**
Milton Av. *Alf* 6J **45**
Milton Av. *Stre* 5C **34**
Milton Clo. *Sut A* 5F **39**
Milton Ct. *R'hd* 1G **61**
Milton Cres. *R'hd* 1F **61**
Milton Dri. *R'hd* 1F **61**
Milton St. *Kirk A* 5F **49**
Milton St. *Mans* 2A **40**
Minster Clo. *Kirk A* 4D **48**
Minster Way. *Swanw* 4E **54**
Minton Pastures. *For T* 7G **31**
Misterton Ct. *Mans* 7B **30**
Misterton Cres. *R'hd* 2F **61**
M1 Commerce Pk. *Duck* 1D **4**
Monk Rd. *Alf* 1H **55**
Monk Rd. Ind. Est. *Alf* 1J **55**
Monsal Cres. *Tib* 3B **36**
Monsal Dri. *S Norm* 5B **46**
Montague St. *Mans* 3E **40**
Montrose Sq. *Mans W* 2B **30**
Monument La. *Iron* 2A **64**
Monyash Way. *Belp* 2F **67**
Mooracre La. *Bsvr* 5A **6**
Moore Clo. *Hlmwd* 6K **13**
Moorfield Av. *Bsvr* 5K **5**
Moorfield La. *Lang* 2K **7**
Moorfield Pl. *Wars* 2J **19**
Moorfield Rd. *Holb* 7G **67**
Moorfield Sq. *Bsvr* 5K **5**
Moorgate Av. *N Hou* 1D **28**
Moorgreen Ind. Pk. *Newt* 7K **65**
Moorhaigh La. *Ple* 5D **28**
Moorland Clo. *Sut A* 3E **38**
Moorland Dri. *Heath* 5B **14**
Moorland Way. *Mans* 3G **41**
Moor La. *Bsvr* 5K **5**
Moor La. *Mans* 3K **39**
Moor La. *Scarc* 6D **6**
Moor Ri. *Holb* 7G **67**
Moor Rd. *Brins* 4G **65**
Moorside La. *Holb* 7G **67**
Moor St. *Mans* 3A **40**
Moorview Clo. *Wing* 4B **12**
Moray Sq. *Mans* 4H **39**
Morley Clo. *Belp* 1J **67**
Morley Clo. *Mans* 4H **41**
Morleyfields Clo. *Rip* 3F **63**
Morley Park. 6A 62
Morley St. *Kirk A* 6F **49**
Morley St. *Stan H* 3A **38**
Morley St. *Sut A* 6D **38**
Mornington Rd. *Hlmwd* 7K **13**
Morrell Wood Dri. *Belp* 2H **67**
Morton. 4G 35
Morton Av. *Clay C* 4B **24**
Morton Clo. *Mans* 3H **41**
Morton Rd. *Pils* 2J **35**
Morton Rd. *Stre* 3C **34**
Morton St. *Mans* 7J **29**
Morven Av. *Bsvr* 5K **5**
Morven Av. *Mans W* 6B **30**
Morven Av. *Sut A* 7C **38**
Morven Rd. *Kirk A* 5F **49**
Morven Ter. *Wars* 4H **19**
Mosborough Rd. *Huth* 1J **47**
Moseley Rd. *Ann* 3G **59**
Moseley St. *Rip* 2D **62**
Mosscar Clo. *Wars* 6F **19**
Mosscar La. *Wars* 5E **18**
Mossdale Rd. *For T* 1E **40**
Moss La. *Rip* 1D **62**
Moulton Clo. *Belp* 2H **67**
Moulton Clo. *Swanw* 3F **55**
Mount Cres. *S Norm* 7C **46**
Mount Cres. *Wars* 4J **19**
Mount Milner. *Mans* 3D **40**
Mount Pleasant. 1B 66
(Belper)
Mount Pleasant. 7B 36
(Blackwell)
Mount Pleasant. 4J 19
(Market Warsop)
Mount Pleasant. *Kirk A* 2D **58**
Mount Pleasant. *Mans* 2A **40**
Mount Pleasant. *Ridd* 6K **55**

80 A-Z Mansfield

Mount Pleasant—Ollerton Rd.

Mount Pleasant. *Rip* 2D **62**
Mount Pleasant. *Sut A* 5D **38**
Mt. Pleasant Dri. *Belp* 2C **66**
Mount St. *Mans* 7A **30**
Mount, The. *For T* 5K **31**
Mt. View Clo. *Mans* 3D **40**
Mowlands Clo. *Sut A* 7F **39**
Muirfield Clo. *Kirk A* 3C **48**
Muirfield Way. *Mans W* 2E **30**
Mulberry Clo. *Belp* 4F **67**
Mulberry Clo. *Wing* 3A **12**
Mulberry M. *Rip* 6C **62**
Murray St. *Mans* 4B **40**
Muschamp Ter. *Wars* 4H **19**
Muskham Ct. *Mans* 7B **30**
Musters Rd. *News V* 5H **59**
Musters St. *Shire* 3A **18**
Mynd, The. *Mans W* 3E **30**
Myrtle Clo. *Shire* 1H **17**

N

Nailers Way. *Belp* 2G **67**
Naseby Rd. *Belp* 3H **67**
Needham St. *Cod* 4H **63**
Nesbit St. *Bsvr* 6K **5**
Nesbitt St. *Sut A* 1D **48**
Nest Av. *Kirk A* 6G **49**
Nest Cres. *Kirk A* 6G **49**
Nether Clo. *Swanw* 4E **54**
Nether Clo. *Wing* 5A **12**
Nethercroft La. *Dane* 5E **24**
Nethercross Dri. *Wars* 2J **19**
Netherfield Grange. *Sut A* 1B **48**
Netherfield La. *Chur W* 7J **9**
Nether Green. 7H 65
Nether Langwith. 4A 8
Nether Moor. 6A 12
Nethermoor Rd. *Old T* 1C **24**
Nethermoor Rd. *Wing & New T* 5A **12**
Nether Pilsley. 7K 25
Nether Springs Rd. *Bsvr* 3H **5**
Newark Clo. *Mans* 7F **41**
Newark Dri. *Mans* 7F **41**
Newark Rd. *New O* 4E **22**
Newark Rd. *Sut A* 1G **49**
Newark Rd. *W'low* 5H **23**
Newark Way. *Mans* 7G **41**
New Bagthorpe. 7K 57
Newbarn Clo. *Shire* 5H **17**
Newbery Clo. *Edwin* 5J **21**
New Birchwood. 2A 56
New Bolsover. 5G 5
New Bolsover. *Bsvr* 5G **5**
Newbound La. *Sut A* 5K **27** (in two parts)
Newboundmill La. *Ple* 5D **28**
New Breck Rd. *Belp* 4E **66**
New Brinsley. 3G 65
New Bldgs. Dri. *Wars* 1J **31**
Newcastle St. *Huth* 6H **37**
Newcastle St. *Mans* 2A **40**
Newcastle St. *Mans W* 5B **30**
Newcastle St. *Wars* 3H **19**
New Clo. *Blid* 5C **52**
New Clo. *Kirk A* 5E **48**
New Cotts. *Cuc* 3F **9**
New Cross. 6D 38
New Cross St. *Sut A* 5D **38**
New England Way. *Ple* 5G **29**
New Fall St. *Huth* 6H **37**
Newgate La. *Mans* 3C **40**
Newhaven Av. *Mans W* 5B **30**
New Higham. 7D 34
New Houghton. 1D 28
New Hucknall Waye. *Huth* 1J **47**
Newlands. 6K 31
Newlands Av. *Boug* 2J **23**
Newlands Clo. *Rip* 3E **62**
Newlands Cres. *Nwtn* 6C **36**
Newlands Dri. *For T* 6K **31**
Newlands Dri. *Ridd* 6J **55**
Newlands Rd. *For T* 1G **41** (in two parts)
Newlands Rd. *Ridd* 1J **63**
New La. *Blid* 4K **51**
New La. *Hilc* 7E **36**
New La. *Stan H* 3B **38**
New Linden St. *Shire* 3A **18**
New Line Rd. *Kirk A* 6C **48**
Newlyn Dri. *S Norm* 4E **46**
Newmarket. 5A 24
Newmarket La. *Clay C* 5A **24**
Newmarket St. *Mans* 3E **40**
New Mill La. *For T* 5C **30**
Newnham Av. *Rip* 3C **62**
New Ollerton. 3G 23
Newport Cres. *Mans* 7H **29**
New Rd. *Belp* 4D **66**
New Rd. *Blid* 5C **52**
New Rd. *Heage* 1G **67**
New Rd. *Iron* 2J **63** (Alfreton Rd.)
New Rd. *Iron* 1B **64** (Monument La.)
New Row. *Jack* 6C **56**
New Scott St. *Lang* 4A **8**
New Sta. Rd. *Bsvr* 5H **5**
Newstead. 5H 59
Newstead Abbey. 3C 60 (Remains of)
Newstead Clo. *Kirk A* 5G **49**
Newstead Clo. *Sels* 4K **57**
Newstead St. *Mans* 2H **39**
New St. *Alf* 6F **45**
New St. *Bsvr* 3J **5**
New St. *Gras* 4E **12**
New St. *Hghm* 7C **34**
New St. *Hilc* 2E **46**
New St. *Huth* 6H **37**
New St. *Kirk A* 6F **49**
New St. *Mort* 4F **35**
New St. *Nwtn* 6C **36**
New St. *N Wing* 2E **24**
New St. *Pils* 7K **25**
New St. *Rip* 3E **62**
New St. *Som* 3J **55**
New St. *S Norm* 3C **46**
New St. *Sut A* 7C **38**
New St. *Swanw* 4D **54**
New Ter. *Ple* 3D **28**
Newton. 6C 36
Newton Clo. *Belp* 1G **67**
Newtondale Av. *For T* 7E **30**
Newton Green. 5C 36
Newton Rd. *Tib* 4B **36**
Newton St. *Mans* 3C **40**
Newton Town. 1K 39
Newtonwood La. *Nwtn* 5D **36**
New Wessington. 2A 44
New Westwood. 7F 57
Nicholson's Row. *Shire* 4K **17**
Nightingale Av. *Ple* 4E **28**
Nightingale Clo. *Dane* 6E **24**
Nightingale Clo. *Rip* 3D **62**
Nightingale Cres. *Sels* 5K **57**
Nightingale Dri. *Mans* 7J **29**
Ninth Av. *For T* 1G **41**
Nix's Hill. *Nix H* 1H **55**
Nix's Hill Ind. Est. *Nix H* 1G **55**
Noel St. *Mans* 2A **40**
Nook, The. *Holb* 7G **67**
Nook, The. *Los* 7J **63**
Nook, The. *Shire* 4H **17**
Norbury Dri. *Mans* 5E **40**
Norbury Way. *Belp* 1G **67**
Norfolk Av. *Gras* 5F **13**
Norfolk Clo. *Wars* 3G **19**
Norfolk Ct. *Mans W* 3E **30**
Norfolk Dri. *Mans* 1B **40**
Norman Av. *Sut A* 1E **48**
Norman Rd. *Rip* 2C **62**
Norman Rd. *Som* 4A **56**
Normanton Av. *Alf* 7J **45**
Normanton Brook Rd. *S Norm* 3F **47**
Normanton Clo. *Edwin* 4H **21**
Normanton Common. 5C 46
Normanton Dri. *Mans* 3E **40**
Northam Dri. *Rip* 2C **62**
North Av. *Rain* 1C **52**
North Clo. *S Norm* 5B **46**
North Cres. *Clip V* 5C **32**
North Cres. *Duck* 1C **4**
Northern Bri. Rd. *Sut A* 6D **38**
Northern Vw. *Sut A* 6D **38**
Northfield. *Klbrn* 5K **67**
Northfield Av. *Ple V* 4K **29**
Northfield Dri. *Mans* 3E **40**
Northfield La. *Mans W* 4J **29** (in four parts)
Northfield La. *Pal* 2K **15**
Northfield Pk. *Mans W* 3B **30**
Northfields Clo. *Sut A* 6C **38**
North Gro. *Duck* 1C **4**
North La. *Belp* 5B **66** (in two parts)
North Pk. *Mans* 6E **40** (in two parts)
Northrowe. *Kirk A* 3C **58**
North Side. *New T* 6C **12**
North St. *Alf* 7H **45**
North St. *Clay C* 3A **24**
North St. *Doe L* 6F **15**
North St. *Huth* 5J **37**
North St. *Kirk A* 1F **59**
North St. *Lang* 4A **8**
North St. *Nwtn* 7B **36**
North St. *N Wing* 2E **24**
North St. *Pinx* 7F **47**
North St. *Ridd* 5K **55**
North St. *S Norm* 5B **46**
North St. *Sut A* 6D **38**
North St. *Wars V* 2D **18**
North Ter. *Belp* 3E **66**
North Vw. St. *Bsvr* 5G **5**
North Wingfield. 1G 25
N. Wingfield Rd. *Gras* 2D **12**
Northwood Av. *Sut A* 5B **38**
Norton. 1J 9
Norton La. *Cuc* 3H **9**
Norwell Ct. *Mans* 7B **30**
Norwich Clo. *Mans W* 3D **30**
Norwood Av. *Has* 1D **12**
Norwood Clo. *Has* 1E **12**
Norwood Clo. *Sut A* 6K **37**
Norwood La. *Sut A* 5J **27**
Nottingham Clo. *Wing* 4B **12**
Nottingham Dri. *Wing* 4B **12**
Nottingham La. *Ridd & Iron* 5A **56**
Nottingham Rd. *Alf* 6G **45**
Nottingham Rd. *Belp* 3E **66**
Nottingham Rd. *Cod* 5J **63**
Nottingham Rd. *Kirk A* 1F **59**
Nottingham Rd. *Mans* 4B **40**
Nottingham Rd. *R'hd* 7E **50**
Nottingham Rd. *Rip* 2E **62**
Nottingham Rd. *Sels* 5G **57**
Nuncar Ct. *Kirk A* 2E **58**
Nuncargate. 2E 58
Nuncargate Rd. *Kirk A* 2D **58**
Nunn Brook Ri. *Huth* 1G **47**
Nunn Brook Rd. *Huth* 7G **37**
Nunn Clo. *Huth* 1G **47**
Nursery Av. *Sut A* 7A **38**
Nursery Ct. *Mans* 1C **40**
Nursery Dri. *Bsvr* 4H **5**
Nursery Gdns. *S Norm* 6E **46**
Nursery St. *Mans* 1C **40**
Nuttall Clo. *Alf* 7F **45**
Nuttall St. *Alf* 7F **45**
Nuttall Ter. *Doe L* 6F **15**
Nuttals Park. 3E 62

O

Oadby Dri. *Ches* 1C **12**
Oak Av. *Blid* 6D **52**
Oak Av. *Lan M* 7D **64**
Oak Av. *Mans* 1C **40**
Oak Av. *New O* 3H **23**
Oak Av. *Rain* 1E **52**
Oak Av. *Rip* 5D **62**
Oak Av. *Shire* 3H **17**
Oak Bank Clo. *Mans* 1B **40**
Oak Bank Mnr. *Mans* 1B **40**
Oak Clo. *Pinx* 7E **46**
Oakdale Clo. *Dane* 6E **24**
Oakdale Rd. *Mans* 2K **39**
Oakdale Rd. *S Norm* 6C **46**
Oak Dri. *Alf* 6H **45**
Oakerthorpe. 7B 44
Oakes Clo. *Som* 4J **55**
Oakes's Row. *Iron* 6B **56**
Oakfield Av. *Kirk A* 2B **48**
Oakfield Av. *Wars* 5H **19**
Oakfield Clo. *Mans* 7F **41**
Oakfield La. *Wars* 6G **19**
Oakham Bus. Pk. *Mans* 6K **39**
Oakham Clo. *Mans* 5B **40**
Oakham Dri. *Sels* 4J **57**
Oakhurst Clo. *Belp* 1B **66**
Oakland Av. *Huth* 7H **37**
Oakland Cres. *Ridd* 6K **55**
Oakland Cft. *Huth* 6H **37**
Oakland Rd. *For T* 1E **40**
Oaklands, The. *S Norm* 6C **46**
Oakland St. *Alf* 6H **45**
Oakleaf Cres. *Sut A* 1A **48**
Oaklea Way. *Old T* 2B **24**
Oakleigh Av. *Mans W* 4E **30**
Oakmeadows. *S Norm* 6D **46**
Oakridge Clo. *For T* 7F **31**
Oak Rd. *Gras* 4F **13**
Oaks, The. *Mans* 6C **40**
Oak St. *Kirk A* 5F **49**
Oak St. *Sut A* 2B **38**
Oak Tree Av. *Edwin* 5J **21**
Oak Tree Av. *Glap* 1K **27**
Oak Tree Bus. Pk. *Mans* 5H **41**
Oak Tree Clo. *Mans* 2H **41**
Oak Tree Clo. *Swanw* 3G **55**
Oak Tree Cres. *Mans W* 4B **30**
Oak Tree La. *Mans* 2G **41**
Oak Tree Leisure Cen. 4H 41
Oaktree Rd. *Hilc* 1E **46**
Oak Tree Rd. *Sut A* 5E **38**
Oak Vw. Dri. *Har W* 3D **50**
Oakwood Ct. *Ann* 5E **58**
Oakwood Dri. *R'hd* 2G **61**
Oakwood Gro. *Edwin* 7K **21**
Oakwood Rd. *Mans* 5H **41**
Oberon Retail Pk. *Belp* 4D **66**
Observatory Way. *Kirk A* 2F **49**
Occupation La. *Edwin* 6K **21**
Occupation La. *Kirk A* 4D **48**
Occupation La. *N Wing* 2E **24**
Occupation Rd. *N Hou* 1D **28**
Oddicroft La. *Sut A* 1E **48**
Off the Avenue. *Sut A* 1B **48**
Ogston. 4A 34
Ogston La. *Hghm* 5A **34**
Old Barn Ct. *Old C* 2D **32**
Old Chapel Clo. *Kirk A* 5C **48**
Old Chapel La. *Und* 2J **65**
Old Clipstone. 2E 32
Old Colliery La. *Hlmwd* 7A **14**
Old Fall St. *Huth* 6H **37**
Old Hall Clo. *Pils* 6J **25**
Old Hall Clo. *Wars* 2J **19**
Old Hartshay Hill. *Rip* 2C **62**
Old Hill. *Bsvr* 4J **5**
Old Mnr. Rd. *Mans W* 5B **30**
Old Mkt. Pl. *Mans* 2B **40**
Old Mkt. Pl. *S Norm* 4C **46**
Old Mill La. *Cuc* 3H **9**
Old Mill La. *Mans W* 6C **30**
Old Mill La. Ind. Est. *Mans W* 7C **30**
Old Newark Rd. *Mans* 1D **50** (in three parts)
Old Peverel Rd. *Duck* 1C **4**
Old Rd. *Sut A* 2D **38**
Old Rufford Rd. *B'thpe* 7K **43**
Old Rufford Rd. *Ruff* 7C **22**
Old School Clo. *Doe L* 6F **15**
Old School La. *Ple* 3E **28**
Old Sookholme La. *Wars* 3G **19**
Old Stone Bri. *Iron* 7B **56**
Old Storth La. *S Norm* 6D **46**
Old Swanwick Colliery Rd. *Swanw* 2F **55**
Old Ter. *Ple* 4D **28**
Old Tupton. 1C 24
Olive Av. *Shire* 1H **17**
Olive Ct. *Sut A* 5D **38**
Olive Gro. *For T* 1F **41**
Ollerton. 4E 22
Ollerton Rd. *Edwin* 5K **21**
Ollerton Rd. *New O* 3E **22**
Ollerton Rd. *Oll* 1F **11**
Ollerton Rd. *Oxt* 7J **53**

Ollerton Watermill—Plainspot Rd.

Ollerton Watermill. 4E 22
Omberley Av. Sut A 3F 39
Ontario Dri. Sels 4J 57
Opal Clo. Rain 1E 52
Openacre. Iron 7B 56
Openwoodgate. 4H 67
Openwoodgate. Belp 4H 67
Openwood Rd. Belp 4H 67
Orange Clo. Shire 1H 17
Orange St. Alf 6H 45
Orchard Clo. Bsvr 5K 5
Orchard Clo. Holb 7F 67
Orchard Clo. Mans 7C 40
Orchard Clo. Shire 2J 17
Orchard Clo. Wain 5G 63
Orchard Ct. S Norm 6B 46
Orchard Cres. Glap 7K 15
Orchard Cres. Swanw 4D 54
Orchard Rd. Kirk A 5C 48
Orchard Rd. Ridd 5J 55
Orchards, The. Jack 7D 56
Orchard St. Mans 7B 30
Orchard, The. Belp 3D 66
Orchard, The. Cod 3H 63
Orchard, The. Sut A 7F 39
Orchard Vw. Bsvr 6G 5
Orchard Vw. Mans W 5B 30
Orchard Wlk. Kirk A 5C 48
Orchard Way. Sut A 2A 48
Orchid Clo. Kirk A 3D 48
Orchid Dri. Sut A 1E 48
Orchid Way. Shire 4H 17
Ormonde Fields Golf Course. 5K 63
Ormonde St. Lan M 7D 64
Ormonde Ter. Lan M 7D 64
Orton Way. Belp 1F 67
Osbourne St. Kirk A 3D 58
Osbourne Yd. Wars 3H 19
Osier Dri. Ann 4E 58
Osmaston Wlk. Mans 4H 41
(off Oak Tree La.)
Ossington Clo. Med V 6K 9
Oundle Dri. Mans 7H 29
Outgang La. Mans W 4D 30
(in two parts)
Outgang La. Ple V 2F 29
Out La. Heath 2A 26
Outram Ct. Rip 2E 62
Outram St. Rip 2E 62
Outram St. Sut A 7D 38
Outseats Dri. Alf 7H 45
Oval, The. Sut A 5B 38
Ovencroft La. Bsvr 3A 6
Overdale Av. Sut A 2C 38
Over La. Belp 4H 67
Over La. Shot G & Haz 6A 66
Overmoor Vw. Tib 2D 36
Overstone Clo. Belp 3H 67
Overstone Clo. Sut A 4D 38
Over Woodhouse. 3H 5
Owlcotes Vw. Bsvr 6J 5
Ox Clo. Clay C 4D 24
Oxclose La. Mans 5H 29
(in two parts)
Oxclose La. Mans W 5A 30
Oxcroft Estate. 1A 6
Oxcroft La. Bsvr 4J 5
Oxford Clo. Rain 2C 52
Oxford St. B'wll 1A 46
Oxford St. Doe L 6H 15
Oxford St. Kirk A 6F 49
Oxford St. Mans 7C 30
Oxford St. Rip 3D 62
Oxford St. Sut A 7B 38
Oxpasture La. Lang 1F 7
Oxton Clo. Mans 2J 39

P

Packhorse Row. Nor 2J 9
Packman's Rd. Mans W & For T 4H 31
Packman's Rd. Wars 1G 31
Paddock Clo. Edwin 4J 21
Paddock Clo. Wing 4A 12
Paddocks Clo. Pinx 5E 46
Paddocks, The. Huth 7H 37
Paddocks, The. Mans W 3E 30
Paddocks, The. Pils 6J 25
Paddock, The. B'wll 1B 46
Paddock, The. Bsvr 5K 5
Paddock, The. Kirk A 6C 48
Paddock, The. Ple 3E 28
Paddock, The. Stan H 4A 38
Padley Clo. Rip 1C 62
Padley Hill. Mans 3A 40
Padley Way. N Wing 3F 25
Padley Wood La. Pils 1G 35
Padley Wood Rd. Pils 6J 25
Palace Theatre, The. 2C 40
Paling Cres. Sut A 6C 38
Palmer Dri. Swanw 4E 54
Palmerston St. Und 2H 65
Palmerston St. W'wd 6E 56
Palterton. 2J 15
Palterton La. Sut S 1E 14
(Mill Hill)
Palterton La. Sut S 1C 14
(Shire La.)
Pankhurst Pl. Clay C 5C 24
Papplewick. 7D 60
Pargate Clo. Mare 7D 62
Park Av. Blid 5D 52
Park Av. Glap 6A 16
Park Av. Kirk A 3F 59
Park Av. Mans 1C 40
Park Av. Mans W 3B 30
Park Av. Rip 3F 63
Park Av. Shire 3J 17
Park Clo. Ches 1A 12
Park Clo. Klbrn 7K 67
Park Clo. Pinx 1E 56
Park Clo. Shirl 1E 44
Park Ct. Mans 1C 40
Park Dri. Swanw 5F 55
Parker's La. Mans W 5C 30
Parkers Row. Cuc 3G 9
Park Gdns. Huth 6J 37
Park Hall Gdns. Mans W 3C 30
Park Hall Rd. Mans W 2C 30
Parkhouse Clo. Clay C 4B 24
Parkhouse Dri. S Norm 5A 46
Parkhouse Green. 4G 25
Parkhouse Rd. Lwr P 3G 25
Parkin St. Alf 6H 45
Parkland Clo. Mans 7E 40
Parkland Dri. Wing 5A 12
Park La. Heage 4A 62
Park La. Lang 1C 8
Park La. Mans 4B 40
Park La. Pinx 7E 46
Park La. Sels & Kirk A 3J 57
Park La. Shirl 1E 44
Park La. S Wing 3A 54
Park La. W'low 5H 23
Park M. Mans W 4C 30
Park M. Ridd 5K 55
Park M. Sut A 4D 38
Pk. Mill Dri. Westh 3J 45
Park Rd. Belp 5E 66
Park Rd. Hlmwd 6K 13
Park Rd. Mans W 5B 30
Park Rd. Old T 1C 24
Park Rd. Rip 3E 62
Park Rd. Shire 2J 17
Park Row. Clay C 4D 24
Parks Av. S Wing 7A 44
Park Side. Belp 4E 66
Parkside. Huth 6J 37
Park Side. Som 4K 55
Parkside Clo. Iron 7B 56
Parkside Dri. Iron 7B 56
Parkside Rd. Edwin 5H 21
Parkstone Av. Rain 7B 42
Park St. Alf 7F 45
Park St. Ches 1A 12
Park St. Kirk A 5D 48
Park St. Mans W 5B 30
Park St. Rip 3E 62
Park St. Sut A 6D 38
Park, The. 1C 40
Park, The. Iron 1A 64
Park, The. Mans 1C 40
Park, The. Tev 2J 37
Park Vw. Lang 4K 7
Park Vw. N Wing 1F 25
Park Vw. Ple 3E 28
Park Vw. Ridd 6K 55
Park Vw. Way. Mans 4B 40
Park Wlk. Klbrn 6K 67
Parkway. For T 5K 31
Parkway. Sut A 6K 37
Parliament Rd. Mans 1J 39
Parliament St. Sut A 7D 38
Parthenon Clo. Ple 3D 28
Parwich Rd. N Wing 2F 25
Paschall Rd. Kirk A 2F 59
Pasteur Av. Rip 2C 62
Pasture Clo. Stan H 4A 38
Pasture La. Hilc 1E 46
Pasture La. Ston 6G 35
Pastures, The. Mans W 3D 30
Patchills Cen., The. Mans 2F 41
Patchills, The. Mans 2F 41
Patchwork Row. Shire 3K 17
Patterson Pl. Mans 2D 40
Paul Av. Mans 3G 41
Paulson's Dri. Mans 1B 40
Pavilion Clo. Wars 3H 19
Pavilion Gdns. N Hou 7D 16
Pavilion Gdns. Sut A 3E 38
Pavilion Rd. Kirk A 4F 49
Pavilion Workshops. Hlmwd 6K 13
Peach Av. Sels 5H 57
Peach Av. S Norm 3D 46
Peacock St. Mans 3B 40
Peacock Way. Swanw 3F 55
Peafield La. Mans W & Wars 4E 30
Peak Av. Ridd 5H 55
Peakdale Clo. Rip 6D 62
Peak, The. Shire 4J 17
Peak Vw. S Norm 5B 46
Pearl Av. Kirk A 7F 49
Pearl Clo. Rain 1E 52
Pear Tree Av. Rip 4D 62
Pear Tree Dri. Shire 1H 17
Pear Tree La. Sut A 7K 27
Pear Tree Rd. Pils 7J 25
Pease Clo. Alf 7H 45
Peasehill. 4F 63
Pease Hill. Alf 7H 45
Peasehill. Rip 4F 63
Peasehill Rd. Rip 4E 62
Pecks Hill. Mans 2E 40
Peel Cres. Mans 6H 29
Peel Rd. Mans 1J 39
Peel St. S Norm 4D 46
Peel St. Sut A 6E 38
Pegasus Ct. Bsvr 4K 5
Peggy La. Hghm 5A 34
Pelham Rd. Kirk A 5E 48
Pelham St. Mans 2C 40
Pelham St. Sut A 7B 38
Pelham Way. For T 5K 31
Pemberley Chase. Sut A 2B 48
Pemberton, The. S Norm 6D 46
Pembleton Dri. Mans 7H 29
Pendean Clo. B'wll 1A 46
Pendean Way. Sut A 1B 48
Pendine Clo. S Norm 4E 46
Penfold Way. Mort 4H 35
Penistone Gdns. Dane 6D 24
Penncroft Dri. Dane 5D 24
Penncroft La. Dane 5D 24
Pennine Av. Ridd 4H 55
Pennine Clo. Huth 5G 37
Pennine Clo. Mans W 4C 30
Pennine Clo. Nwtn 6C 36
Pennine Clo. Tib 3B 36
Pennine Dri. Kirk A 6B 48
Pennine Dri. Sels 4H 57
Pennine Dri. S Norm 5B 46
Pennine Vw. Pal 2J 15
Pennine Wlk. Gras 4F 13
(off Wenlock Wlk.)
Pennine Way. Gras 4F 13
Penn St. Belp 3E 66
Penn St. Sut A 6D 38
Pennytown Ct. Som 2J 55
Penrith Pl. Mans 1H 39
Penrose Ct. Sels 4J 57
Penrose Cres. Ark T 3A 4
Penryn Clo. S Norm 4E 46
Pentland Ct. Mans 4H 39
Pentrich. 6B 54
Pentrichlane-end. 7A 54
Pentrich Rd. Rip 2D 62
Pentrich Rd. Swanw 4D 54
Pentrich Wlk. Mans 4H 41
Penzance Pl. Mans 2H 41
Pepper St. Sut A 7E 38
Percival Clo. Sut A 6C 38
Percival Cres. Sut A 6C 38
Percy St. Sut A 7B 38
Perlethorpe Av. Mans 7K 29
Perlethorpe Av. Med V 7K 9
Perlethorpe Clo. Edwin 4H 21
Perth Clo. Mans W 3C 30
Peters Av. Clay C 4B 24
Petersfield Clo. Mans 2H 39
Petersmiths Clo. New O 1G 23
Petersmiths Cres. New O 1G 23
Petersmiths Dri. New O 2G 23
Peterway. Som 3K 55
Petticoat La. Bsvr 3C 6
Pettifor Ter. Westh 1J 45
Peveril Clo. Ridd 5J 55
Peveril Ct. Rip 3C 62
Peveril Dri. Ridd 5J 55
Peveril Dri. Sut A 7A 38
(in two parts)
Peveril Rd. Bsvr 3H 5
Peveril Rd. Tib 3B 36
Pewit Clo. Hlmwd 7K 13
Pewit La. Mort 2J 35
Pheasant Hill. Mans 7A 30
Philip Av. Kirk A 1F 59
Philip Clo. Rain 2E 52
Philipway. Som 3K 55
Phoenix Rd. Newt 7K 65
Phoenix St. Sut A 5F 39
Pickard St. Mans 2E 40
Pickburns Gdns. Klbrn 7K 67
Pickman Cotts. New T 7D 12
Pierpoint Pl. Kirk A 4D 48
Pilgrim Clo. R'hd 1F 61
Pilsley. 7J 25
Pilsley Clo. Belp 1G 67
Pilsley Green. 1J 35
Pilsley Rd. Dane 5D 24
Pilsley Rd. Mort 4H 35
Pinchom's Hill Rd. Belp 4F 67
Pine Av. New O 3H 23
Pine Clo. Kirk A 4D 48
Pine Clo. Mans W 3C 30
Pine Clo. Rain 1B 52
Pine Clo. Rip 3D 62
Pine Clo. Shire 1J 17
Pines Way. Har W 3D 50
Pine Vw. Dane 5E 24
Pineview Clo. Mans 7F 41
Pinewood Av. Cod 5H 63
Pinewood Av. Edwin 7A 22
Pinewood Clo. Alf 7J 45
Pinewood Clo. Kirk A 4G 49
Pinewood Dri. Mans 7F 41
Pinewood Rd. Belp 1C 66
Pinfold Gdns. For T 6F 31
Pinfold, The. Belp 2G 67
Pinfold, The. Glap 6K 15
Pingle Cres. Belp 2D 66
Pingle La. Belp 2D 66
Pinxton. 1F 57
Pinxton Ct. Mans 4H 41
Pinxton Grn. Pinx 7G 47
Pinxton La. Kirk A 4H 47
Pinxton La. Pinx 6K 47
Pinxton La. S Norm 5E 46
Pinxton Rd. Kirk A 7B 48
Pinxtonwharf. 2E 56
Piper Av. Clay C 4E 24
Pipers Ct. Iron 7B 56
Pit Hill. Lang 4K 7
Pit Hill. Ple 3E 28
Pit La. Dane 5E 24
Pit La. Mort 4G 35
Pit La. Rip 3E 62
Pit La. Shirl 1D 44
Pit La. Wain 5G 63
Plains La. Black 3A 66
Plain Spot. 2G 65
Plainspot Rd. Brins 3G 65

82 A-Z Mansfield

Platt St. *Pinx* 1E **56**
Pleasant Av. *Bsvr* 7K **5**
Pleasley. 3E **28**
Pleasleyhill. 4F **29**
Pleasley Rd. *Skeg* 3E **38**
Pleasley Rd. *Tev* 2K **37**
Pleasley Springs. *Ple* 3F **29**
Pleasley Va. *Ple V* 2H **29**
Pleasley Va. Bus. Pk. *Ple V* . .2H **29**
Plough Yd. *Wars* 2H **29**
Plumptre Rd. *Lan M* 7D **64**
Plum Tree Av. *For T* 7H **31**
Plymouth Av. *Pinx* 1G **57**
Pollard Dri. *Mans* 2C **40**
Polyfields La. *Bsvr* 6K **5**
Pond La. *New T* 7D **12**
Pond St. *Kirk A* 5E **48**
Pool Clo. *Pinx* 1F **57**
Poolsbrook Rd. *Duck* 1C **4**
Poplar Av. *Kirk A* 4G **49**
Poplar Av. *Rip* 4D **62**
Poplar Dri. *Glap* 7K **15**
Poplar Dri. *New T* 6C **12**
Poplar Dri. *Ple* 4F **29**
Poplar Gro. *Chur W* 1G **19**
Poplar Gro. *For T* 7H **31**
Poplar Rd. *S Norm* 3D **46**
Poplars, The. *Gras* 4E **12**
      (off Mill La.)
Poplars, The. *Sut A* 6E **38**
Poplar St. *Mans W* 5C **30**
Poplar St. *New O* 3H **23**
Poplars Way. *Har W* 3D **50**
Poplar Ter. *Sels* 5G **57**
Poppy Clo. *Shire* 4H **17**
Poppy Gdns. *Tib* 2D **36**
Porterhouse. 3F **63**
Porterhouse Rd. *Rip* 3E **62**
Portland Av. *Bsvr* 5K **5**
Portland Av. *Kirk A* 2E **58**
Portland Clo. *Sut A* 7D **38**
Portland Ct. M. *Mans W* 4C **30**
Portland Cres. *Bsvr* 5K **5**
Portland Cres. *Mans W* 5D **30**
Portland Cres. *Med V* 5A **10**
Portland Ind. Est. *Kirk A* 3E **48**
Portland Pk. 7D **48**
Portland Pk. *Kirk A* 7D **48**
Portland Pk. Vis. Cen. 7D **48**
Portland Pl. *Mans* 3A **40**
Portland Rd. *Lang* 4A **8**
      (Cockshut La.)
Portland Rd. *Lang* 3K **17**
      (King Edward St.)
Portland Rd. *Sels* 3J **57**
Portland Row. *Edwin* 7A **22**
Portland Sq. *Sut A* 7D **38**
Portland St. *Kirk A* 5E **48**
Portland St. *Mans* 3B **40**
Portland St. *Mans W* 5C **30**
Portland St. *N Hou* 1D **28**
Portland St. *Sut A* 7D **38**
Portland St. *Wars* 3H **19**
Portland Ter. *Lang* 4A **8**
Postmans La. *Temp N* 3J **13**
Post Office Rd. *Kirk A* 5F **49**
Potter La. *W'low* 7H **23**
Potter St. *Sut A* 5E **38**
Pottery Clo. *Belp* 2G **67**
Poulter St. *Lang* 5K **7**
Poulterwell La. *Pal* 2K **15**
Pratt Clo. *Mans* 7H **29**
Precinct Rd. *Kirk A* 5F **49**
Prest Av. *Med V* 6A **10**
Preston Av. *Alf* 6H **45**
Preston Rd. *Rain* 2C **52**
Prestwold Av. *For T* 7H **31**
Prestwold Way. *Ches* 1C **12**
Priestley Av. *Stre* 5C **34**
Priestsic Rd. *Sut A* 6C **38**
Primary Clo. *Belp* 3E **66**
Primrose Av. *Und* 2H **65**
Primrose Clo. *Kirk A* 3D **48**
Primrose Clo. *S Norm* 3D **46**
Primrose Ct. *Mans W* 4F **31**
Primrose Ct. *Sut A* 1F **49**
Primrose Hill. *B'wll* 1A **46**
Primrose Way. *Lang J* 1K **17**
Primrose Way. *Sut A* 1A **48**

Primula Clo. *Shire* 4H **17**
Princess Av. *For T* 1G **41**
Princess Av. *S Norm* 5C **46**
Princess Av. *Wars* 3J **19**
Princess Pl. *Clay C* 6C **24**
Princess St. *Kirk A* 7B **48**
Princess St. *Mans* 4A **40**
Prior Clo. *Sut A* 5F **39**
Priory Av. *Kirk A* 3F **59**
Priory Av. *R'hd* 2H **61**
Priory Ct. *Mans W* 5B **30**
Priory Gdns. *Swanw* 3G **55**
Priory Gro. *Kirk A* 5H **49**
Priory Rd. *Alf* 6H **45**
Priory Rd. *Blid* 5C **52**
Priory Rd. *Mans W* 5B **30**
Priory Rd. *Nwtn* 6C **36**
Priory Sq. *Mans W* 5B **30**
Privet Av. *Kirk A* 4E **48**
Promenade, The. *Kirk A* 4H **49**
Prospect Av. *S Norm* 5B **46**
Prospect Clo. *Kirk A* 3F **49**
Prospect Ct. *Huth* 1G **47**
Prospect Dri. *Belp* 5D **66**
Prospect Dri. *Shire* 4J **17**
Prospect Gdns. *Swanw* 4E **54**
Prospect Pl. *Sut A* 7C **38**
Prospect Rd. *Den* 6K **67**
Prospect Rd. *Pils* 7J **25**
Prospect St. *Alf* 6H **45**
Prospect St. *Mans* 3D **40**
Prospect Units. *Kirk A* 3G **49**
Providence Pl. *Alf* 7F **45**
Providence Rd. *Jack* 7C **56**
Providence St. *Rip* 4E **62**
Pump Hollow Rd. *For T* 1G **41**
      (in three parts)
Purbeck Clo. *Mans W* 2C **30**
Pye Av. *Mans* 2H **39**
Pye Bridge. 5A **56**
Pye Bri. Ind. Est. *Pye B* 5A **56**
Pye Hill. 7C **56**
Pye Hill Rd. *Jack* 7C **56**
Pytchley Clo. *Belp* 3H **67**
Python Hill Rd. *Rain* 1D **52**

Quadrangle, The. *Blid* 5C **52**
Quadrangle, The. *Mans* 1B **40**
Quadrangle, The. *News V* 5H **59**
Quaker La. *Mans* 2B **40**
Quaker Way. *Mans* 2B **40**
Quarries Way. *Kirk A* 6C **48**
Quarry Clo. *R'hd* 3G **61**
Quarrydale Av. *Sut A* 4C **38**
Quarrydale Dri. *Sut A* 4C **38**
Quarrydale Rd. *Sut A* 5D **38**
Quarry Dale Vw. *Mans* 4E **40**
Quarry Dri. *Kirk A* 7F **49**
Quarry La. *L'by* 6B **60**
Quarry La. *Mans* 5A **40**
Quarry La. *Ston* 5F **35**
Quarry Rd. *Belp* 5D **66**
Quarry Rd. *Bsvr* 3J **5**
Quarry Rd. *R'hd* 3G **61**
Quarry Rd. *Som* 4J **55**
Quarry Yd. *Sut A* 7C **38**
Queen's Ct. *For T* 5K **31**
Queens Dri. *Belp* 2C **66**
Queens Dri. *Brins* 5G **65**
Queen St. *Belp* 4E **66**
Queen St. *Clay C* 6C **24**
Queen St. *Iron* 7A **56**
Queen St. *Kirk A* 6E **48**
Queen St. *Mans* 2B **40**
Queen St. *Pils* 7J **25**
Queen St. *Pinx* 7E **46**
Queen St. *Som* 3D **46**
Queen St. *S Norm* 5B **46**
Queen St. *Sut A* 5K **39**
Queen St. *Wain* 5F **63**
Queen St. *Wars* 2G **19**
Queens Vw. Dri. *Wain* 5G **63**
Queens Wlk. *Hlmwd* 6A **14**
Queens Wlk. *Mans* 5B **30**
      (off Queen St.)
Queen's Wlk. *Neth L* 5A **8**

Queen's Wlk. *New T* 6D **12**
      (off Ward St.)
Queensway. *For T* 7G **31**
Queensway. *Hlmwd* 6A **14**
Queensway. *Kirk A* 1F **59**
Queen's Way. *New T* 6D **12**
Queensway. *Pils* 7J **25**
Queensway. *Ston* 6F **35**
Queen Victoria Rd. *New T* 6C **12**
Quenby La. *Rip* 3E **62**
Quines Hill Rd. *For T* 6H **31**

Racecourse Rd. *Mans* 4E **40**
Radbourne St. *Mans W* 4E **30**
Radford St. *Mans* 3B **40**
Radmanthwaite. 5H **29**
Radmanthwaite La. *Ple* 3F **29**
Radmanthwaite Rd. *Ple* 5H **29**
Radnor Pl. *Ple* 4G **29**
Raglan St. *Alf* 6G **45**
Railway Cotts. *Cor* 2F **13**
Railway Cotts. *Hlmwd* 6B **14**
Railway Row. *Iron* 7B **56**
Railway Ter. *Has* 1B **12**
Rainworth. 1C **52**
Rainworth By-Pass. *Rain* 6K **41**
Rainworth Water Rd. *Rain* 1B **52**
Raleigh Rd. *Mans* 1H **39**
Ralph Dri. *Som* 4J **55**
Ramsden Cft. *Rain* 1C **52**
Ramsey Clo. *For T* 6G **31**
Randol Clo. *Mans* 5H **39**
Rangewood Rd. *S Norm* 6B **46**
Rannoch Dri. *Mans* 4H **39**
Ransom Rd. *Rain* 6K **41**
Ransom Wood Bus. Pk.
     Rain 6K **41**
Ratcher Way. *For T* 1H **41**
Ratcliffe Ga. *Mans* 3C **40**
Raven Av. *Tib* 4B **36**
Raven Clo. *Ridd* 5J **55**
Raven Oak Clo. *Belp* 5E **66**
Ravensdale. 1E **40**
Ravensdale Av. *Mans* 1D **40**
Ravensdale Rd. *Mans* 1D **40**
Ravenshead. 1F **61**
Ravenshead Leisure Cen.
  . . . . .3G **61**
Rawson Green. 6K **67**
Rawson Grn. *Klbrn* 6K **67**
Rawson St. *Sels* 5J **57**
Raylawn St. *Mans* 3G **41**
Raymond Clo. *Kirk A* 3B **48**
Recreation Clo. *B'wll* 1A **46**
Recreation Dri. *Shire* 5K **17**
Recreation Rd. *Ann* 3G **59**
Recreation Rd. *Lang J* 7J **7**
Recreation Rd. *N Hou* 1D **28**
Recreation St. *Mans* 2C **40**
Recreation St. *Sels* 5K **57**
Recreation Vw. *Lang J* 1J **17**
Rectory Clo. *Duck* 3C **4**
Rectory La. *Kirk A* 6C **48**
Rectory Rd. *Chur W* 1J **19**
Rectory Rd. *Duck* 3C **4**
Redacre Clo. *Bsvr* 5A **6**
Red Barn Clo. *Mans* 6D **36**
Redbarn La. *Nwtn* 6D **36**
Redbarn Way. *Sut A* 1A **48**
Redcar Clo. *Mans* 4E **40**
Redcliffe Rd. *Mans* 3D **40**
Redcliffe St. *Sut A* 5D **38**
Redcroft Clo. *Edwin* 5H **21**
Redfern Av. *Rip* 2E **62**
Redfern St. *New T* 1C **24**
Redgate Clo. *Mans* 1J **39**
Redgate St. *Mans* 1J **39**
Redgate St. *Pinx* 1F **57**
Redhill Ct. *Belp* 5F **67**
Red La. *Brins* 4G **65**
Red La. *S Norm* 7A **46**
      (in two parts)
Redmoor Clo. *Cod* 3H **63**
Redruth Dri. *Mans* 7H **41**
Reform St. *Kirk A* 3D **58**
Reform St. *Sut A* 7D **38**

Reform St. Ind. Est. *Sut A* 7D **38**
      (off Reform St.)
Regent Ct. *Iron* 7B **56**
Regent St. *Kirk A* 6D **48**
Regent St. *Mans* 2B **40**
Regent St. *Sut A* 7B **38**
Regina Cres. *R'hd* 2F **61**
Reindeer St. *Mans* 3D **40**
Renfrew St. *Mans* 4J **39**
Repton Ct. *Mans W* 4E **30**
Reservoir Houses. *Hghm* 4A **34**
Retford Rd. *Boug* 1K **23**
Revill Ct. *Kirk A* 3C **48**
Reynolds Av. *Rip* 3F **63**
Rhodes Wlk. *Mans* 3J **39**
Ribbledale Clo. *Mans* 4G **41**
Riber Av. *Som* 3K **55**
Riber Clo. *Kirk A* 2E **58**
Riber Cres. *Old T* 3B **24**
Richardsons La. *Ridd* 6J **55**
Richmond Dri. *Mans W* 6D **30**
Richmond Rd. *Kirk A* 5H **49**
Richmond St. *Mans* 4F **41**
Ricket La. *Blid* 6E **50**
Riddings. 5K **55**
Ridd Way. *Wing* 4A **12**
Ridge Clo. *Sut A* 6B **38**
Ridgedale Rd. *Bsvr* 5J **5**
Ridgedale Vw. *Rip* 2D **62**
Ridge, The. *B'wll* 1A **46**
Ridgeway. *Lang J* 2K **17**
Ridgeway Av. *Bsvr* 4A **6**
Ridgeway La. *Wars* 4H **19**
Ridgeway Ter. *Wars* 3G **19**
Ridgewood Gro. *R'hd* 1G **61**
Riding Hill Av. *Shire* 4H **17**
Ridings, The. *For T* 7F **31**
Riley Av. *Sut A* 6A **38**
Riley Clo. *Sut A* 6A **38**
Riley La. *Rip* 4A **54**
Ringwood Av. *Mans* 5C **40**
Ripley. 3D **62**
Ripley Heritage Cen. 3D **62**
      (off Market Pl.)
RIPLEY HOSPITAL. 3D **62**
Ripley Leisure Cen. 3D **62**
Ripley Rd. *Heage* 3A **62**
      (Bridle La.)
Ripley Rd. *Heage & Lwr H* 7A **54**
      (Chesterfield Rd.)
Rise Hill. 2D **58**
Riverside Clo. *Cuc* 3G **9**
Riverside Way. *Bsvr* 4G **5**
Riverside Way. *Mans W* 3D **30**
River Vw. *Pye B* 5C **56**
River Vw. *Wars* 2H **19**
Robert Av. *Mans* 4K **39**
Roberts Av. *Huth* 7H **37**
Roberts Dri. *Alf* 6H **45**
Robertson's Av. *Duck* 2C **4**
Robey Clo. *For T* 7H **31**
Robin Down Clo. *Mans* 7D **40**
Robin Down Ct. *Mans* 7C **40**
Robin Down La. *Mans* 7C **40**
Robin Gro. *R'hd* 2G **61**
Robin Hood Av. *Edwin* 7A **22**
Robin Hood Av. *Wars* 5H **19**
Robin Hood Rd. *Blid* 5D **52**
Robin Hood Rd. *Kirk A* 3F **59**
Robin Hood Ter. *R'hd* 7H **51**
Rob La. *Farn* 7K **53**
Rocester Way. *N Wing* 2F **25**
Rochdale Ct. *Mans* 4G **41**
Rochester Rd. *Rain* 2C **52**
Rock Av. *Mans* 2C **40**
Rock Cres. *Clay C* 3A **24**
Rock Hill. *Mans* 3D **40**
Rock Hill Gdns. *Mans* 3D **40**
Rock Ho. Clo. *Tib* 4B **36**
Rocklands, The. *Shire* 3J **17**
Rock La. *Sut S* 1A **14**
Rockley Way. *Shire* 3J **17**
Rock St. *Mans* 3D **40**
Rock Ter. *Blid* 6A **52**
Rock, The. *Wars V* 2E **18**
Rock Valley. *Mans* 2C **40**
      (in two parts)
Roderick Av. *Kirk A* 2F **59**
Rodery, The. *Mans* 4E **40**

Rodger's La.—Sherwood Pines Forest Walks Cycle Route

Rodger's La. *Alf* 6G 45
Roebuck Dri. *Mans* 6B 40
Roewood Clo. *Kirk A* 3D 48
Roger Clo. *Sut A* 4D 38
Rolaine Clo. *Mans W* 4C 30
Roman Bank. *Mans W* 5D 30
Romsey Pl. *Mans* 3H 39
Rona Clo. *Mans* 4J 39
Roods Clo. *Sut A* 2B 48
Rookery La. *Sut A* 2J 47
Rookery, The. *Mans* 1A 40
Rookwood Clo. *Blid* 5C 52
Rooley Av. *Sut A* 6A 38
Rooley Dri. *Sut A* 6A 38
Rooley La. *Stan H* 5K 37
Roosevelt Rd. *Sut A* 5F 39
Rooth St. *Mans* 3B 40
Rope Wlk. *Rip* 4E 62
Ropeway, The. *Kirk A* 5C 48
Roseberry St. *Kirk A* 6F 49
Rosebery Hill. *Mans* 3C 40
Rose Cottage Dri. *Huth* 7H 37
Rose Ct. *Clay C* 4A 24
Rosedale Gdns. *Sut A* 2B 48
Rosedale La. *R'hd* 7F 51
Rosedale Way. *For T* 6F 31
Rosehill Ct. *Bsvr* 5J 5
Roseland La. *Shire* 3F 17
(in two parts)
Rose La. *Mans W* 4C 30
Rosemary Av. *Mans* 1A 40
Rosemary Cen. *Mans* 2A 40
Rosemaryhill. 4H 57
Rosemary St. *Mans* 1A 40
Rosemont Clo. *Sut A* 3D 38
Rosewood Clo. *S Norm* 3D 46
Rosewood Ct. *Kirk A* 4G 49
Rosewood Dri. *Kirk A* 4G 49
Rosier Cres. *Swanw* 3G 55
Rosings Ct. *Sut A* 1C 48
Rosling Way. *Ark T* 4A 4
Roston Clo. *Mans* 4H 41
Rother Cft. *New T* 7D 12
Rotherham Rd. *Bsvr* 6B 6
Rotherham Rd. *N Hou* 3B 16
Rother St. *Pils* 6J 25
Rothwell La. *Belp* 3F 67
Round Hill. 1G 49
Roundhill Clo. *Sut A* 1G 49
Rouse St. *Pils* 7K 25
Rowan Av. *R'hd* 2G 61
Rowan Av. *Rip* 4D 62
Rowan Clo. *For T* 7D 30
Rowan Clo. *Kirk A* 5C 48
Rowan Cft. *Huth* 5H 37
Rowan Dri. *Kirk A* 4D 48
Rowan Dri. *Sels* 4F 57
Rowan Dri. *Shire* 2H 17
Rowan Dri. *Shirl* 1D 44
Rowland Ct. *Alf* 5F 45
Rowland St. *Alf* 6G 45
Rowthorne. 1K 27
Rowthorne Av. *Swanw* 3G 55
Rowthorne La. *Glap* 2J 27
Royal Ga. *Belp* 4H 67
Royal Oak Ct. *Edwin* 5K 21
Royal Oak Dri. *Sels* 4K 57
Royston Dri. *Belp* 2H 67
Ruby Gdns. *Kirk A* 6H 49
Ruby Gro. *Rain* 1E 52
Ruddington Ct. *Mans* 7G 41
Ruddington Rd. *Mans* 7G 41
Rufford. 1J 43
Rufford Av. *Mans* 2C 40
Rufford Av. *Med V* 5A 10
Rufford Av. *New O* 3G 23
Rufford Av. *Rain* 1D 52
Rufford Clo. *Sut A* 4D 38
Rufford Colliery La. *Rain* 1C 52
Rufford Country Pk. 7C 22
Rufford Ct. *Rain* 1E 52
Rufford Dri. *Mans W* 5E 30
Rufford La. *W'low* 7D 22
Rufford Mill Cotts. *Ruff* 7D 22
Rufford Mill Heritage Cen. 7D 22
Rufford Rd. *Edwin* 6K 21
Rugby Av. *Alf* 7J 45
Rugby Rd. *Rain* 2C 52
Rupert St. *Lwr P* 4H 25
Rushes, The. *Mans W* 3D 30
Rushley Vw. *Sut A* 1A 48
Rushpool Av. *Mans W* 4D 30
Ruskin Rd. *Mans* 6H 29
Russell Gdns. *Old T* 2B 24
Russell St. *Sut A* 6D 38
Rutherford Av. *Mans* 4E 40
Rutland. *Kirk A* 5H 49
Rutland Av. *Bsvr* 5J 5
Rutland Av. *Wain* 5G 63
Rutland Clo. *Wars* 3G 19
Rutland Rd. *W'wd* 7D 56
Rutland St. *Mans* 4B 40
Rydal Way. *Clay C* 5B 24
Rye Ct. *Dane* 5D 24
Rye Cres. *Dane* 5D 24
Ryedale Av. *Mans* 4G 41
Ryegrass Clo. *Belp* 3H 67
Rykneld Ct. *Clay C* 5C 24
Rykneld Ri. *Wing* 4A 12
Rylah. 2H 15
Rylah Hill. *Pal* 2H 15

S

Sacheverall Av. *Pinx* 7E 46
Saddlers Clo. *For T* 7F 31
Sadler St. *Mans* 1K 39
St Albans Clo. *Hlmwd* 7A 14
St Andrews Clo. *Swanw* 4G 55
St Andrews Cres. *Sut A* 3D 38
St Andrew's Dri. *Swanw* 4E 54
St Andrews St. *Kirk A* 4F 49
St Andrews St. *Sut A* 3C 38
St Andrew St. *Mans* 4C 40
St Catherine St. *Mans* 4C 40
St Chads Clo. *Mans* 6C 40
St Edmund's Av. *Mans W* 5C 30
St Edwin's Dri. *Edwin* 5J 21
St George's Pl. *Belp* 3D 66
St Helens Av. *Pinx* 6E 46
St Helen's Dri. *Sels* 4F 57
St James Clo. *Belp* 3H 67
St James Dri. *Brins* 4F 65
St John's Av. *Kirk A* 6F 49
St John's Clo. *Brins* 3F 65
St Johns Clo. *Rip* 2F 63
St John's Dri. *Klbrn* 7K 67
St John's Pl. *Mans* 2A 40
St John's Rd. *Belp* 3E 66
St John St. *Mans* 2A 40
St Judes Way. *Rain* 1C 52
St Lawrence Av. *Bsvr* 5A 6
St Lawrence Rd. *N Wing* 1F 25
St Leonards Pl. *Shirl* 1E 44
St Leonards Way. *For T* 7H 31
St Margaret St. *Mans* 4C 40
St Marks Ct. *Sut A* 2K 47
St Mary's Ct. *Sut A* 5B 38
St Mary's Dri. *Edwin* 5J 21
St Mary's Rd. *Sut A* 5B 38
St Mary's Wlk. *Jack* 1D 64
St Mellion Way. *Kirk A* 4C 48
St Michael Ct. *Sut A* 6E 38
St Michaels Dri. *S Norm* 3C 46
St Michael St. *Sut A* 6E 38
St Modwens Ct. *Sut A* 7D 38
St Pauls Av. *Has* 1D 12
St Peters Av. *Chur W* 1H 19
St Peter's Clo. *Belp* 3D 66
St Peters Clo. *Duck* 2C 4
St Peters Clo. *New O* 3F 23
St Peter's Cft. *Belp* 3E 66
St Peters Dri. *Rain* 1C 52
St Peters Retail Pk. *Mans* 3B 40
St Peter's Way. *Mans* 2B 40
St Thomas Av. *Kirk A* 6F 49
St Thomas Clo. *Tib* 4A 36
St Wilfrids Dri. *Kirk A* 5B 48
St Wilfrids Pk. *Kirk A* 6B 48
Salcey Clo. *Swanw* 4F 55
Salcombe Rd. *Alf* 5H 45
Sales Av. *New T* 7C 12
Salisbury Clo. *Mans W* 4D 30
Salisbury Dri. *Belp* 2H 67
Salisbury Rd. *Mans* 1J 39
Salmon La. *Kirk A* 4A 58
Sampson's La. *Ple* 5F 29
Sampson St. *Kirk A* 3D 58
Sampsons Yd. *Huth* 6H 37
Samuel Brunts Way. *Mans* 1C 40
Samuel Clo. *Mans* 1K 39
Samuel Ct. *Rip* 4D 62
Sandalwood Clo. *Mans* 5H 41
Sandalwood Dri. *Kirk A* 4G 49
Sandbed La. *Belp* 6G 67
Sanders Av. *Mans* 1E 40
Sandfield Av. *R'hd* 3H 61
Sandfield Clo. *Mans* 5H 41
Sandfield Rd. *Kirk A* 3D 58
Sandgate Av. *Mans W* 4D 30
Sandgate Rd. *Mans W* 4D 30
Sandham La. *Rip* 3C 62
Sandhill Rd. *Und* 1K 65
Sandhills Rd. *Bsvr* 5K 5
Sandhurst Av. *Mans* 5B 40
Sandown Rd. *Mans* 5H 41
Sandown Rd. *Sut A* 6F 39
Sandringham Ct. *Mans W* 2B 30
Sandringham Dri. *Mans W* 2B 30
Sandringham Rd. *Mans W* 3E 30
Sandstone Pl. *Mans* 4E 40
Sandwich Clo. *Kirk A* 4C 48
Sandwood Clo. *Nwtn* 6C 36
Sandycliffe Clo. *For T* 7F 31
Sandy La. *Cuc* 5H 9
Sandy La. *Edwin* 7K 21
Sandy La. *Mans* 2D 40
Sandy La. *R'hd* 6H 51
Sandy La. *Wars* 2H 19
(in two parts)
Santon Clo. *For T* 6G 31
Santon Rd. *For T* 6G 31
Sapphire Clo. *Rain* 2E 52
Sapphire Dri. *Kirk A* 6G 49
Sarah Clo. *Som* 4J 55
Sartfield Rd. *For T* 6H 31
Saundby Av. *Mans* 7H 29
Savile Row. *New O* 3G 23
Saville Rd. *Sut A* 3D 38
Saville St. *Blid* 5C 52
Saville Way. *Wars* 3G 19
Sawley Dri. *Mans* 5H 41
Saw Pit Ind. Est. *Tib* 2E 36
Saw Pit La. *Tib* 4D 36
Saxby Dri. *Mans* 5H 41
Scarcliffe. 1D 16
Scarcliffe Ct. *Sut A* 6D 38
Scarcliffe Lanes. *Up L* 7F 7
Scarcliffe St. *Mans* 3D 40
Scarcliffe Ter. *Lang* 4A 8
Scarrington Ct. *Mans* 7G 41
Scarsdale St. *Bsvr* 6G 5
School Clo. *Heath* 6B 14
School Clo. *Nwtn* 6C 36
School Clo. *Shirl* 7D 34
School Clo. *Ston* 6F 35
School Clo. *Westh* 1J 45
School Cft. *Ridd* 5K 55
Schoolfield Clo. *Bsvr* 5A 6
School Hill. *Ann* 3F 59
School La. *Cuc* 3G 9
School La. *Mans W* 5C 30
School La. *Oll* 4F 23
School La. *Rip* 3C 62
School La. *S Norm* 6D 46
School Rd. *Sels* 4J 57
School Rd. *Und* 7J 57
School St. *Kirk A* 5F 49
Scotches. 2D 66
Scotches, The. *Belp* 2D 66
Scotswood Rd. *Mans W* 2B 30
Scott Clo. *Gras* 3E 12
Scott Cres. *Ston* 6F 35
Scott Dri. *Belp* 2J 67
Scott Dri. *Som* 3K 55
Scotts Way. *Kirk A* 2F 59
Scotts Yd. *Rip* 2D 62
Seaforth Sq. *Mans* 4H 39
Seagrave Av. *Kirk A* 2F 59
Seagrave Dri. *Ches* 1C 12
Seanor La. *Lwr P* 3G 25
Searby Rd. *Sut A* 1G 49
(in two parts)
Searson Av. *Bsvr* 5J 5
Searston Av. *Hlmwd* 7K 13
Searwood Av. *Kirk A* 3C 48
Second Av. *Clip V* 5C 32
Second Av. *Edwin* 5J 21
Second Av. *For T* 7G 31
Second Av. *Rain* 7B 42
Sedgebrook St. *Mans W* 5E 30
Sedgwick St. *Jack* 1D 64
Selston. 4J 57
Selston Common. 5J 57
Selston Golf Course. 5F 57
Selston Green. 5F 57
Selston Rd. *Jack* 7D 56
Selwyn St. *Bsvr* 6A 6
Selwyn St. *Mans* 4E 40
Setts Way. *Wing* 3B 12
Seventh Av. *Clip V* 5A 32
Seventh Av. *For T* 1G 41
Severn Cres. *N Wing* 3F 25
Severn Sq. *Alf* 6G 45
Shaftesbury Av. *Mans* 7H 29
Shafton Clo. *Clay C* 4E 24
Shafton Wlk. *Clay C* 4E 24
Shakespeare Av. *Mans W* 4B 30
Shakespeare Av. *Stre* 5C 34
Shakespeare Clo. *Old T* 2B 24
Shakespeare Dri. *Alf* 6H 45
Shakespeare St. *Gras* 4E 12
Shakespeare St. *Hlmwd* 6K 13
Shardlow Way. *Mans* 5H 41
Sharrard Clo. *Und* 2J 65
Sharratt Ct. *Mans* 7G 41
Shaw Cft. *Sut A* 4D 38
Shawcroft Av. *Ridd* 6J 55
Shaw La. *Milf & Holb* 7D 66
Shaw St. *Hlmwd* 6K 13
Shaw St. *Mans* 2E 40
Shaw St. *Ridd* 5J 55
Shaw's Yd. *Klbrn* 7K 67
Shearsby Dri. *For T* 6F 31
Sheepbridge La. *Mans* 4K 39
Sheep La. *Shirl* 2C 44
Sheepwalk La. *R'hd* 7F 51
Sheepwash La. *Sut A* 6F 39
(in two parts)
Sheldon Rd. *Los* 7J 63
Shelford Av. *Kirk A* 4B 48
Shelford Hill. *Mans* 3J 39
Shelley Av. *Mans W* 4B 30
Shelley Clo. *Kirk A* 3G 49
Shelley Gro. *Ston* 6G 35
Shelley St. *Hlmwd* 6K 13
Shelton Clo. *Mans* 7J 29
Shelton Rd. *Mans* 7G 41
Shepherd's La. *Sut A* 7G 27
Shepherds Oak. *Sut A* 3C 38
Shepherds Way. *Sut A* 7F 39
Sherbourne Dri. *Belp* 2H 67
Sheringham Dri. *Mans* 4C 40
Sherview Av. *Mans* 2G 41
Sherwood Av. *Blid* 5E 52
Sherwood Av. *Edwin* 5J 21
Sherwood Av. *Pinx* 7F 47
Sherwood Av. *Shire* 3J 17
Sherwood Clo. *Mans* 2E 40
Sherwood Ct. *Kirk A* 5F 49
Sherwood Ct. *Mans W* 6B 30
Sherwood Dri. *New O* 3G 23
Sherwood Dri. *Shire* 4J 17
Sherwood Forest Art & Craft Cen. 4J 21
Sherwood Forest Cvn. Pk. *Mans* 1C 32
Sherwood Forest Country Pk. 2H 21
Sherwood Forest Farm Pk. 1A 32
Sherwood Forest Golf Cen. 2K 41
Sherwood Forest Vis. Cen. 3K 21
Sherwood Grange. *Mans* 1F 41
Sherwood Hall Gdns. *Mans* 1F 41
Sherwood Hall Rd. *Mans* 2E 40
Sherwood Heath Nature Reserve. 3D 22
Sherwood Pde. Rain 1D 52
(off Kirklington Rd.)
Sherwood Park. 4D 58
Sherwood Pines Forest Pk. 5G 33
Sherwood Pines Forest Walks Cycle Route. 3G 33

84 A-Z Mansfield

Sherwood Pines Vis. Cen. . . .4G 33
Sherwood Pl. Clip V 4D 32
Sherwood Pl. Kirk A 2E 58
Sherwood Ri. Kirk A 2E 58
Sherwood Ri. Mans W 6A 30
Sherwood Rd. Rain 1D 52
Sherwood Rd. Sut A 1C 48
Sherwood St. Bsvr 6H 5
Sherwood St. Huth 6H 37
Sherwood St. Kirk A 3E 58
(Glebe St.)
Sherwood St. Kirk A 5F 49
(Low Moor Rd.)
Sherwood St. Lea 3J 55
Sherwood St. Mans 3B 40
Sherwood St. Mans W 5B 30
Sherwood St. Nwtn 5D 36
Sherwood St. Stre 4C 34
Sherwood St. Wars 3H 19
Sherwood Way. Sels 5K 57
Shetland Clo. For T 7F 31
Shetland Rd. Tib 4B 36
Shirburn Av. Mans 1C 40
Shirebrook. 3K 17
Shirebrook Bus. Cen.
Shire 4A 18
Shirebrook Town Farm. 2H 17
Shireoaks. Belp 2B 66
Shireoaks Ct. Mans 7G 41
Shires, The. For T 7F 31
Shires, The. Sut A 1B 48
Shirland. 7D 34
Shirland Dri. Mans 5H 41
Shirland Golf Course. 2D 44
Shirley Rd. Rip 3D 62
Shirley Rd. Swanw 4F 55
Short Lands. Belp 3E 66
Short Row. Belp 3D 66
Short St. Belp 3F 67
Short St. Sut A 6E 38
Short St. Wars 3H 19
Shoulder of Mutton Hill.
Kirk A 2F 59
Shropshire Av. W'wd 7E 56
Shuttlewood Rd. Bsvr 1H 5
Sibthorpe St. Mans 4A 40
Siddalls Dri. Sut A 6K 37
Sidings Rd. Kirk A 3G 49
Sidings Way. Westh 1J 45
Siena Gdns. For T 6G 31
Silken Holme. S Norm 6D 46
Silk St. Sut A 7C 38
Silver Birch Cres. Westh 2J 45
Silverdale Av. Mans W 4B 30
Silverhill Cotts. Sut A 1J 37
Silverhill La. Tev 7G 27
Silverwood Av. R'hd 2G 61
Simpson Rd. Mans 2H 39
Singleton Av. Mans 1E 40
Siskin Ct. Mans 5H 41
Sitwell Dri. Klbrn 7K 67
Sitwell Grange La. Pils 7K 25
Sitwell Vs. Mort 4E 34
Sixth Av. Clip V 5A 32
Sixth Av. Edwin 6J 21
Sixth Av. For T 1G 41
Skegby. 3B 38
Skegby Hall Gdns. Skeg 3C 38
Skegby La. Sut A & Mans 3F 39
Skegby Mt. Mans 4J 39
Skegby Rd. Huth 6J 37
Skegby Rd. Kirk A 2C 58
Skegby Rd. Sut A 5E 38
Skegness. 5K 57
Skerry Hill. Mans 2D 40
Skye Gdns. Tib 4B 36
Slack Av. Rip 3D 62
Slack La. Heath 4B 14
Slack La. Ridd 7H 55
Slack La. Rip 3D 62
Slack's La. Pils 6J 25
Slade Clo. S Norm 6D 46
Slant La. Mans W 3B 30
Slant La. Shire 2H 17
Slater St. Clay C 5D 24
Slater St. Sut A 5D 38
Sleet Moor. 2F 55
Sleetmoor La. Swanw 2F 55

Sleights La. Pinx 1E 56
Smalley Clo. Und 2J 65
Small Ga. Mans W 2E 30
Smeath Rd. Und 2H 65
Smedley Av. Som 2K 55
Smiths La. Stre 2C 34
Smithson Av. Bsvr 5K 5
Smithy Clo. Und 3E 40
Smithy Av. Clay C 4C 24
Smithymoor. 2A 34
Smithy Pl. Gras 5F 13
Smithy Row. Sut A 7B 38
Snaefell Av. For T 6G 31
Snowberry Av. Belp 4F 67
Snowdrop Dri. Mans W 4F 31
Somercotes. 3J 55
Somercotes Hill. Som 3J 55
Somersall St. Mans 1J 39
Somersby Ct. Mans 4H 41
(off Thornton Clo.)
Sookholme. 5C 18
Sookholme Clo. Shire 3K 17
Sookholme Dri. Wars 4G 19
Sookholme La.
Sook & Wars 5D 18
(in three parts)
Sookholme Rd. Shire 4K 17
(in two parts)
Sookholme Rd. Sook 5D 18
Sotheby Av. Sut A 1G 49
Sough Rd. S Norm 3C 46
South Av. Rain 1C 52
South Av. Shire 4K 17
South Cres. Bsvr 5K 5
South Cres. Clip V 5C 32
South Cres. Duck 1C 4
Southcroft. Alf 6G 45
South End. 6F 13
Southend. Gras 5F 13
Southfield Av. Has 1D 12
Southfield Dri. S Norm 5E 46
Southfields Av. Pinx 7F 47
Southfields Clo. Kirk A 2C 58
Southgate Rd. Wars 2J 19
Southgreen Clo. Mans 7E 40
Southgreen Hill. Mans 7E 40
South Hill. 3A 34
S. Hill La. Hghm 3A 34
South Normanton. 4C 46
Southpark Av. Mans 7F 41
South Pl. Rip 3D 62
S. Ridge Dri. Mans 6D 40
South St. Nwtn 7B 36
South St. Pils 7K 25
South St. Ridd 6K 55
South St. S Norm 4D 46
South St. Swanw 5D 54
South Vw. Milf 7E 66
Southview Gdns. R'hd 1G 61
Southwell Clo. Kirk A 4E 48
Southwell La. Kirk A 5C 48
Southwell La. Ind. Est.
Kirk A 4E 48
Southwell Rd. E. Rain 7K 41
Southwell Rd. W. Mans 3D 40
Southwood Av. Sut A 5B 38
Sovereign Way. Mans 5H 41
Sowter Av. Sut A 5C 38
Spa Clo. Sut A 2D 48
Spa Cft. Tib 4A 36
Spa La. Mans W 4H 31
Spang La. Huth 5G 37
Spencer Av. Belp 3F 67
Spencer Dri. Som 4K 55
Spencer Rd. Belp 3E 66
Spencer St. Bsvr 6H 5
Spencer St. Mans 3A 40
Sperry Clo. Sels 5H 57
Spinners Way. Belp 1G 67
Spinney Clo. Kirk A 4C 48
Spinney Clo. Mans W 2E 30
Spinney, The. Belp 1E 66
Spinney, The. Har W 3D 50
Spinney, The. Rip 1D 62
Spinney, The. Shire 4H 17
Spire Clo. Kirk A 3C 58
Spittal Grn. Bsvr 6J 5
Sporton Clo. S Norm 3C 46

Sporton La. S Norm 3C 46
Spring Clo. Belp 1C 66
Springfield Av. Los 7H 63
Springfield Av. Shire 2J 17
Springfield Clo. Mans 4G 41
Springfield Cres. Bsvr 3H 5
Springfield Cres. Som 4K 55
Springfield Rd. Hlmwd 7K 13
Springfield Ter. Rip 3E 62
Springfield Vw. Rip 2D 62
Springfield Way. Kirk A 4H 49
Spring Hill. Mans W 5B 30
Springhill Way. Cod 4G 63
Spring Hollow. Haz 7A 66
Spring La. Lang 1C 6
Spring La. Tib 5E 26
Spring La. Wars V 4D 18
(Bully La.)
Spring La. Wars V 1C 18
(William Wood La.)
Spring Rd. Ridd 5A 56
Spring Rd. Sut A 7C 38
Springvale Clo. Dane 6D 24
Springvale Rd. Dane 6D 24
Springwell St. Huth 7H 37
Springwood Gdns. Belp 3E 66
Springwood St. Temp N 3H 13
Springwood Vw. Clo. Sut A . . .6A 38
Spruce Av. Sels 5F 57
Spruce Gro. Kirk A 4G 49
Square, The. Dane 5E 24
Square, The. Rain 1D 52
Squires Cft. Old C 2E 32
Squires La. Old C 2C 32
Stables Ct. Bsvr 5A 6
Stacey Rd. Mans 6H 29
Stafford Dri. Tib 4B 36
Staffa Dri. Tib 4B 36
Stafford St. Mans 1K 39
Stafford St. Mans W 6C 30
Stainforth St. Mans 6C 40
Stainsby. 7E 14
Stainsby Clo. Hlmwd 7B 14
Stainsby Common. 2A 26
Stainsby Dri. Mans 2G 41
Stainsby Gro. Huth 7H 37
Stainsby Mill. 1F 27
Stamper Cres. Sut A 3D 38
Stanage St. Mans 4H 41
Stanhope St. Doe L 6G 15
Stanley. 7G 27
Stanley Av. Rip 2E 62
Stanley Clo. R'hd 7G 51
Stanley La. Sut A 5F 27
Stanley Rd. For T 7H 31
Stanley Rd. Mans 5B 40
Stanley St. Som 4K 55
Stanton Av. Belp 3F 67
Stanton Cres. Sut A 5B 38
Stanton Hill. 3A 38
Stanton Pl. Mans 2K 39
Stanton Pl. N Hou 1E 28
Stanton St. N Hou 1D 28
Starr Av. Sut A 6B 38
Statham Av. New T 7C 12
Station Av. News V 5K 59
Station Cotts. Ple 2E 28
Station Hill. Mans W 5B 30
Station La. Cod 6H 63
Station La. Edwin 6J 21
Station La. Iron 1B 64
Station New Rd. Old T 1C 24
Station Rd. Bsvr 4G 5
Station Rd. Clip V 6A 32
Station Rd. Lang J 1J 17
Station Rd. Mans 3B 40
Station Rd. Mort 4H 35
Station Rd. News V 5J 59
Station Rd. N Wing 1E 24
Station Rd. Oll 4E 22
Station Rd. Pils 7K 25
Station Rd. Rain 2C 52
Station Rd. Scarc 1D 16
(in two parts)
Station Rd. Sels 2G 57
Station Rd. Shire 3K 17
Station Rd. Sut A 7D 38
Station Rd. Tib 3B 36
Station St. Kirk A 5E 48
Station St. Mans 3B 40
Station St. Mans W 5B 30

Station St. Sut A 7D 38
Station Vw. Shire 4J 17
Station Yd. Sut A 2D 38
Staunton Clo. Ches 1A 12
Staveley Rd. Ark T 1A 4
Steam Mill La. Rip 4F 63
Steel La. Bsvr 4K 5
Steel's La. Pal 1K 15
Stella St. Mans 4B 40
Stenson Ct. Rip 3F 63
Stephenson Pl. Clay C 4A 24
Stepnall Heights. Boug 1J 23
Stevenson Cres. Sut A 7B 38
Stewart St. Ridd 6K 55
Stinting La. For T 6E 30
Stinting La. Shire 4H 17
Stirland St. Cod 3H 63
Stirling Av. Mans 4J 39
Stockley. 3G 15
Stockley Clo. Glap 5H 15
Stockley Vw. Bsvr 6K 5
Stocks La. Duck 3C 4
Stockwell Ct. Mans 3A 40
Stockwell Ga. Mans 2B 40
(Crown Wlk.)
Stockwell Ga. Mans 3A 40
(Padley Hill)
Stockwell Ho. Mans 2A 40
(off Connexion, The)
Stoke Clo. Belp 3H 67
Stokes Trad. Est. Mans 5J 39
Stollard St. Clay C 4D 24
Stonebridge La. Wars 3F 19
Stonebridge Rd. Mans 3G 19
Stonebroom. 5H 35
Stonebroom Ind. Est. Ston 5H 35
Stonebroom La. Ston 5H 35
Stonechurch Vw. Ann 3F 59
Stone Cres. Mans 2H 39
Stone Cross Ct. Mans 1B 40
Stone Cross La. Mans 1B 40
(in two parts)
Stonehills Way. Sut A 5F 39
Stoneholes Dri. Dane 6E 24
Stonehouse Ter. News V 5H 59
Stone Leigh Clo. Mans 4E 40
Stoneleigh Way. Swanw 3F 55
Stonemason M. Kirk A 5F 49
Stoneyford. 5C 64
Stoneyford Ct. Sut A 5D 38
Stoneyford Rd. Sut A 4B 38
Stoney La. Belp 3E 66
Stoney La. Brins 7E 64
(in two parts)
Stoney La. Rip 5G 63
Stoney La. Sels 4G 57
Stoney St. Sut A 6D 38
Stony Houghton. 5C 16
Stormont Clo. S Norm 6D 46
Storthfield Way. S Norm 6D 46
Storth La. S Norm 5D 46
Stort Sq. Mans W 6D 30
Stow Ct. Mans W 5E 30
Stranfaer Clo. Swanw 4F 55
Stranraer Clo. Mans W 2C 30
Stratton Rd. Bsvr 4J 5
Strawberry Bank. Huth 5F 37
Strawberry Way. For T 1H 41
Straw La. Stre 1C 34
Street Lane. 7B 62
Street La. Den 4A 62
Strelley Av. Rip 4C 62
Strettea La. Hghm 7C 34
Stretton. 1C 34
Stretton Hillside. 4C 34
Stretton Rd. Clay C 6C 24
Stretton Rd. Mort 3E 34
Stride, The. Ches 1A 12
Strutt St. Belp 4D 66
Stuart Av. For T 1F 41
Stuart Av. New O 1H 23
Stuart St. Mans 2E 40
Stuart St. Sut A 1C 48
Stubbins Wood. Lang J 1J 17
Stubbins Wood La. Lang J 1J 17
Studland Clo. Mans W 2D 30
Sudbury Ct. Mans 4H 41
Sudbury Dri. Huth 7G 37
Suff La. Pinx 7E 46

Sulby Clo. *For T* 6G 31
Summercourt Dri. *R'hd* 7F 51
Summerfield Rd. *Kirk A* 3C 48
Summerhill Ct. *Huth* 6H 37
   (off Swanson Av.)
Summit Clo. *Kirk A* 4E 48
Summit Dri. *Mans* 3J 17
Sunflower Clo. *Shire* 4H 17
Sunningdale Clo. *Kirk A* 3C 48
Sunningdale Pk. Cvn. Pk.
   New T 6C 12
Sunny Bank. *Mans* 6C 40
Sunny Bank. *Tib* 4B 36
   (in two parts)
Sunny Bank Gdns. *Belp* 5D 66
Sunnycroft. *Sut A* 1A 48
Surgery La. *Blid* 6C 52
Surrey Dri. *Mans* 1K 39
Sutton Clo. *Sut A* 3E 38
Sutton Forest Side. 6E 38
Sutton Hall Rd. *Bsvr* 6G 5
Sutton in Ashfield. 7C 38
Sutton La. *Sut S* 5A 4
Sutton Middle La. *Kirk A* 3D 48
   (in two parts)
Sutton Rd. *Huth* 6J 37
Sutton Rd. *Kirk A* 5C 48
Sutton Rd. *Mans* 5H 39
Sutton Scarsdale. 1C 14
Sutton Scarsdale Hall. 1C 14
Sutton Spring Wood. 1H 13
Sutton Vw. *Bsvr* 6K 5
Swallow Clo. *Mans* 5H 41
Swan La. *Mans W* 5B 30
Swann Yd. *Huth* 6H 37
Swanson Av. *Huth* 6H 37
Swanwick. 4E 54
Swanwick Av. *Shire* 4K 17
Swanwick Ct. *Alf* 1F 55
Swanwick Hill. *Swanw* 5E 54
Swanwick Rd. *Lea* 4H 55
Swinecot Rd. *Edwin* 4K 21
Swinfen Broun. *Mans* 6C 40
Swinney Bank. *Belp* 2E 66
Swinney La. *Belp* 2E 66
Swinton Copse. *Boug* 1J 23
Swinton Ri. *R'hd* 1F 61
Sycamore Av. *Glap* 7K 15
Sycamore Av. *Kirk A* 4C 48
Sycamore Av. *Rip* 4D 62
Sycamore Clo. *Bsvr* 4A 6
Sycamore Clo. *Pinx* 7F 47
Sycamore Clo. *Rain* 1D 52
Sycamore Clo. *Sels* 4F 57
Sycamore Clo. *Stre* 5C 34
Sycamore Gro. *Mans* 4F 41
Sycamore Rd. *Mans W* 3C 30
Sycamore Rd. *New O* 3H 23
Sycamores, The. *S Norm* 5D 46
Sycamore St. *Chur W* 1F 19
Sydney Clo. *Mans W* 2C 30
Syerston Rd. *Mans* 7G 41
Sylvan Cres. *Sut A* 4E 38
Sylvan Dri. *Old T* 2A 24
Sylvester St. *Mans* 4K 39
Sywell Clo. *Sut A* 4D 38
Sywell Clo. *Swanw* 3F 55

T

Talbot St. *Mans* 5B 40
Talbot St. *Pinx* 1E 56
Tall Trees Pk. Cvn. Pk.
   Mans W 6E 30
Tansley Rd. *N Wing* 3F 25
Tantum Av. *Los* 7J 63
Tapton Pk. *Mans* 2H 41
Tattershall Wlk. *Mans W* 4E 30
Tavistock Av. *Rip* 1D 62
Tavistock Sq. *Alf* 5H 45
Taylor Cres. *Sut A* 1D 48
Taylor's Clo. *Mans* 1E 40
Teal Av. *Mans* 5H 41
Tealby Wlk. *Mans W* 4E 30
Teal Clo. *Shire* 4H 17
Tedburn Dri. *Mans* 7G 41
Teignmouth Av. *Mans* 3F 41
Temple Normanton. 4H 13

Temple Normanton Bus. Pk.
   Cor 3G 13
Temple Normanton By-Pass.
   Temp N 3H 13
Tennyson Av. *Mans W* 6C 30
Tennyson St. *Hlmwd* 6K 13
Tennyson St. *Kirk A* 6F 49
Tennyson St. *Mans* 2A 40
Tennyson St. *Stre* 5C 34
Tennyson Way. *Gras* 4E 12
Ten Row. *Cuc* 3G 9
Tenter La. *Mans* 4A 40
Terrace La. *Ple* 3D 28
Terrace Rd. *Mans* 2C 40
Tetford Wlk. *Mans W* *4E 30*
   (off Coton Clo.)
Teversal. 1A 38
Teversal Av. *Ple* 4F 29
Teversal Trail Vis. Cen. 2K 37
Tewkesbury Av. *Mans W* 4D 30
Thackeray Rd. *Ston* 6F 35
Thanet St. *Clay C* 5C 24
Thickley Bank. *Lang J* 3K 17
Thickley Clo. *Shire* 3K 17
Thieves Wood La. *Mans* 2B 50
Third Av. *Clip V* 5B 32
Third Av. *Edwin* 5J 21
Third Av. *For T* 1G 41
Third Av. *Rain* 7B 42
Thirteen Row. *Pal* 1J 15
Thistle Pk. *Mans W* 4F 31
Thompson Cres. *Sut A* 1D 48
Thomson Dri. *Cod* 4H 63
Thomson Wlk. *Cod* *4G 63*
   (off Thomson Dri.)
Thoresby Av. *Edwin* 5J 21
Thoresby Av. *Kirk A* 6H 49
Thoresby Av. *Shire* 3J 17
Thoresby Clo. *Med V* 7K 9
Thoresby Clo. *Rip* 3E 62
Thoresby Cres. *Stan H* 3A 38
Thoresby Dri. *Edwin* 5H 21
Thoresby Rd. *Mans W* 4A 30
Thoresby Rd. *Rain* 1B 52
Thoresby St. *Mans* 2A 40
Thoresby St. *Sut A* 5E 38
Thorn Av. *Mans* 7K 29
Thornbridge Cres. *Ches* 1A 12
Thornbury Dri. *Mans* 1H 39
Thorney Abbey Rd. *Blid* 5D 52
Thorney Ct. *Mans* 7G 41
Thorneywood Av. *Kirk A* 3C 58
Thornham Cres. *Kirk A* 3D 58
Thornhill Dri. *Boug* 2J 23
Thorn Ter. *Mans* 2A 40
Thornton Clo. *Mans* 4H 41
Thornton St. *Sut A* 1D 48
Thorntree Ct. *Ches* 1A 12
Thorpelands Av. *For T* 7E 30
Thorpe Rd. *Mans* 7G 41
Thorpe Way. *Belp* 2F 67
Three Gates. *Belp* 5D 66
Three Thorn Hollow. 7K 41
Thurcaton Way. *Nwtn* 6C 36
Thurlby Ct. *Mans W* 4E 30
Thurley Wlk. *Mans* 5H 41
Thurston Av. *Som* 3K 55
Tibshelf. 4B 36
Tibshelf Rd. *Hlmwd* 7K 13
Tibshelf Rd. *Ston* 7J 35
Tibshelf Rd. *Sut A* 2J 37
Tideswell Clo. *R'hd* 7G 51
Tideswell Ct. *Mans* 2D 40
Tilford Rd. *News V* 5H 59
Timber La. *Pils* 3K 25
Tintern Clo. *Kirk A* 6G 49
Tiree Clo. *Tib* 4B 36
Tissington Av. *Chur W* 7J 9
Titchfield Av. *Mans W* 5D 30
Titchfield Av. *Sut A* 7C 38
Titchfield St. *Mans* 1A 40
Titchfield St. *Wars* 4H 19
Titchfield St. *Mans* 7G 41
Toadhole. 5E 56
Toadhole Furnace. 4B 44
Tom La. *Duck* 1A 4
Tom Wass Rd. *Sut A* 2C 48
Toothill La. *Mans* 2B 40
Toothill Rd. *Mans* 2B 40

Top Farm Ct. *Klbrn* 7K 67
Top La. *Ple* 6D 28
Top Row. *Jack* 6C 56
Top Row Cotts. *Oll* 5G 23
Top Sandy La. *Wars* 4J 19
Top St. *Rain* 1D 52
Tor Av. *Ridd* 5J 55
Torksey Wlk. *Mans W* 4E 30
Tor La. *Oll* 4E 22
Torrani Way. *N Wing* 1F 25
Tourist Info. Cen.
   Mansfield 2B 40
   Ollerton 3E 22
   Ripley 2D 62
Tower Bus. Cen. *Clay C* 4C 24
Tower Clo. *Som* 3J 55
Tower Cres. *Bsvr* 6K 5
Town End. *Bsvr* 5J 5
Town End. *Shirl* 6D 34
Town La. *Mans* 6D 36
Townroe Dri. *Mans* 1H 39
Town St. *Pinx* 6F 47
Tranmere Av. *Clay C* 5D 24
Transvaal Ter. *Pal* 2K 15
Tree La. *Mans* 4G 41
Trelawney Rd. *Clay C* 5D 24
Trent Gro. *Alf* 1G 55
Trent Rd. *Boug* 3K 23
Trent Wlk. *Mans W* 4E 30
Treswell Ct. *Mans* *7G 41*
   (off Wilford Rd.)
Triangle, The. *Belp* 3C 66
Trowell Ct. *Mans* 7G 41
Trusley Wlk. *Mans W* 5E 30
   (Calver St.)
Trusley Wlk. *Mans W* 4E 30
   (Radbourne St.)
Tuckers La. *Mans* 1K 39
Tudor Av. *For T* 1F 41
Tudor Cres. *Rain* 2C 52
Tudor Dri. *Mans* 5C 40
Tudor St. *Sut A* 1C 48
Tudsbury Ter. *Sut A* 6E 38
Tupton. 7D 12
Tupton Moor Clo. *Old T* 6D 12
Tupton Way. *Hlmwd* 6K 13
Turnberry Av. *Kirk A* 3C 48
Turner La. *Boug* 1J 23
Turners La. *Swanw* 4G 55
Turnley Rd. *S Norm* 4E 46
Turnoaks Bus. Pk. *Ches* 1B 12
Turnoaks La. *Ches* 1A 12
   (in two parts)
Turnstone Cres. *Mans* 5H 41
Turton Ct. *News V* 5J 59
Tuxford Av. *Med V* 6K 9
Tuxford St. *Mans* 7G 41
Tuxford Rd. *Boug* 3H 23
Twin Oaks Dri. *Sut A* 7A 38
Twinyards Clo. *Sut A* 1A 48
Twitchell, The. *Sut A* 7D 38
Twitchell Vw. *Sut A* 1D 48

U

Underwood. 3J 65
Underwood Green. 2H 65
Underwood Hill. 2G 65
Union St. *Mans* 2A 40
Union St. *Sels* 4J 57
Union St. *S Norm* 6B 46
Union St. *Sut A* 7D 38
Unity Rd. *Kirk A* 3F 49
Unwin Rd. *Sut A* 6F 39
Unwin St. *Huth* 6J 37
Upper Birchwood. 1B 56
Upper Cft. *Dane* 5D 24
Upper Cft. *New T* 7D 12
Up. Cross La. *Wars* 3J 19
Up. Dunstead Rd. *Lan M* 7D 64
Upper Hartshay. 3A 62
Upper Langwith. 7H 7
Up. Mantle Clo. *Clay C* 4C 24
Up. Marehay Rd. *Rip* 6C 62
Up. Mexborough Rd. *Sels*
   . . . . .4J 57
Upper Pilsley. 6J 25
Upper Pleasley. 3D 28

Upton Mt. *Mans* 7J 29
Urban Rd. *Kirk A* 5E 48

V

Vale Av. *Wars* 3G 19
Vale Clo. *Bsvr* 5J 5
Vale Clo. *Mans* 5E 40
Vale Dri. *Shire* 5K 17
Vale Rd. *Mans W* 5B 30
Vale Vw. *Mans* 5E 40
Valentine Av. *Sels* 4F 57
Vale Rd. *Mans W* 4A 30
Vallance St. *Mans W* 4B 30
Valley Clo. *Lwr P* 4H 25
Valley Rd. *Bsvr* 6J 5
Valley Rd. *Clay C* 4A 24
Valley Rd. *Shire* 2J 17
Valley Vw. *Belp* 5E 66
Valley Vw. *Bsvr* 7K 5
Valley Vw. *Mans* 5E 40
Valley Vw. *N Wing* 7J 55
Valmont Av. *Mans* 3G 41
Vanguard Trad. Est. *Ches* 1B 12
Vaughan Pl. *Lang J* 1J 17
Vellus Ct. *Sut A* 7F 39
Ventura Ct. *Kirk A* 3G 49
Venture Cres. *Nix H* 1G 55
Vera Cres. *Rain* 2D 52
Vere Av. *Sut A* 5C 38
Verney St. *N Hou* 1D 28
Verney Way. *N Hou* 1D 28
Vernon Av. *R'hd* 2F 61
Vernon Ct. *Shire* 3A 18
Vernon Cres. *R'hd* 2F 61
Vernon Ri. *Gras* 5F 13
Vernon Rd. *Kirk A* 5D 48
Vernon St. *Shire* 3A 18
Vernon St. Ind. Est. *Shire* 3A 18
Verona Ct. *Mans* 6G 41
Veronne Dri. *Sut A* 3E 38
Vesper Ct. *For T* 1F 41
Vexation La. *Ruff* 7B 22
Vicarage Clo. *Belp* 3E 66
Vicarage Clo. *Heath* 5D 14
Vicarage Clo. *Shire* 4J 17
Vicarage Clo. *Swanw* 4E 54
Vicarage Ct. *Mans* 6J 29
Vicarage Ct. *Skeg* 2C 38
Vicarage Gdns. *Clay C* 6C 24
Vicarage La. *Iron* 7B 56
Vicarage M. *Ridd* 5A 56
Vicarage Rd. *Milf* 7D 66
Vicarage Way. *Kirk A* 3D 58
Vicar La. *Tib* 3C 36
Vicars Ct. *Clip V* 6B 32
Vicar Water Country Pk.
   . . . . .6C 32
Vicar Way. *For T* 2H 41
Vickers St. *Wars* 3H 19
Victoria Clo. *Boug* 2K 23
Victoria Ct. *Mans* 4A 40
Victoria Cres. *Iron* 7B 56
Victoria Dri. *B'wll* 1A 46
Victoria Rd. *Kirk A* 5D 48
Victoria Rd. *Pinx* 6F 47
Victoria Rd. *Rip* 2D 62
Victoria Rd. *Sels* 5H 57
Victoria Rd. *Alf* 7H 45
Victoria St. *Bsvr* 6K 5
Victoria St. *Clay C* 5C 24
Victoria St. *Iron* 7B 56
Victoria St. *Mans* 4A 40
Victoria St. *Rip* 2F 63
Victoria St. *Sels* 4J 57
Victoria St. *Shire* 3K 17
Victoria St. *Som* 3J 55
Victoria St. *S Norm* 4C 46
Victoria St. *Stan H* 3A 38
Victoria St. *Sut A* 7C 38
Victoria St. *Wars* 2G 19
Victoria Ter. *Sels* 2G 57
Victoria Ter. *Tib* 2D 36
Victoria Wlk. *New T* 6D 12
Victory Av. *Rip* 3F 63
Victory Clo. *For T* 7G 31
Victory Clo. *Kirk A* 4F 49
Victory Dri. *For T* 7F 31
Villas Rd. *Bsvr* 4G 5

Gas, The. *Lang* 3K 7
illiers Rd. *Mans* 2E 40
Violet Clo. *Shire* 4H 17
Violet Hill. *For T & Mans* 1G 41

W

Wade Clo. *Mans* 6C 40
Wagstaff La. *Jack* 7D 56
Wain Av. *N Wing* 1G 25
Waingroves. **5G 63**
Waingroves Rd. *Rip* 4F 63
Waingroves Rd. *Wain* 6H 63
Wain Way. *N Wing* 1G 25
Wainwright Av. *Mans* 7H 29
Walcote Clo. *Belp* 2G 67
Walesby Ct. *Mans* 6G 41
Walesby Dri. *Kirk A* 5H 49
Walesby La. *New O* 3F 23
Walgrave Clo. *Belp* 1F 67
Walkden St. *Mans* 5H 29
Walker Av. *Rip* 2E 62
Walkers Clo. *For T* 7H 31
Wallis Rd. *Mans* 2E 40
Wall St. *Rip* 2D 62
Walnut Rd. *Belp* 4H 17
Walnut Tree Cres. *For T* 6K 31
Walters Av. *Brins* 6G 65
Walters Cres. *Sels* 5F 57
Waltham Rd. *R'hd* 1G 61
Walton Clo. *For T* 1H 41
Walton Dri. *Sut A* 2B 48
Walton St. *Sut A* 6E 38
Wansley La. *Bagt* 1G 65
Ward Dri. *Som* 4K 55
Ward Pl. *Mans* 3J 39
Ward St. *New T* 7D 12
Warmwells La. *Rip* 5D 62
Warnadene Rd. *Sut A* 2C 48
Warren Av. *Ann* 3G 59
Warren Clo. *Huth* 7J 37
Warren Clo. *Pils* 6J 25
Warren Rd. *Kirk A* 2F 59
Warren Way. *For T* 2J 41
Warsop Enterprise Cen.
  Wars 2H 19
Warsop Hill. **5H 9**
Warsop La. *Blid & Rain* 4D 82
Warsop Rd. *Mans W* 5C 30
Warsop Vale. **3D 18**
Warwick Clo. *Kirk A* 5H 49
Warwick Dri. *Mans* 2E 40
Warwick Gdns. *Belp* 2H 67
Warwick Rd. *Som* 2H 55
Washington Dri. *Mans* 4J 39
Watchorn Cotts. *Alf* 7F 45
  (off Gladstone Rd.)
Watchorn La. *Alf* 1F 55
Watercress La. *Dane* 6D 24
Waterdown Clo. *Mans W* 3D 30
Water La. *Bsvr* 6G 5
Water La. *Mans* 6C 16
  (in two parts)
Water La. *Ple* 4F 29
Water La. *S Norm* 4D 46
Waterloo. **4J 25**
Waterloo Clo. *Hilc* 2E 46
Waterloo St. *Clay C* 4C 24
Waterloo St. *Doe L* 6H 15
Water Meadows Swimming &
  Fitness Cen. 3B 40
Waterside. *Iron* 7B 56
Waterson Av. *Mans* 6F 41
Waterson Clo. *Mans* 6G 41
Waterson Oaks. *Mans* 5F 41
Waterworks Dri. *Clip V* 3E 32
Watnall Cres. *Mans* 2J 39
Watson Av. *Mans* 2C 40
Watson St. *Wars* 3H 19
Waverley Clo. *Kirk A* 5H 49
Waverley Rd. *Mans* 5B 40
Waverley St. *Tib* 2C 36
Wayside Clo. *N Wing* 1G 25
Weavers Clo. *Belp* 2G 67
Weavers Cft. *Rip* 4D 62
Weaver's La. *Und & Ann* 7D 58
Webb St. *News V* 5J 59
Webster Clo. *Rain* 1D 52

Weetman Av. *Chur W* 1H 19
Weighbridge Rd. *Mans* 3C 40
Welbeck Clo. *Sut A* 4D 38
Welbeck Dri. *Edwin* 5H 21
Welbeck Rd. *Bsvr* 5K 5
Welbeck Rd. *Mans W* 5C 30
Welbeck Sq. *Stan H* 3A 38
Welbeck St. *Kirk A* 6F 49
Welbeck St. *Mans* 2A 40
Welbeck St. *Wars* 3H 19
Welbeck Vs. *Bsvr* 4K 5
Welburn Clo. *For T* 6F 31
Welfare Clo. *Shire* 4J 17
Welfitt Gro. *Neth L* 4B 8
Welford Clo. *Skeg* 4F 39
Wellbeck St. *Sut A* 7D 38
Wellcroft Clo. *Mans* 4K 39
Wellington Clo. *Wars* 4H 19
Wellington Ct. *Belp* 3D 66
Wellington M. *Shirl* 7D 34
Wellington Pk. *Shirl* 7D 34
Wellington St. *Rip* 3E 62
Well La. *Hghm* 6C 34
Wellow. **6H 23**
Wellow Clo. *Mans* 1H 39
Wellow Clo. *Sut A* 1G 49
Wellow Grn. *W'low* 5H 23
Wellow Rd. *Oll* 4F 23
Wellow Wood Vw. New O *3G 23*
  (off Rufford Av.)
Wells Clo. *Mans W* 4D 30
Wellspring Clo. *Wing* 3B 12
Wells St. *Bsvr* 6A 6
Well St. *Rip* 3D 62
Welshcroft Clo. *Kirk A* 4E 48
Welton Av. *Belp* 1F 67
Welwyn Av. *Mans W* 4E 30
Wenham La. *Huth* 5H 37
Wenlock Dri. *Gras* 4F 13
Wenlock Wlk. *Gras* 4F 13
Wensleydale Clo. *For T* 7E 30
Wensley Rd. *N Wing* 3F 25
Wentbridge Dri. *Mans* 5G 41
Wentworth Clo. *For T* 6F 31
Wentworth Rd. *Kirk A* 3C 48
Wesley Rd. *Ston* 6F 35
Wesley St. *Kirk A* 3E 58
Wessington La. *S Wing* 5A 44
West Av. *Rip* 3C 62
W. Bank Av. *Mans* 1B 40
W. Bank Lea. *Mans* 7B 30
W. Bank Link. *Mans* 7B 30
W. Bank Wynd. *Mans* 1B 40
Westbourne Av. *Ston* 5G 35
Westbourne Clo. *Mans W* 4E 30
Westbourne Clo. *Sut A* 6B 38
Westbourne Rd. *Sut A* 7B 38
Westbourne Rd. *Und* 2J 65
Westbourne Vw. *Sut A* 6B 38
Westbrook Av. *R'hd* 7F 51
Westbrook Dri. *Rain* 2D 52
Westbury Gdns. *Belp* 2G 67
West Cres. *Duck* 1C 4
Westdale Av. *Sut A* 4E 38
Westdale Rd. *Jack* 7D 56
Westdale Rd. *Mans* 7B 30
West Dri. *Edwin* 5J 21
West End. *Alf* 7G 45
West End. *Pinx* 6E 46
West End. *Sut A* 7C 38
West End. *Und* 7G 45
W. End Ct. Sut A *7B 38*
  (off Willowbridge La.)
Western Av. *Kirk A* 7F 49
Western Av. *Mans* 4K 39
Western Av. *Swanw* 4D 54
Westfield Clo. *Mans* 1K 39
Westfield Clo. Sut A *7C 38*
  (off Church La.)
Westfield Dri. *B'wll* 1K 45
Westfield Dri. *Mans* 1J 39
Westfield La. *Mans* 7H 29
Westfield Rd. *Kirk A* 2F 59
West Ga. *Mans* 2B 40
West Hill. *Cod* 5H 63
West Hill. *Mans* 1A 40
West Hill. *Sut A* 3B 38
W. Hill Av. *Mans* 2B 40
W. Hill Dri. *Mans* 2B 40

Westhill La. *Gras* 4E 12
W. Hill Pk. *Mans W* 5B 30
W. Hill Way. *Mans* 2B 40
Westhouses. **1J 45**
Westland Dri. *Pinx* 7E 46
West La. *Edwin* 5J 21
Westleigh. *Mans W* 2D 30
Westminster Av. *Kirk A* 5G 49
Westminster Ct. *Mans W* 5D 30
Westmorland Way. *Jack* 1D 64
Weston Clo. *Sut A* 2G 49
Weston Spot Clo. *Rip* 5D 62
West St. *Clay C* 4A 24
West St. *Doe L* 6F 15
West St. *Lang* 3A 8
West St. *Ridd* 5J 55
West St. *S Norm* 5B 46
West St. *Ston* 5F 35
West St. *Wars V* 3D 18
West Vw. *Bsvr* 6K 5
West Vw. *Tib* 4B 36
West Way. *Som* 2J 55
Westwood. **7E 56**
Westwood Gdns. *Mort* 4H 35
Westwood Gdns. *W'wd* 7E 56
Westwood La. *Tib* 2B 36
  (in two parts)
Whaley. **2G 7**
Whaley Bri. Clo. *Mans* 4J 41
Whaley Common. **2H 7**
Whaley Rd. *Bsvr* 3C 6
Whaley Rd. *Lang* 2H 7
Whaley Thorns. **3A 8**
Whaley Thorns Country Pk.
  . . . . .4J 7
Whaley Thorns Heritage Cen.
  . . . . .3A 8
Whaley Thorns Ind. Est.
  Lang 3K 7
Wharfedale Gdns. *Mans* 4G 41
Wharf La. *Tib* 2E 36
Wharf Rd. *Mans* 3B 40
Wharf Rd. *Pinx* 1E 56
Wharf Rd. *Stan H* 3A 38
  (in two parts)
Wharf Rd. Ind. Est. *Pinx* 7G 47
Wharf Yd. *Kirk A* 2C 58
Wharmby Av. *Mans* 5H 29
Whatton Ct. *Mans* 6G 41
Wheatcroft Clo. *Dane* 6D 24
Wheatcroft Clo. *Wing* 3A 12
Wheatfield Cres. *Mans W* 3E 30
Wheatfield Way. *Sut A* 2C 38
Wheatley Av. *Kirk A* 5D 48
Wheatley Av. *Som* 2J 55
Wheatley Clo. *For T* 7F 31
Wheatsheaf Ter. *Wars V* 3D 18
Wheeldon Av. *Belp* 3F 67
Wheeler Ga. *Und* 2J 65
Wheelwrights, The. *Edwin* 5K 21
Whilton Clo. *Sut A* 4E 38
Whilton Ct. *Belp* 3H 67
Whinney Bank. *Mans W* 4D 30
Whinney Hill. **4E 30**
Whinney Hill. *Mans W* 4D 30
Whinney La. *New O* 1H 23
Whitcombe Pl. *Rip* 2D 62
White Gates. *Cod* 4H 63
Whitegates Way. *Huth* 7G 37
White Hart St. *Mans* 3B 40
White Hart Yd. *Mans* 2B 40
  (off Stacey Rd.)
White Lion Yd. Mans *6H 29*
  (off Church St.)
White Moor. **2H 67**
Whitemoor Hall. *Belp* 2H 67
Whitemoor La. *Belp* 3G 67
White Post. **3K 53**
White Post Modern Farm Cen.
  . . . . .3K 53
Whites Clo. *Alf* 1H 55

White's La. *Som* 2H 55
Whitestone Clo. *Mans* 5G 41
Whitewater Clo. *New O* 2G 23
Whitewater Rd. *New O* 2G 23
Whitmore Av. *Gras* 5E 12
Whitney Clo. *For T* 7G 31
Whittaker Rd. *Rain* 2C 52
Whitton Pl. *Duck* 1C 4
Wichal Farm Clo. *Rip* 5D 62
Wickerwood Dri. *Kirk A* 4C 48
Wicksteed Clo. *Belp* 2H 67
Widmerpool St. *Pinx* 1E 56
Wilberforce Rd. *Mans* 6H 29
Wilcox Av. *Mans W* 3B 30
Wilcox Dri. *Und* 3J 65
Wilde Cres. *Sels* 5J 57
Wilders Lea Ct. *Belp* 5E 66
Wildflower Gro. *Sut A* 1B 48
Wild Hill. *Sut A* 2F 37
Wilford Rd. *Mans* 6G 41
Wilhallow La. *Jack* 1G 65
Wilkinson Clo. *Ches* 1A 12
Wilkinson Clo. *Ple* 3E 28
  (in two parts)
Willetts Ct. *Sut A* 1D 48
Willey La. *Und* 3J 65
Williams Clo. *Ridd* 5K 55
Williamson St. *Mans* 2K 39
William St. *Belp* 3D 66
Williamthorpe. **7K 13**
Williamthorpe Clo. *N Wing* 1G 25
Williamthorpe Ponds
  (Nature Reserve) 5K 13
Williamthorpe Rd. *N Wing* 1G 25
William Wood La. *Wars V* 1C 18
Willingham Ct. *Mans* 4H 41
Willoughby Ct. *Mans* 7G 41
Willow Av. *For T* 7G 31
Willow Av. *Kirk A* 4C 48
Willow Av. *Rip* 5D 62
Willow Av. *Shire* 2H 17
Willowbridge Ct. Sut A *7B 38*
  (off Willowbridge La.)
Willowbridge La. *Sut A* 1A 48
Willow Clo. *Alf* 5G 45
Willow Clo. *Pils* 7J 25
Willow Clo. *Sels* 4K 57
Willow Clo. *S Norm* 5D 46
Willow Clo. *Und* 3J 65
Willow Cres. *Sut A* 6B 38
Willow Dri. *Ann* 5D 58
Willow Gro. *Belp* 5E 66
Willows Av. *Alf* 5G 45
Willows Ct. *Rip* 2D 62
  (off Cromford St.)
Willows, The. *Ple* 2E 28
Willows, The. *Wars* 2H 19
Willow St. *Shirl* 1C 44
Willow Tree Clo. *For T* 6K 31
Willson Dri. *Ridd* 5H 55
Wilmore Way. *Sut A* 4H 39
Wilmot Rd. *Belp* 3E 66
Wilson Av. *B'wll* 1A 46
Wilson Av. *Kirk A* 5D 48
Wilson Clo. *Dane* 6D 24
Wilson La. *Heath* 5D 14
Wilson St. *Alf* 6H 45
Wilson St. *Mans* 5H 29
Wilson St. *Pinx* 7F 47
Wiltshire Av. *Jack* 7D 56
Wimsey Way. *Som* 1G 55
Winborne Clo. *Mans* 3H 39
Winchester Clo. *Mans* 6G 41
Winchester Clo. *N Wing* 2F 25
Winchester Dri. *Mans W* 4D 30
Windermere Rd. *Clay C* 5B 24
Windlea Rd. *Ridd* 5J 55
Windmill Clo. *Bsvr* 3J 5
Windmill La. *Belp* 3E 66
Windmill La. *Mans* 1C 40
  (in two parts)
Windmill Ri. *Belp* 2E 66
Windmill Ri. *Som* 4K 55
Windmill Ri. *S Norm* 5B 46
Windrush Clo. *Sut A* 7C 38
Windsmoor Rd. *Brins* 3F 65
Windsor Av. *Sut A* 6K 37
Windsor Clo. *Swanw* 4G 55
Windsor Ct. *Mans* 3B 30

Windsor Dri. *Wars* 3G **19**
Windsor Gdns. *Mans* 4D **40**
Windsor Rd. *For T* 5K **31**
Windsor Rd. *Mans* 4D **40**
Windsor Rd. *Sels* 3J **57**
Windy Ridge. *Wars* 4J **19**
Wingerworth. 4A **12**
Wingerworth Cotts. *Gras* 4E **12**
Wingerworth Hall. *Wing* 4A **12**
Wingerworth Hall Est. Wing . . .4A *12*
(off Lodge Dri.)
Wingerworth St. *Gras* 4E **12**
Wingfield Rd. *Alf* 7E **44**
Wingfield Rd. *Mans* 5G **41**
Wingfield Rd. *New T* 7D **12**
Wingfield Vw. *Clay C* 4E **24**
Winkburn Rd. *Mans* 1K **39**
Winkpenny La. *Tib* 4B **36**
Winsick. 1E **12**
Winster Av. *R'hd* 7H **51**
Winster Clo. *Belp* 2F **67**
Winster Clo. *Old T* 3A **24**
Winster Way. *Mans* 4H **41**
Winterbank Clo. *Sut A* 1A **48**
Winter Closes. *Und* 3H **65**
Winthorpe St. *Mans* 3H **39**
Wire La. *Nwtn* 6D **36**
Withorn M. *Mans* 2J **39**
Woburn Av. *Kirk A* 5G **49**
Woburn Clo. *B'wll* 1A **46**
Woburn Clo. *Swanw* 4F **55**
Woburn Ct. *B'wll* 1A **46**
Woburn La. *Ple* 3F **29**
Woburn Rd. *Ple* 4G **29**
Wolfcote Clo. *Dane* 7D **24**
Wollaton Clo. *Mans* 2H **41**

Wollaton Rd. *Kirk A* 5G **49**
Wolseley Ct. *Sut A* 6D **38**
Wolsey Dri. *Kirk A* 3F **49**
Woodborough Rd. *Mans* 7J **29**
Wood Clo. *For T* 1F **41**
Woodend. 1C **8**
Wood End Dri. *R'hd* 1G **61**
Woodfield Dri. *Rip* 4G **63**
Woodfield Rd. *Pinx* 6F **47**
Woodfield Rd. *S Norm* 6B **46**
Woodhall Clo. *Kirk A* 3C **48**
Woodhall Clo. *Mans* 1F **41**
Woodhall Gdns. *Mans* 1F **41**
Woodhead Clo. *Edwin* 6K **21**
Woodhouse Clo. *Mans W* 6C **30**
Woodhouse La. *Bsvr* 2G **5**
Woodhouse La. *S Norm* 5A **46**
Woodhouse La. *Sut A* 2D **38**
Woodhouse Rd. *Bsvr* 4H **5**
Woodhouse Rd.
Klbrn & Hors W 7K **67**
Woodhouse Rd. *Mans* 1B **40**
Woodhouse Sta. Enterprise Cen.
Mans W 5A **30**
Woodland Av. *Huth* 5G **37**
Woodland Clo. *Clip V* 4D **32**
Woodland Cres. *Mans* 5F **41**
Woodland Dri. *Mans* 5F **41**
Woodland Gro. *Mans W* 4C **30**
Woodland Gro. *Old T* 1B **24**
Woodland Gro. *Wars* 3H **19**
Woodland Ri. *R'hd* 1G **61**
Woodland Rd. *For T* 7F **31**
Woodlands Pk. Homes.
Rain 7B **42**
Woodlands, The. *Lang* 2A **8**
Woodlands, The. *Mans* 7B **30**

Woodlands Way. *Sut A* 1A **48**
Woodland Vw. *Lang* 3A **8**
Woodland Wlk. *Kirk A* 5H **49**
Woodland Way. *Old T* 3B **24**
Wood La. *Chur W* 7E **8**
Wood La. *Ple V & Shire* 6G **17**
(in two parts)
Wood La. *Rip* 7A **54**
Wood La. *Scarc* 1D **16**
(in two parts)
Woodlinkin. 6A **64**
Woodnook. 5J **57**
Wood Nook Clo. *Sels* 5H **57**
Woods Hill. *Sut A* 7C **38**
Woodside. *Sut A* 2C **38**
Woodside Av. *Mans* 6D **40**
Woodside Av. *Rip* 4D **62**
Woodside Gdns. *R'hd* 7G **51**
Woodside Pl. *Clay C* 4B **24**
Woodside Rd. *R'hd* 7F **51**
Woodside Rd. *Shire* 2J **17**
Wood St. *Alf* 5J **45**
Wood St. *Cod* 4H **63**
Wood St. *Hlmwd* 6A **14**
Wood St. *Lea* 3H **55**
Wood St. *Mans* 2A **40**
Wood St. *Rip* 2D **62**
Wood St. *Wars* 2H **19**
Wood St. N. *Alf* 5J **45**
Woodthorpe Av. *Clay C* 4A **24**
Woodview Clo. *Wing* 5A **12**
Woodview Gdns. *For T* 6J **31**
Woolley Clo. *Old T* 1B **24**
Worcester Av. *Mans W* 3C **30**
Worcester Clo. *Dane* 4E **24**
Worcester M. *Mans W* 2C **30**
Wordsworth Av. *Mans W* 4B **30**

Wordsworth Av. *Sut A* 6K **3**
Worksop Rd. *Cuc* 2G **5**
Worksop Rd. *Oll* 5H **11**
Worsborough Clo. *Mans* 4K **39**
Wren Pk. Clo. *Belp* 2B **66**
Wright Av. *Rip* 3F **63**
Wrightson Clo. *Sut A* 6E **38**
Wright St. *Cod* 4H **63**
Wycliffe Rd. *Alf* 6G **45**
Wynndale Dri. *Mans* 4G **41**
Wysall Clo. *Mans* 7J **29**
Wyver. 1C **66**
Wyver La. *Belp* 1D **66**

Y

Yardley Clo. *Swanw* 3F **55**
Yardley Way. *Belp* 3H **67**
Yeoman Av. *Mans* 7G **41**
Yeovil Ct. *Mans* 5H **41**
Yew Tree Av. *For T* 6K **31**
Yew Tree Av. *Kirk A* 4D **48**
Yew Tree Clo. *New O* 2G **23**
Yew Tree Dri. *Huth* 7H **37**
Yew Tree Dri. *Old T* 2B **24**
Yew Tree Dri. *Shire* 2H **17**
Yew Tree Rd. *New O* 3G **23**
York Av. *Jack* 7D **56**
York Cres. *Doe L* 6G **15**
York St. *Mans W* 6B **30**
York Pl. *N Wing* 1H **25**
York Rd. *Shire* 4J **17**
York St. *Mans* 4A **40**
York St. *Sut A* 6C **38**
York Ter. *Pinx* 2E **56**
York Ter. *Wars* 3H **19**
Young Cres. *Sut A* 7F **39**